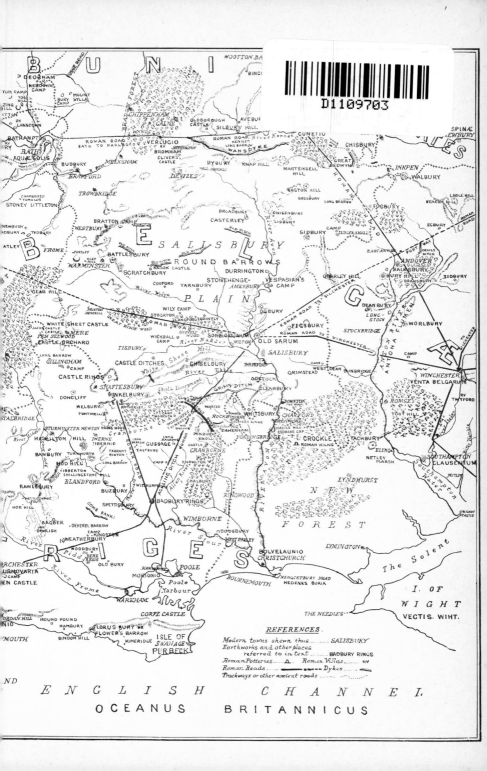

Early Wars of Wessex

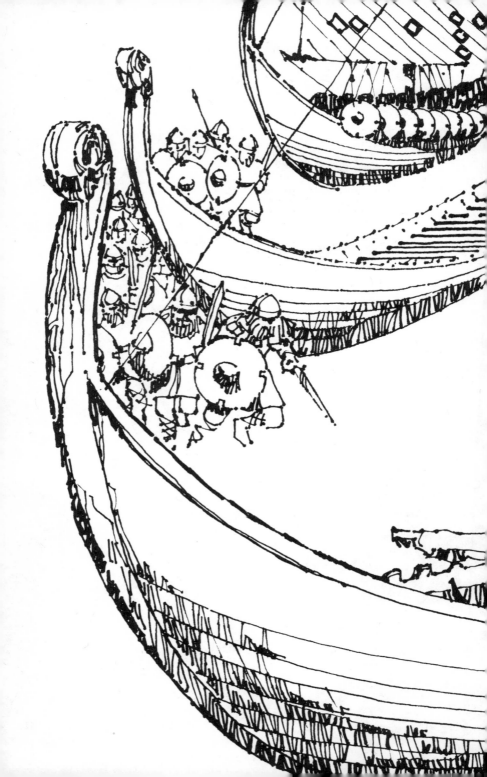

Early Wars of Wessex

Albany Major

BLANDFORD PRESS
Poole Dorset

First published in Great Britain
by **Blandford Press**, Link House, West Street, Poole, Dorset. BH15 1LL

ISBN 0 7137 2068 9

This Revised and illustrated edition 1978

Printed and bound in Great Britain
by Biddles of Guildford

Contents

5

Publisher's Note

The Early Wars of Wessex was first published in 1913. At that time it presented an entirely new look at the Saxon and Viking incursions into southern Britain, replacing speculation by an account based on detailed field work and archaeology and sound historical research. The result was a superb piece of scholarship and a highly readable book, which illuminated, as far as possible in the light of knowledge then available, a period of British history which had remained virtually a blank in all histories published up to that time.

Over sixty years later the book still remains a highly readable account of this fascinating period. The reader must, however, bear in mind that scholarship has advanced, and some suggestions made by the author are no longer valid, but in order to retain the flavour of the original work, Albany Major's text has not been altered. In many cases archaeology has filled in many of the gaps noted by the author, in others it has confirmed or disproved his hypotheses.

The Early Wars of Wessex is still the only book that reconstructs in detail this amazing period of British history. Read in conjunction with a modern archaeology, bearing in mind that some of the county boundaries have been changed since the book was written, it will provide a fascinating and exciting reconstruction of Wessex during the formation of what became the Kingdom of England.

BOOK 1

Chapter 1

A study of the early history of Wessex inevitably leads to the conclusion that the warfare which took place in the west of England in the early Saxon period must have had an influence which made itself felt far beyond local limits, and materially helped to shape the destiny of the kingdom at large. The record is one of steady advance of a united and determined people in the face of an equally united and steady enemy, in a war carried on from generation to generation almost without intermission, until the last trace of British resistance in the furthest west was overcome, long after the midland kingdom had ceased to be harassed by wars with the Welsh.

The result of this warfare is seen in the successful stand which Wessex alone, habituated to arms as she was, could make against the Danes in the time of Alfred and even later. There is no doubt that the active practice of arms in Wessex long after the other kingdoms had settled into something like peace and stagnation, explains the overlordship of her kings from the days when Ecgberht came as a leader, fresh from the camps of Charlemagne, after his long exile.

There are two sources from which the history of the earliest wars of Wessex are to be gathered. The former is the British account, and in it we are told that some few years after a terrible defeat at Mount Badon, Cerdic's warfare with Arthur ended by an oath of fealty on the part of the Saxon to the British king, Cerdic receiving the grant of Somerset and Hampshire, which became the kingdom of Wessex accordingly. The story is evidently nothing but a court panegyric on the personal valour of Arthur, and the writers are anxious to give the impression that there was warfare all over England at the period.

Turning to the other authority, the *Anglo-Saxon Chronicle,* we can trace the West Saxon advance as given in their traditions from point to point across the country, until they first reach the Somerset border after the battle of Deorham and capture of Bath in 577. There is nothing in

Lappenberg (England under the Anglo-Saxon Kings). *See also* The Conquest of Britain by the Saxons *(D. Haigh, London, 1861, pp.312-16). Both these writers accept the British account.*

It is now the fashion to discredit the account in the Chronicle *on various grounds and to suggest for Wessex an origin for which there is not the slightest evidence in any of the ancient authorities on the subject. An examination of this theory in the text would be outside our scope. Originally propounded by Sir Henry Howorth in* The English Historical Review *(Vol. VIII), it has received some countenance from Professor H. M. Chadwick and is adopted by Professor C. Oman* (England before the Norman Conquest, *pp. 224-7).*

the story that clashes with military anɑ strategical requirements and where we are able to check it by topographical and archaeological evidence, we find it confirmed and explained in a curious and striking way. The further record of the struggle in which the greater part of Somerset was subdued in the latter half of the seventh century is precise, and can be supported by documentary evidence from other sources. With these definite facts before us, it is impossible to accept the British romance which ascribes the origin of Wessex to a cession of Somerset and Hampshire to the defeated Saxons, while the claim by Somerset enthusiasts that the battle of Llongborth, sung by a Welsh bard, was fought at Langport, near Bridgwater, in the heart of their county, is equally untenable.

Like the later Scandinavians, the Saxons had been a terror on the English coast long before they came in the middle of the fifth century with the definite intention of settling in new-won lands. At the end of the fourth century the Saxon ships had, equally with the Picts and Scots, been the watched-for terror of the northern garrisons, and the poet Claudian names these three races as among those whom the victories of Stilicho had rendered harmless for a time. Their restlessness was part of the great "folk-wanderings," and it was a foregone conclusion that sooner or later a seafaring race would find its way across the channel; and it must not be forgotten that long before England was invaded, the opposite coasts of France were more or less settled by Saxons. For some reason they seem to have left the shores of northern England where they were first heard of, and by the fifth and sixth centuries had passed southward to raid the richer coasts of the Channel. The later Roman writers speak of the Saxons always as sea-rovers of the most desperate sort. They came, according to Orosius, who is perhaps the best authority, from the coasts and coastal marshes on the borders of the Roman empire, and seem never to have owned the sway of Rome.

An archer of the 11th century.

Orosius, VII, 32.

The early Saxon was a precursor of the Vikings as a hardy seaman, and the mention of the Saxon vessels and Saxon knowledge of the sea by the Latin writers contemporary with their raids is constant. We cannot claim for them the possession of such splendid craft as those of the north in the Viking age, but that they had seagoing vessels in which they raided even to the western coast of Gaul, is certain. By the fifth century they had colonised in the north of France, and as Freeman says, "Bayeux was a Saxon city before Winchester." But there was to be a difference.

In Gaul, the Saxon settlements were small and scattered, and they were gradually merged in the greater Teutonic elements in this country. In Britain they were also small and scattered, but there was nothing to interfere with their growth, except the resistance which they might meet from the Roman and Celtic elements in the country. . .the Teutonic kingdoms in Britain were the work of generations. . . they did not fall, but were merged into a single kindred whole. The main difference is that in Britain the Teutonic conquerors displaced the Celtic and Roman inhabitants in a way which they never did in Gaul. . .they became the people of the land itself.

How this came to pass in the case of Wessex we can trace step by step, both from the chronicles and from the well-marked physical characters of the country. The latter indicate lines which the frontiers marked out by the successive stages of the advances recorded must of necessity have followed.

In tracing these lines we have to take into account the importance of the ancient earthworks which are so numerous throughout Wessex. Whatever their date may have been, they were each and all available to the British, and had to be reckoned with by the invaders. Their importance in any case would be great when held by any large body of men, but it was all the greater while any trace of Roman methods and organisation remained. At the date of the landing of Cerdic there would still be some attempt to carry out Roman traditions and the arms and

The well-known Nydam boat, found in the heart of the district from which the invaders came and illustrated in Du Chaillu's Viking Age (Vol. 1, p. 220) is supposed to be of or about this date. Her length is 75 feet, and though not fitted for sailing, she is quite capable of long coasting voyages. Her crew, on the later viking reckoning of three men to an oar, would be about 100. Ships of greater length than this were exceptional until the late viking age, and it is not likely that Cerdic's ships carried more men. Of course we do not accept the landings in "three" or "five" ships, as recorded by the chroniclers, literally. They probably copied blindly from earlier records in which three or five ships, perhaps represented pictorially, stood for a fleet.

Western Europe in the Fifth Century, *Prof. E. A. Freeman, Chapters 1 and 2.*

A 10th century archer.

general military arrangements of the British would be of the Roman type, though debased and passing into a mere fashion without any real knowledge of the importance of the legionary model.

Against this decayed organisation we have to set, as in the case of the later Viking invasions, the discipline of the sea, and the close cohesion of the crews of each ship under their tried leaders. It is more than possible that the very attempt at a cumbersome, because misused and misunderstood, military method was the cause of actual disaster to the British, at least in the open field. In the defence of earthworks the reverse would be the case. The ordered Roman ranks and their relief system had full effect. The heavy armour and the weighty "pilum" were in their places, behind the square shields.

The ancient earthworks are imposing even now. They were more so when the ditches were of their full depth, and the sides of the vallum were sheer and smooth. Probably too they were stockaded, and the entrances, which are now but gaps, were certainly filled with heavy gates. What the taking of a hill fort at its full strength meant is best seen in records of the taking of the Maori "Pahs" in the wars of our own days. The enterprise must have been exactly that of the Saxons, if every they attempted to storm a well-mannered Wessex hill fort. Putting aside the effects of modern weapons, it is doubtful if either the Saxon spear or the bayonet could have won a way into the strongholds.

Cerdic's men were more lightly armed than the Romanised Britons. The spear and short heavy "seax" were the universal weapons, and the sword occurs seldom with these in Saxon graves. Either it was the weapon of the chiefs, or it was too valuable to bury—probably the latter, as the sword is the weapon of all races. Mail was scarce in the Saxon ranks, but the hard leathern jacket was usual, with an iron-bound round shield and helm, the whole Saxon war gear hardly seeming

Badbury Rings, Dorset, the supposed site of Mons
Badonicus.

to alter for centuries—until the coming of the
viking hosts in fact.

An examination of the recorded names or
positions of the early battles between Briton and
Saxon throws a vivid light on the nature of the
struggle and the character of the British
resistance. Out of sixteen battles in South Britain
recorded in the *A.-S. Chronicle* four are stated to
have been fought at the landing-place on the
coast; four, if not five, occurred at river-fords
and another on the banks of a stream; three were
fought in defence of fortresses; while there is no
clear indication of the position of the remaining
three. Taking the four battles or campaigns of
Vortimer (Guorthemer) recorded by Nennius, we
find that two are placed on the coast in the
attempt to drive back the invaders to Thanet or
their ships. The other two took place on the river
Derwent and at Episford. These names point
clearly to an almost entirely defensive warfare on
the part of the Britons. Apart from attempts to
prevent a landing, or to force the invaders to re-
embark, their efforts were mainly directed to
holding the successive lines of defence presented
by their rivers, or by fortified positions. The long
resistance they were able to offer with other
indirect evidence shows that they were able to
carry on this mode of warfare with no small
measure of skill and success.

According to the *Chronicle* Cerdic and Cynric,
who founded the kingdom of the West Saxons,
first landed at "Cerdices-ora" in the year 495.

They were reinforced in 501 by the landing of

*One at Cymenesora,
one at Portsmouth,
two at Cerdicesora;
Aeglesthrep (ford),
Crecganford,
Wippedesfleet,
Mearcredesburn,
Cerdicesford;
Andredesceaster,
Searoburh, Beranburh;
the defeat of the
Britons in 473, the
war with Natanleod,
the battle of
Cerdicesleaga.*

*The list of Arthur's
twelve battles given
by Nennius also
points in the same
direction. Seven of
them are upon rivers,
viz. four on the
Duglas and one each
on the rivers Glein,
Lussas and Trat
Treuriot; four occur
at castles or other
strongholds,
Guinnion castle,
Caerleon, Mount
Breguoin and Mount
Badon, while the
remaining one takes
place in the wood of
Celidon.*

13

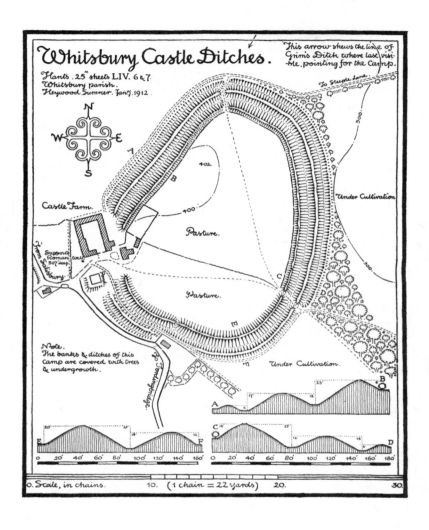

Plan of Whitsbury Castle in Hampshire.

the chiefs Port, Bieda and Maegla at Portsmouth. In 508 Cerdic and Cynric won a victory over a king called Natanleod, or possibly at a place of that name (Netley or Nately?), which gave them the dominion over a wide stretch of territory, and in 514 the *Chronicle* records the landing of the West Saxons under Stuf and Wihtgar, Cerdic's nephews, at the original haven Cerdices-ora. The actual position of this place, is not known, but it must have been either on the sea-coast of Hampshire or in Southampton Water. The distances involved are, however, so small that the identification of the exact spot is of no great moment. Five years later, in 519, Cerdic and Cynric established the kingdom of Wessex and in the same year the *Chronicle* records a battle at Cerdicesford.

Nothing is said as to the nationality of the first two bands of invaders, but from Bede's evidence as to the presence of Jutes in Hampshire and the Isle of Wight, we may infer that the host that came in 501 consisted largely of Jutes. The invaders of 514 are distinctly stated to have been West Saxons. Whether the names of the various chiefs recorded are genuine has little bearing on the argument. Bede's statements are amply borne out by archaeological evidence, which shows that there was a large Jutish element on the mainland of Hampshire, especially in the valley of the Hamble, as well as on the Isle of Wight. But the assumption of many writers that this fact disproves the story of the landing of the West Saxons does not follow. Apart from Henry of Huntingdon's statement that in the war of 508 "Cerdic and his son entreated aid from Aesc, the king of Kent, and from Aella, the great king of the South Saxons, and from Port and his sons, the last who had come over," there is nothing incredible in this account of the arrival at intervals of successive bands of invaders of different though kindred nationalities, who united to found the kingdom of Wessex.

The original frontiers of that kingdom are no

The statement in the **Chronicle** *that after this battle the land was named "Natahleag" as far as Cerdicesford (Charford) has been regarded with suspicion. But though its exact import may be doubtful, we find traces of the name over a wide area. It occurs in North Hampshire at Nately near Mapledurwell; again on opposite sides of Southampton Water at Netley near Hamble on the east, and Netley Marsh and Netley Down near Eling on the west, while in the immediate neighbourhood of Charford we seem to see it at Natanbury near the Moot at Downton.*

Henry of Huntingdon, Book II.

If the name of the founders of Wessex, "Gewissa," means "confederates," it is at least as likely to have been derived from such a combination as this, as from the hypothetical confederacy of war-bands from Berkshire and North Hampshire which Professor Oman suggests as its origin. But the origin of the name is by no means certain.

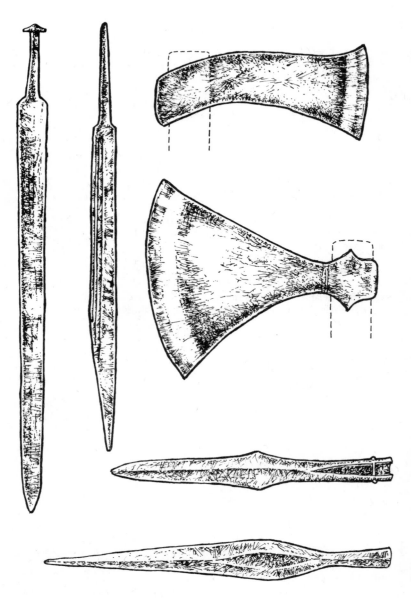

Saxon and Viking weapons.

doubt represented more or less accurately by the ancient boundaries of the county of Hampshire and a study of these leads to some interesting results. The district east of the line of Southampton Water, forming the bulk of the county, consists mainly of the country drained by the rivers Meon, Hamble, and Itchen, is roughly oblong and fairly homogeneous. Its northern boundary follows generally the line of the Roman road that ran east and west through Silchester, but it is deflected to the north in a rough semicircle in such a way as to include the whole of the district round that town. It has been argued from this that the capture of Silchester, of which no record has come down to us, was the work, not of Mercian Angles but of the West Saxons, acting probably in co-operation with a force that had pushed up the Thames to Reading, and was subduing the district along the river now represented by Berkshire. Silchester was undoubtedly left waste and desolate after its fall and it is most improbable that any regard would have been paid to its side had the fixing of the county boundary dated from some later period. Its only value was as a trophy of victory. We have, therefore, in the way the county boundaries are drawn at this point, almost a proof that they date back to the time of the Anglo-Saxon conquest. This, as we shall see below, is supported by other evidence.

Military dress of the 9th centur

Further west the boundary between the two counties follows the southern edge of the Kennet valley, till it meets the Wiltshire boundary close to Inkpen Beacon. A mile east of the point where the three counties meet it passes through the centre of a considerable camp called Walbury. To the west of Inkpen Wansdyke reaches its eastward termination, so far at any rate as it can be traced, while in the neighbourhood there are other indications of ancient dykes on or near the borders of Wiltshire and Berkshire.

To the west of this main section of Hampshire lie two smaller sections of the county, the one comprising, roughly speaking, the valley of the Anton, the other the district between Southampton Water and the Avon. These appear to be later additions and it would seem that the further west the invaders came the more difficult they found it to penetrate inland so that the northern border of each of these two sections is set back far towards the south, as compared with the county east of it. Old Sarum, the Roman Sorbiodunum, also appears to have had a great influence on the later stages of the conquest, as the Hampshire boundary line is drawn eight miles east and as many south of the British fortress. The approach to it is guarded on the east by Figsbury camp, close to the Roman road from Winchester, which antiquaries have christened Chlorus' Camp, and the southward approach is likewise covered by the chain of fortresses described below. Another approach from the east up a little tributary of the Anton, which may have been navigable for light vessels, is also covered by a camp at West Dean, just beyond the Hampshire border.

All these indications suggest that a combined advance westward after the capture of Silchester along the line of the later county boundaries of Hampshire and Berkshire was checked in the neighbourhood of Inkpen Beacon, probably by defensive works of the Britons. Thenceforward the invaders had to proceed independently, but they held Walbury jointly to guard against a British counterstroke. While the advance of Hampshire from the east was thus checked, an advance up the Anton valley was also checked some ten miles to the south by the camps at Sidbury, Ludgershall and Fosbury. Beyond and behind these and the earthworks already mentioned was the line of Chute and Savernake Forests with connecting dykes and supporting camps, barring the way of Hampshire and Berkshire alike.

North-east of Andover there is another earthwork, the "Devil's Ditch," which originally crossed the line of the Roman road from

Silchester to Old Sarum and appears to have spanned a belt of open country between two tracts of forest. What part, if any, it may have played in these operations is not easy to conjecture.

No exact correspondence can be traced between these divisions of the county and the invasions recorded in the *Chronicle*. That of 501 is connected with Portsmouth according to the text, and Silchester probably did not fall till some time between the years 508 and 514. We are, however, inclined to think that the conquest of the two western sections followed on the arrival of the West Saxons in 514. But we have no data to guide us and only know that the operations in which they took part culminated in the battle of Cerdicesford in 519.

Our enquiries into these and other events in the early history of these islands are too often hampered by uncertainty as to the precise site of events recorded; rendering it impossible to draw definite conclusions as to their significance. Fortunately we now come to an instance where no such uncertainty exists. Cerdices-ford is undoubtedly Charford on the Avon, about four miles above Fordingbridge, and this knowledge and a close study of the topography of the district throw a flood of light on the events that determined the boundary in this quarter.

Charford lies just south of the county boundary. Across the Wiltshire border, a mile or more to the north, lies Downton with earthworks generally supposed to be the remains of a Saxon moothill and place of assembly. They have, however, been much altered and cut about before assuming their present shape and may have been formed out of an earlier entrenchment commanding the river. Across the river, about eight miles to the west of Charford, Ackling Dyke, an old Roman road, runs in a south-westerly direction from Old Sarum to Badbury Rings. Across Cranborne Chase this road runs for the most part over open down and here on the river side it is covered by a chain of camps.

General Pitt-Rivers shows this dyke as only extending south of the Roman road and with the ditch to the east, but Dr. J. P. Williams-Freeman tells us that it has been traced for a long distance north of the road and that the ditch is on the west. It is now very much wasted and in many parts ploughed out, but must originally have been little inferior in size to Bokerly Dyke.

Compare the camps at West Dean and Dudsbury.

We of course do not suggest that these camps had originally any connection with the road or were meant to cover it. But with the exception of Odstock they were probably all in existence before the coming of the Saxon. Odstock may be of later date.

The most important of these, now known as Whitsbury Castle Ditches, lies about eight miles south of Old Sarum and almost due west of Charford, some two and a half miles beyond the Avon. It crowns the summit of Whitsbury Down, one of the highest points in the neighbourhood, which rises to a height of four hundred feet above the sea, with imposing defences formed of three great banks and ditches covering an area of eighteen acres. Nearly two miles off, lying about W. by S., is a small camp covering some three and a half acres on Damerham or Rockbourne Knoll, a point which rivals Whitsbury Castle Ditches in height, while Clearbury Ring, five acres in extent and over 450 feet above the sea, lies about three miles N.N.W. of the latter stronghold, between it and Old Sarum. Lastly in a copse on Odstock Down, which rises from the valley of the Ebble, facing Clearbury Ring and half a mile N.W. of it, there are the remains of a camp, which judging from the fragment left must have been bigger than Clearbury. This, however, from its position may be of a different origin from the three first mentioned.

In the campaign which ended with the battle of Charford the Saxons were evidently endeavouring to push westward across the Avon, their ultimate object being the cutting of the road between Old Sarum and Badbury, a dangerous line of British concentration. The choice of Charford as the point of attack was not accidental.

To the south of it the right bank of the river was covered with impenetrable forest, and it was the furthest point from Old Sarum at which access could be gained to the open downland. Probably there was a simultaneous advance up the Avon valley.

Between Charford and Fordingbridge there are two camps close to the Avon on the left bank, Castle Hill overlooking the river, and Godmans Cap, or Frankenbury, a little way from it, which may possibly belong to the period immediately preceding the battle.

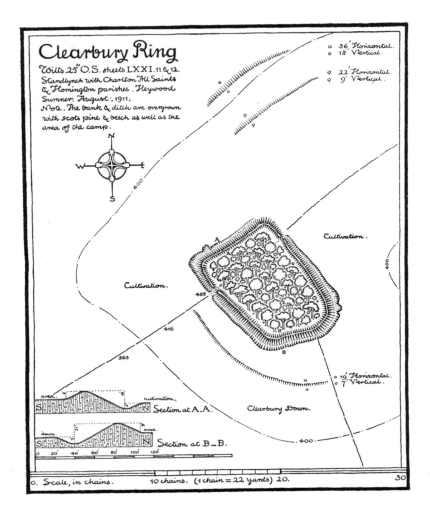

Clearbury Ring

Wilts 25" O.S. sheets LXXI.11.&12.
Standlynch with Charlton All Saints
& Homington parishes. Heywood
Sumner. August. 1911.
N.B. The bank & ditch are overgrown
with scots pine & beech as well as the
area of the camp.

N

W — E

S

400

36 Horizontal.
18 Vertical.

22 Horizontal.
9 Vertical.

Cultivation.

Cultivation.

458

416

363

400

10 Horizontal.
7 Vertical.

area   cultivation.   Section at A.A.

down   area   Section at B_B.

0 20 40 60 80 100 120

Clearbury Down.

400

0. Scale, in chains.   10 chains. (1 chain = 22 yards) 20.   30

Plan of Clearbury Ring, Wiltshire including two sections of the bank and ditches.

The result of the battle remains evident in two tongues of Hampshire territory, which run up north-westward into Wiltshire beyond and opposite Charford. The northernmost of these extends for about two miles and a half beyond the river and comprises North Charford and Breamore Downs. It is bounded at the extremity by a section of Grim's Ditch, an earthwork which may have been an ancient tribal boundary, though its date has not been determined and its exact course and object is uncertain. The name seems to indicate that the Saxons found it already in existence and did not know its makers. The southernmost of these two tongues extends up the valley of the Rockbourne and over Rockbourne Down for some five miles from the river. It cuts the probable course of an eastern section of Grim's Ditch, and its furthest point N.W. just touches the northerly section. Its southern boundary just before reaching Grim's Ditch runs through the centre of the little camp at Damerham Knoll. Between these two strips of Hampshire Whitsbury Down thrusts eastward a finger of land, barely a mile across, crowned with the stronghold already described.

If we are right in supposing that the old boundaries of Hampshire represent the frontier of Cerdic's Wessex and if the boundaries opposite Charford date from that period, they can have but one explanation. Though the West Saxons succeeded in forcing the river passage and driving the foe before them, the Britons must have rallied on Whitsbury Castle and were able to hold it, though they had to yield possession of the strips of land on either side of it to the foe. The exact local conditions which fixed the boundaries we have described are perhaps not now to be discovered, but pasturage on the downlands was no doubt as important to the earliest West Saxon invaders of the district as it was to their descendants, whose settlements in the neighbouring valleys run up in strips from the wooded river bottoms to the downs.

The Rockbourne valley had undoubtedly a far greater economic importance in Romano-British times that it has at present. The Rockbourne stream broke out much higher up the valley than its present source, and of course carried a greater volume of water. Moreover, on the extreme verge of this strip of Hampshire, just south of the border where for a short distance it follows the western section of Grim's Ditch, Heywood Sumner discovered a large enclosure, and evidence of Romano-British settlement. Adjoining this enclosure is a pond of considerable antiquity, known as Spring Pond, but it is doubtful whether this dates back to the time of the enclosure. Probably there was a watercourse actually running through the latter in Romano-British times.

It would seem that the boundaries in this quarter were drawn so as to include in Saxon Hampshire practically the whole course of the Rockbourne stream, as well as the site of the enclosure discovered by Mr Sumner, while leaving Whitsbury Castle in British territory.

It will of course be urged that it would not have been possible for the Saxons to hold territory dominated by Whitsbury Castle on one side and Damerham Knoll on the other. But it must be remembered that the command of the strongest fortress, if its garrison is unable to take the offensive, is limited to the ground covered by its artillery. Even if the Briton still used the catapult and other engines of the Roman, these are not likely to have been very formidable a hundred and more years after the legions had left, and for all practical purposes we may limit the command of Whitsbury Castle to the ground a bowshot from its walls. Nor did the bow of the sixth century approach in range or power the English longbow of later times.

On the other hand it may be said that, if the Saxons were able to hold such advanced positions on either side of Whitsbury Castle, the Britons would have been obliged to evacuate it.

The ditch has suffered much from cultivation, is ploughed out in parts and reduced everywhere till it appears more than a hollow way. Mr Sumner, however, cut two trenches across it in 1912 to test the theory that it was a covered way connecting Clearbury and the other camps. He found that the bottom of the ditch was only some 18 inches wide, and in neither section did the floor or sides show any sign of wear. (See Report of the Committee on Ancient Earthworks, etc. 1912).

There are only two
known cases of sieges
undertaken by the
Anglo-Saxons up to
this date, the sieges of
Andredesceaster and
of Mount Badon.
From the entries in
the Chronicle under
the years 477 and 491
and the story in
Henry of Huntingdon,
we conclude that
Aella was forced to
undertake the siege of
Andredesceaster by
the persistent menace
of the guerilla bands
in Andredsweald. The
siege of Mount Badon,
according to Gildas
and Nennius, ended
disastrously for the
Saxons.

Both the Clearbury
and the Damerham
Knoll camps are far
inferior to Whitsbury
in size and strength.
They were useful
positions for
connecting links, but
it is doubtful if they
had a water supply or
could have been held
for any length of
time, if isolated.

But threatening as the Saxon position looks on paper, the chain of fortresses—Old Sarum, Clearbury, Whitsbury—remained virtually intact, with the Roman road to Badbury behind them still unbroken. Whitsbury was a very formidable fortress to carry by assault and it had its own water supply, a well under the ramparts marked as a "Roman" well in the Ordnance maps. Further evidence goes to show that the Saxon invaders knew that fortresses standing solely on the defensive must fall sooner or later, and that it was against their practice to waste their strength in trying to carry them by storm.

Our conclusion is that Charford was in its result a drawn battle and brought about a position of stalemate. The West Saxons could not advance beyond the point they had won nor could the Britons drive them back. But by holding on to the commanding fortress on Whitsbury Down they were in a measure secure, as any preparations for a further advance would at once be observed. We have designedly left out of account the camp on Damerham Knoll. In itself it was of no great strength, and, if the earliest frontier, like the later county boundary, ran through its centre, the only possible conclusion we can come to is that both sides agreed to neutralise it, which harmonises entirely with the result arrived at on other grounds.

Turning to other quarters, the fixing of the Wessex boundary just north of Charford was perhaps determined by the presence of entrenchments at Downton commanding the river. In any case the position of Clearbury, with the strong and important city of Sorbiodunum (Old Sarum) beyond it at the junction of several Roman roads, was sufficient reason for the halt in the advance of Wessex which there seems to have been at this point.

South-east of Downton the boundary for some distance follows a road, which is probably on the line of a track called the "herepath" by the *Codex Wintoniensis*, a 12th century cartulary.

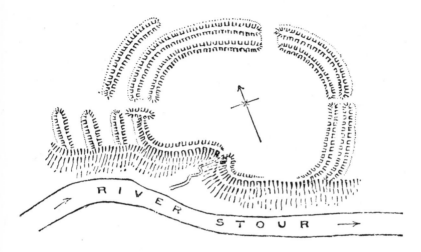

Plan of Dudsbury Camp, near West Parley.

The name seems again directly to link the frontier at this point with days of warfare between Saxon and Briton.

Southward from the Rockbourne territory the boundary ran almost parallel with the Avon at a distance of about three miles west of the river, following for part of the distance the Moors River, a tributary of the Stour. Cerdic in fact had command of and could hold the river valley, but that was all. Any further advance was stayed by a belt of forest, backed by a line of strong camps. The forest belt along the Avon reaches south to the Stour, which the frontier line crosses at a ford below West Parley. Thence it swerves westward as it nears the sea, finally reaching the coast at a point a little to the east of Poole Harbour. There is a tendency among some modern historians to discount the value of a woodland frontier. They judge rather by the woods of to-day, but there is no doubt that a wide stretch of primaeval forest, uncleared, undrained and full of the enemy, was as impassable a barrier to Cerdic and his men as the German forests were to the Romans.

On the left bank of the Stour, about a mile
west of the border, is Dudsbury camp, a strong
fortress on a bluff rising sixty or seventy feet
above the river. Warne's plan shows the unusual
and commanding character of this camp, but
some of his details are now hard to trace and
there seems to have been a slight landslip on the
river face that has carried away part of the
ramparts. The plan, however, gives no idea of the
height of the camp above the river and fails to
show that along the river front some twenty feet
below the crest of the vallum there runs a broad
and comparatively level platform, or berm, which
overhangs the river and its narrow bank at the
foot of the bluff, commanding them absolutely.
The hollow way shown on the south-west leads
down to this platform, the descent from it to the
river brink being very steep and difficult. South
of the river opposite the camp are broad and
perfectly level fields, which must once have been
marsh or lagoon. The channel must always have
run under the bluff, and, as long as the camp was
held and the river platform manned by a hostile
force, the passage of ships would be impossible,
even if the waterway were left clear. A very slight
obstruction in the channel below the camp
would have made it still more hopeless to try and
force a passage. The fixing of the frontier at this
point was evidently determined by the existence
of this camp.

Chapter 2

In 519, the year of the battle of Charford, Cerdic and Cynric, as already stated, assumed the kingship of Wessex, and at this point, so far as our records go, the further extension of the kingdom was stayed for some thirty years. The reason for this pause in the advance is not far to seek. Apart from the certainty that there must have been heavy losses during the last advance, ⁺he evidence we have drawn from the extraordinary character of the frontier opposite Charford shows that the final campaign must have ended in a drawn battle and an agreement that left each side in possession of the ground it held. Moreover there is no record in the *Chronicle* of the arrival of any further reinforcements. But beyond all this there was the imperative need to settle, consolidate and cultivate the new-won lands. The earlier stages of the Saxon conquest were precisely similar in detail to the later Danish occupations of parts of England, and we have very definite statements that Danish advances ceased while the chiefs were apportioning and tilling their conquered districts. Wessex at this time had reached a frontier which was defensible against the Britons, and at the same time hard to pass. The land within it was sufficient for the time, and there was no reason why the hazard of a further extension of territory should be incurred. The statement of the definite assumption of kingship at this time is clear evidence that the period of aggression had been succeeded by the wished-for period of organisation.

It is noteworthy that a full generation elapsed before any further advance on the part of Wessex is recorded. In that time the natural increase of the fighting force may have been greatly augmented by reinforcements from beyond the sea, as the British writers state was the case, but in any case the increase of population in the thirty years would make expansion as imperative to the Saxons of Wessex as to any overpopulated Danish district, which must needs send its sons

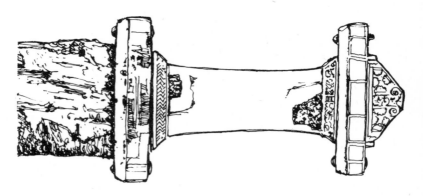

Sword-hilt from a burial at Coombe, Kent.

on the Viking path. This feature of the long inactivity of Wessex between 519 and the victory at Searobyrig in 552 has been very largely overlooked, but it is most important—so important indeed that there is no need to seek for a British victory to account for the halt. It must be realised that the Wessex hosts were by no means enormous, that they were only able to win their way onward step by step, and that they were at a very great distance from any reinforcements. They had come to win a new home, and had won it. They were able to hold what they had won—Hampshire—but any immediate attempt at extension of territory must have been out of the question.

The inactivity of the thirty years was broken only by a fight whose result is not given, at "Cerdicesleaga," in 527; and there was also the occupation of the Isle of Wight in 530. It is doubtful whether this was not rather a matter of subjection of the kindred Jutes, who seem to have already acquired the island, than a fresh conquest from the Britons.

According to British authorities there was also a battle between the Britons and West Saxons at the "Mons Badonicus," both date and place being doubtful though there is some evidence that the period might be about 520. Gildas records it as a crushing defeat of the Saxons, which stayed their advance for many years, and Nennius associates it with the name of Arthur. It finds no place in the *Chronicle,* which at this early period records little beyond the main phases in the advance of the conquerors, unless indeed it could be identified with the already mentioned "Cerdicesleaga." The date of "Mons

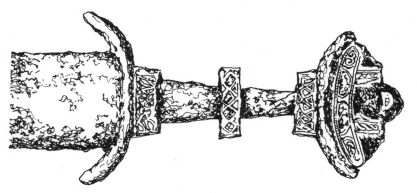

Badonicus" is so uncertain that this is not impossible, and the silence of the *Chronicle* as to the result suggests that "Cerdicesleaga" may have been a British victory. But there is no evidence on the point and our ignorance as to date and place makes any speculation as to the place of "Mons Badonicus" in the story of the conquest pure guess-work.

The long pause in the advance which followed the battle of Charford gave time for the consolidation of Wessex within its first frontiers, and for those frontiers to be definitely fixed. When the new generation pushed forward some thirty years later, under Cynric, their veteran leader, it was to add a new province to the kingdom already won. There is some evidence available from which we can conjecture what were the first steps in this fresh advance. We know that the first stage of the campaign culminated in the capture of Searobyrig, Old Sarum, the Roman Sorbiodunum, in 552. Moreover the name of the new province was Wiltunscire, Wiltshire, and its inhabitants were known as the Wilsaetas, the dwellers on the Wylye. We deduce from this that the forward movement began with an advance up the Avon and the occupation of the valley of the Wylye, where Wilton became the new capital. We can show on other grounds that such an advance must have preceded the capture of Old Sarum, for the occupation of the Cranborne Chase, district, with the reduction of Whitsbury, Clearbury and other fortresses and the cutting of the road to Badbury, was a necessary preliminary to the attack on that city. No attempt on such an important stronghold could have been possible, till the country in rear of the advance was securely held.

The obvious route for the West Saxon advance was up the Avon and its tributaries, the Ebble and Nadder, any British position defending the river at Downton being forced, or turned.

Whether the well-known "Moot" at Downton is formed out of earlier earthworks it is impossible to say, and it is doubtful whether excavation would enable this point to be determined. But its position suggests that it was chosen as the meeting-place of Wessex while the conquest of Wiltshire was in progress. Its place as the centre of the national life during such a period of rapid growth, culminating in the battle of Deorham in 577, would explain the importance that appears always to have been attached to The Moot at Downton even when the facts connected with its early history became blurred and forgotten.

There is another earthwork, on Odstock Down, overlooking the Ebble valley, which may date from an early period in this advance.

The name Odstock (D.B. *Odestoche*) almost certainly indicates that there was a stockaded Saxon camp, the advanced base of operations. The fragment of a camp still left in Odstock Copse stands on lower ground than Clearbury Ring, which it faces across the head of an intervening valley. It is less than a mile from it in a north-westerly direction and in a position which would threaten the line of communications between Clearbury and the Roman road, and cover an advance up the Ebble valley. The occupation of this valley would absolutely sever all direct communication between Clearbury and Old Sarum and open up the way to an advance westward to cut the Roman road, which the West Saxons had failed to accomplish thirty years before. An inevitable consequence to this latter operation would be the fall of Clearbury and Whitsbury and the occupation by the Saxons of the district southwards from the Ebble valley as

A trackway, apparently ancient, runs past it and points towards Britford, but is not evident to the north of the Ebble. The site has been thickly planted and it is impossible to conjecture what may have been the original plan of these earthworks, but Mr Sumner has called our attention to the apparent remains of a remarkable berm defence on the side facing Clearbury Ring.

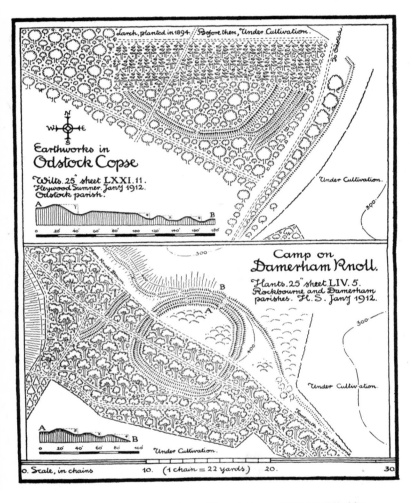

Top: Plan of the earthworks in Odstock Copse, Odstock, Wiltshire.
Bottom: Plan of the camp on Damerham Knoll, Hampshire.

far as Bokerly Dyke and the forests covering Dorsetshire. Eastwards of course the occupation extended to the old Wessex frontier already described.

Westwards there are on the downland ridges certain dykes, that seem as if they may at one time have prolonged the Bokerly line, e.g. Half-Mile Ditch on White Sheet Hill, the bank and ditch on Charlton Down, Tennerley Ditch, etc. Heywood Sumner, who closely examined all these, states that they resemble Bokerly Dyke superficially, and that the inner banks at Whitsbury and Hod Hill are very similar in appearance. General Pitt-Rivers' conclusion from his investigations of Bokerly Dyke is that it dates beyond doubt as late as the departure of the Romans from Britain, and he would assign it to a period not much earlier than A.D. 520. It has evidently been altered and reconstructed subsequently to its original construction and if we are correct in our conclusions that the Saxons held the strip of territory stretching up Rockbourne Valley and over Rockbourne Down, the road into Dorset over Martin Down would have lain open to them, had not some obstacle barred their way. The evidence suggests that all these fortifications were thrown up, or reconstructed, by the Britons as a defence against the advancing Saxon and without attempting to fix a precise date we should assign them to the period between the battle of Charford and the capture of Old Sarum, during which this district was debateable ground. The various dykes above mentioned may mark the western limit of the earliest Saxon advance into Cranborne Chase.

Excavations in Cranborne Chase, *Vol. III, p. 28.*

If Britford on the Avon (D.B. *Bretford* and *Bredford*), just below its junction with the Wylye and the modern town of Salisbury, means the "ford of the Britons," as some antiquaries consider, it marks another stage in the advance. But the derivation is uncertain. In any case, the occupation of the country south of the Ebble and Nadder valleys would open the way for a further advance up the Wylye valley, severing the communications between Old Sarum and the west and completing its isolation on every side but the north. The capture of Old Sarum in 552 carried forward the Wessex frontier to the edge of Salisbury Plain, or possibly to the line of Wansdyke, but the exact stages by which the boundary was pushed westwards to the forest of Selwood and the Frome valley must we fear remain uncertain. A knowledge of local topography and archaeological remains might throw a doubtful ray of light upon it, but there is no historical evidence remaining on which investigation could be based, such as has enabled us to unravel with comparative certainty the story of the advance between the battle of Charford and the capture of Old Sarum.

Four years later (556) another victory was won by Cynric and Ceawlin at Beranburh, which is admitted to be Barbury Hill, a camp of considerable size and strength on the Ridgeway, some six miles north-west of Marlborough, looking north from the edge of the downs. The Saxons had apparently by this time mastered the art of reducing fortified positions, as both here and at Old Sarum the British strongholds would appear to have been captured. This further success must have advanced the frontier to the Thames and the borders of Gloucestershire. Berkshire, if not already united to Wessex was probably absorbed peaceably after this battle, as it was now enveloped on the south and west by Wessex territory: and in 568 Ceawlin of Wessex won Surrey from Aethelberht of Kent at the battle of Wibbandun (Wimbledon).

In 571 Cuthwulf or Cutha, Ceawlin's brother, crossed the Thames, and after defeating the Brito-Welsh at Bedford, took four towns, and occupied the vale of Aylesbury. An advance westward, three years later, carried the kingdom of Wessex to the shores of the Severn by way of the eastern edge of what is now the county of Somerset.

There are remains of ancient dykes of unknown date and origin on Salisbury Plain between Old Sarum and Wansdyke and the date of the construction of Wansdyke is not determined. Gen. Pitt-Rivers considers it Roman or post-Roman, but as he himself points out, the name is conclusive evidence that the Saxons found it in existence and did not know who built it (Cranborne Chase, Vol. III, pp. 29, 30). In the course of excavations carried out by Mr and Mrs B. H. Cunnington in 1908-9 at Knap Hill camp, which lies about a mile south of Wansdyke and close to the Ridgeway, clear traces of a burnt Roman or Romano-British dwelling were found on a plateau under the eastern rampart. Within its enclosure, and 18 inches deep in surface accumulations, they found the blade of a sixth century Saxon sword, which may be a trace of this or the next stage of the advance ("Knap Hill Camp," by Mr and Mrs Cunnington, Wilts. Arch. and Nat. Hist. Magazine, *Vol. XXXVII).*

This advance, according to the *Anglo-Saxon Chronicle*, took place in 577, when Cuthwine and Ceawlin, kings of the West Saxons, "fought against the Britons and slew three kings, Commail, and Condidan, and Farinmail, at the place which is called Deorham, and took three cities from them, Gloucester, and Cirencester, and Bath."

So far as the written record goes, this conquest only touched the edge of Somerset, and the subsequent northward advance of the Saxons bears this out. In the absence of other evidence it may be taken that the new frontier followed on the north-east the line of the Roman road from Silchester to Cirencester and Gloucester, and on the south the line of the road from Marlborough to Bath, and thence by the Avon to the sea, the actual frontier to the south being marked by the Wansdyke, which after reaching the Avon seems to have followed a line nearly parallel with, and a few miles south of, the river.

The result of this acquisition of territory is important. It severed the land communications between the Britons of the country north of the Severn and those of Dyvnaint, and the campaigns against the Welsh from this time accordingly follow two lines. At the present time, apart from possible encroachments on the country between the Avon and the Mendips, for which there is nothing beyond theory, there was no atempt on the part of the West Saxons to extend their conquest toward the west , or to challenge the power of Dyvnaint. The northward advance was continued up the Severn valley in 584, Ceawlin taking many towns and much booty, but loosing his brother Cutha at the battle of Fethanleag. With this expedition the rapid advance made by Wessex in the thirty-two years following the capture of Old Sarum was brought to a close.

The exact line reached by this advance is not well defined, but Wessex had now reached a point at which she must of necessity meet with the growing expansions of the sister kingdoms.

and had acquired a line of frontier which was too far extended for her to hold. The history of the kingdom for a time is a record of recoil, and of internal trouble consequent on dynastic quarrels between the rival houses of Ceawlin and Cutha. The period is marked by the first alliance between English and Britons also. This was directed against Ceawlin, who was defeated at a place called "Woddesbeorg," or according to William of Malmesbury, at "Wodnesdic." This was in 591, and there is no doubt, from the statement of the *Chronicle* that Ceawlin was "expelled," that some of the newly won territory was lost, probably to the Britons. Ceawlin died in the year following this battle.

Ceolwulf of Wessex is stated to have "fought incessantly against the Angles, or the Welsh, or the Picts and Scots," but we have no details of the results of these wars. The next definite statement is in the year 607, when he fought against the South Saxons. In 614 his successor, Cynegils, fought a great battle with the Welsh at Beandun, or Bampton, on the borders of Oxfordshire and Berkshire, when over 2000 Welsh were slain. A battle of this magnitude, fought at such a point, shows how formidably the power of the Welsh in the Midlands must have pressed on Wessex since the battle of Fethanleag.

The success of Northumbria at Chester in 606, which cut off the Welsh of Strathclyde from the midland Britons, led to the rise of the northern kingdom, and in 617 Eadwine of Northumbria "ravaged all Britain and Kent." In 626, provoked by an attempt on the part of Cwichelm of Wessex to assassinate him, Eadwine "went against the West Saxons with an army and slew five kings and many of the people."

Two years later Mercia under Penda began to take the place held by Northumbria, and in 628 the joint kings of Wessex, Cwichelm and Cynegils, "fought against Penda at Cirencester, and afterwards came to an agreement." The nature of this agreement is not stated, but it is doubtful if it can have been to the advantage of Wessex. One result was probably the transfer of the kingdom of the Hwiccas (Gloucestershire) from Wessex to Mercia, which seems to have taken place about this time.

In the years 635-6 Christianity began to make itself felt in Wessex, and the two kings were baptised, both at Dorchester (Oxon.) though at different times. A short relapse into heathenism followed with the accession of Kenwealh, son of Cynegils, in 643, but he was driven from his kingdom by Penda of Mercia in 645, and converted, or reconverted during his three years' exile in East Anglia. The reasons for his restoration to the throne of Wessex are uncertain, but it was possibly the result of an agreement with Penda which would prevent an attack on the southern border of Mercia during a projected conflict with Northumbria. This conflict ended with the fall of Penda at the battle of Winwidfield in 655, and from that time forward Kenwealh owned no subjection to Mercia.

The first act of Kenwealh on his restoration was to build a monastery at Winchester, and to found a bishopric for his kingdom, Birinus "the Roman" and Agilbert "the Gaul" being the first two bishops.

The results of the long struggle with Wales, with Northumbria, and with Mercia during the fifty years which followed the battle of Fethanleag appear to have been the loss by Wessex of all the territory which she had gained since the battle of Deorham in 577. Whether by agreement with Mercia, which is probable, or for reasons due to the strength of the midland kingdom, no further advance of Wessex northward is on record. Yet she was still in the stage of growth and expansion, and acquisition of territory was still vital to her. The way was still open to the west, where the Britons of Dumnonia and of the land of the Durotriges still maintained their independence. A new stage of the advance of Wessex commences from the days of Kenwealh, in which the kingdom of Dyvnaint comes into prominence.

Chapter 3

The territory in which for upwards of a century after the battle of Deorham the Britons of the south-west maintained their independence, comprised the ancient Roman Province of Dumnonia, and the district inhabited by the Durotriges. The latter is practically represented by the modern county of Dorset, and for convenience we can use that name. It is not certain that Dorset ever actually formed part of the Roman Dumnonia so that it is possibly incorrect to include it in the kingdom of Dyvnaint which developed out of that province; but as the pressure from the eastward increased, Dorset and Dyvnaint must needs have been forced by the common peril to stand closely together, and for a time at least it is impossible to separate their history. It is certain that the strong natural and artificial defences which Dorset possessed enabled that district to hold out against the advance of Wessex until a comparatively late date.

The British province of Dumnonia under the Romans extended, according to Ptolemy, from Land's End to "Uxella," which represents the great estuary of the rivers under the Mendips at some point between the mouths of the Axe and Brue at the end of the range west of Weston-super-Mare. That it still extended at least as far as the line of the Mendips after the Roman occupation had come to an end, is shown by the charter quoted by William of Malmesbury, by which a king of Dumnonia granted the island of Inysvitryn to the abbot of Glastonbury. Although the authenticity of this charter is doubted, the question of its genuineness does not affect its testomony to a matter of geography or overlordship of the district, which a forger must needs state correctly enough for general acceptance. William of Malmesbury says the charter was so old that the name of the king could not be deciphered, but he accepts without hesitation the statement that a king of Dumnonia could make a grant of the land where Glastonbury now stands, his only doubt being who the king was. He was evidently quite aware that Dumnonia, or Dyvnaint, included Glastonbury in British times.

It is evident then that a great part of the modern Somerset lay in Dumnonia. There would be no need to go further into this question, but that, for the sake of disproving a somewhat secondary point which has some bearing on the site of the battle of Ethandun, it has been contended that the term Dumnonia included only the modern county of Devon. As a matter of fact the actual question is merely how late the term Dumnonia was used as a geographical term to denote the country west of the Mendips, which was once undeniably Dumnonia, and included in the late British kingdom of Dyvnaint, from which the shrunken modern Devon has its name.

There is evidence to prove that late in the Saxon period the term "Devon" or "Devonshire" (Dyvnaint-scir = the shire made out of old Dyvnaint as it were) covered a large part of West Somerset as we now have it defined, while the term Dumnonia (Domnonia or Damnonia) was used irrespective of county boundaries, whatever they were, in the same way precisely as Northumbria is applied generally to the district north of the Humber, or East Anglia to the district between the Thames and the Wash. We read, for instance, in the *Anglo-Saxon Chronicle* that in 988 "Watchet was ravaged, and Goda the Devonshire thane slain," while Florence of Worcester records that in 977 the Danes "entered the mouth of the river Severn, and ravaged sometimes Cornwall, sometimes North Wales, and then Watchet in Devonshire," Florence evidently using "Devonshire" as the equivalent for Dumnonia or Dyvnaint, as a recognised district even in his time. Hoveden records the cry raised at the battle of Sherston in 1016 in order to spread panic among the Wessex levies, in Latin verse, "Fugite Dorsetenses, Domnani, Wiltonienses," where the men of Somerset and Devon are included under the old geographic and

historic "Domnonia." Possibly this is for the sake
of the "hexameter," but the use of the wide term
must have conveyed some definite meaning to
readers, as the term Northumbria would to us
even at the present time.

It appears, therefore, that Florence of
Worcester, who died in 1118, still considered
Watchet as in "Devon." The earlier use of the
provincial name "Dumnonia" in the same wide
sense may be taken for granted. Up to the time
of Alfred, at least, the ancient boundaries of
Dyvnaint were of importance, and recognised for
administrative military purposes. Asser speaks of
the "western part of Selwood," meaning the
whole territory lying to the westward of that
ancient frontier, Somerset, Devon, and Cornwall.
The line of the Parrett, somewhat further west,
was another recognised boundary in the time of
Alfred, as it had been in the days of Kenwealh.
We read in the *A. S. Chronicle* that in the year
894 Alfred gathered his levies "from every town
east of the Parrett, as well west as east of
Selwood." The use under the year 878 of the
term "Devonshire in Wessex," taken with the
other evidence, points unmistakeably to the part
of old Dyvnaint included in the kingdom of
Wessex—the Dumnonia which Florence of
Worcester and the latter chroniclers still
understood as the land extending to the Parrett
estuary.

Somerset, Dorset, and Devon were grouped under one Earl as late as Edward the Confessor's time (Hen. of Hunt.).

We are so much accustomed to the well-defined
county boundaries which we know from our
maps, that it is hard to realise in the altered
conditions of to-day the physical necessities and
peculiarities which originally determined them. A
tract of fen, forest, or a range of hills means little
to us, but their importance in, say, the tenth
century, must be realised before it is possible to
gain any clear idea of the early history of the
country. It comes as a surprise to most people to
find that across such a comparatively small river
as the Parrett the actual dialect and physique of
the villagers alter—the Devon type, still half

The dialect of the
Quantock district was
the subject of a
special journey and
study by Prince L. L.
Bonaparte in 1875.

Celtic, on the west, and a stone's cast across the
water eastward, the Saxon Wessex people and
talk. The river and its fens, which are of little or
no account now, were once practically
impassable save by a journey not lightly to be
undertaken. It is the same with the hills, and a
tract of forest was a bar through which even the
Romans shrank from driving their roads, if it
could be avoided.

Bearing these points in mind, it is quite possible
to recognise what were of necessity some of the
ancient frontier lines as existing between Saxon
and Welsh after the battle of Charford. The later
line, decided after the Saxons had won their way
from sea to sea by the great victory of Deorham,
is not hard to follow in the same way.

This frontier must have followed pretty closely
the boundaries of Somerset and Dorset as we
know them, and they result from it. Starting
from the mouth of the Hampshire Avon on the
shores of the English Channel, we find that to
the west of that river there stretched a belt of
woodland, the remains of which are still to be
seen in Holt Forest, guarding the present county
of Dorset from eastward attack, and backed by
various camps placed on commanding strategic
positions. Further north another forest district,
now represented by Cranborne Chase stretched
along the Dorset border between that county and
Wiltshire to the Frome valley. The gap between
these two woodlands was covered, as General
Pitt-Rivers has shown, by the entrenchment now
known as Bokerly Dyke. Among the principal
camps guarding the line of the Stour south of
Holt Forest are Dudsbury, close to the river just
beyond the Hampshire border, Badbury Rings,
Buzbury, Hod Hill, and Hambledon Hill.

"Excavations in
Bokerly and
Wansdyke" (Vol. III
of Excavations in
Cranborne Chase).

While the forests and these camps covered the
county on the landward side, the only point east
of Weymouth where it was easily accessible from
the sea is Poole Harbour, and it is almost certain
that this was defended by fortifications dating
from Roman times. The present walls of

Wareham at the head of the inlet are said by Allcroft to be mainly Norman and Cromwellian, but the frequent discovery of Roman remains here, the general Roman plan of the town, and the fact that an important Roman road led directly to the shore of the haven in the neighbourhood of Hamworthy are evidence enough that the Romans did not leave the place undefended, the later walls probably covering their work. In any case, the inlet is flanked by Badbury Rings and the natural fastness of Purbeck, while the remains of lesser camps and other lines of earthwork on the heaths in the neighbourhood show that there was here no actual open door to invaders. The walls of Wareham were strong enough in the time of Alfred to be held against him by the Danes in 877, whatever later modifications may have taken place. Landings in Weymouth Bay would be useless, owing to the proximity of the Ridgeway heights, and the danger of attack from Maiden Castle or Dorchester; and later Danish landings at Charmouth were not successful, so far as penetration inland is concerned.

We do not, of course, so much as suggest that the earthworks which we refer to as strengthening this frontier were constructed at this period for the purpose of limiting the Saxon advance. With the exception of Bokerly Dyke, most of them, are undoubtedly older than the Roman period. They were therefore in existence when the Saxons landed and must have served to render the defenders well able to offer a better and more organised, and subsequently effective, resistance. That they were utilised at this period by the Britons is certain, and in some cases apparently were restored or readapted for the emergency. The entrenchment known as Lydsbury Rings which occupies the north-west angle of the strong camp already mentioned on Hod Hill is in all probability, such an adaption of an ancient work by the "Romanised Britons at a date posterior to the departure of the Romans."

Earthwork of England, p. 389.

Ancient Dorset, *Chas. Warne, pp. 180-4;* Roman Roads in Britain, *T. Codrington* p. 312.

Earthwork of England, pp. 361-7. *Mr Sumner, however, who has examined and planned the camp, considers that the inner entrenchment is undoubted Roman work.*

Camps were not only held, but were in some cases taken by the invaders. The British story of the siege of the "Mons Badonicus," wherever that may have been, is another testimony to the fact. The story may be a myth, but it at least proves that it was a known thing that such a siege of a camp might occur. We have already referred to the assignment of the work at Bokerly Dyke by Gen. Pitt-Rivers to post-Roman times, and its resemblance by other earthworks in the neighbourhood.

Altogether, when the natural and artificial barriers to an advance on Dorset are considered, it is not very surprising that there is no record of their being successfully penetrated by the Saxons. The conquest of Dorset is not written. The absorption of the county into Wessex must be inferred from administrative details.

Turning to the Somerset continuation of the frontier, we find the northern woodland barrier continued between that county and Wilts. by Selwood Forest, which filled the whole of the Frome valley up to the northern Avon. Thence the original boundary northward to the Severn was marked by the Wansdyke. Between this line and the Mendips the country is comparatively open, and the next defensible line to the west is that of the fenlands and rivers immediately west of the Mendip range.

The physical characteristics of this district west of the Mendips had a very marked influence on the position held by Somerset in the warfare of early times—a position which has been hardly recognised. For centuries the nature of the country rendered West Somerset the battle-ground between Wessex and the West Welsh, and the struggle between the two races for the mastery of the West of England was fought out across this march. The district reverted to a frontier position again during the struggle between Alfred and the Danes who had made themselves masters of the rest of Wessex to the eastward, and even so late as the Parliamentary wars and Sedgmoor

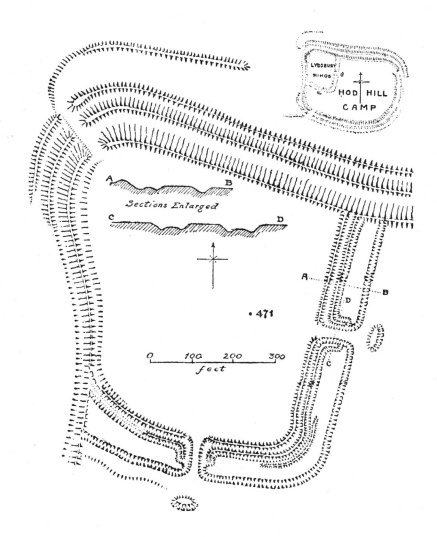

Plan and sections of the earthworks on Hod Hill, Dorset.

it was debateable ground.

The general appearance of the country has been profoundly modified since the tenth century. But it is of course quite possible to reconstruct the conditions which prevailed in Saxon days. These conditions remained unaltered until a far later period, for one may date the general commencement of modern changes to the drainage, enclosure, and extension of cultivation of the time of Charles II.

The main existing changes depend on the felling and disappearance of ancient forests, and the encroachment of land on expanses of water either by silting of river and coast lines, or by modern drainage. This latter feature is particularly evident in North Somerset, where there are large tracts of land, extending from the coast inland along the courses of the rivers debouching into the Severn sea, which are even now hardly above high water level, and are still subject to periodic inundations which to a very great extent reproduce temporarily the ancient appearance of the country.

These low-lying levels, many of which are peat moors, are comparatively narrow, and are bounded in every direction but that of the sea line by ranges of hills of varying but generally abrupt and imposing height, to the base of which the fens extend. It may be said that the campaigning in this district depended for its progress and result on the sudden transition from the bold ridges of hill along its margin to sodden and mere intersected levels at their feet in every direction.

This chain of encircling hills can be practically defined by a line drawn from Weston-super-Mare along the Mendips to Wells: thence by the High Ham and other lesser ranges round Somerton and Ilchester to South Petherton and Ilminster, whence a line drawn through Taunton northwards leads along the eastern foothills of the Quantock range to the small, ancient port and ford on the Parrett, almost at its mouth, at

Combwich.

Almost midway in the tract of country thus marked out, the lesser range of the Polden Hills, running from Street in a north-westerly direction nearly parallel with the Mendips, to within a few miles of the common mouth of the Parrett and Brue rivers, cuts the fenland into two well-defined districts, the one including the levels of the Parrett, Tone, and Cary rivers, and the other those of the Brue and Axe.

The least extensive of these two divisions is that which lies between the Mendip and Polden Hills along the courses of the two last-named rivers. The Axe skirts the base of the Mendips and reaches the sea to the eastward of Brean Down, between that promontory and Weston, and the Brue runs from Glastonbury roughly midway between the two ranges to join the Parrett at its mouth. The marked eminence of Brent Knoll at the estuary, and the long ridge between the two rivers, on which Wedmore stands, are the only elevated points of any size in these fens, most of which are of deep peat. The larger division comprises the fenlands of the Parrett and Cary from the sea to Langport and Somerton, and of the Tone from its junction with the Parrett at Borough Bridge to Taunton. Up to the time of its diversion for drainage purposes at a comparatively late date, the Cary joined the Parrett almost immediately above the confluence of the two large rivers. Its present course is that of the "King's Sedgmoor drain," parallel with the Polden Hills and entering the Parrett at their sudden fall to the level at Downend, about three miles below Bridgwater.

The only elevated point of land on the left bank of the rivers at their confluence is the low Isle of Athelney. On the opposite bank, just below their junction, is another patch of high ground, crowned with the striking terraced fort of Borough Bridge. From near this point a chain of narrow but well-marked elevations runs roughly midway between the Parrett and the

Polden Hills to where they converge at Bridgwater.

The villages occupying these ridges of higher land still bear names which indicate that at one time they stood on actual islands, that nearest to Borough Bridge being Othery, and the rest in order seaward, Middlezoy, Westonzoyland and Chedzoy, a wider stretch of level separating Chedzoy from the other three villages, which though isolated from each other by fen are included under the one name of "Sowi" in Domesday Book. Chedzoy itself is the nearest of these "Islands" both to river and hills, lying just above their closest approximation at Bridgwater. A spur of the Poldens, Pendon Hill, behind which lies Stawell village, reduces the stretch of marsh between island and higher ground to a width of about half a mile, at this point, where the total width of the levels between the Poldens and the riverward slopes of the Quantock foothills is not more than three miles.

From Borough Bridge to Bridgwater on one side and the Poldens on the other the present road through the marshes follows the line of this chain of islands, and it is evident that any trackway between these points must from time immemorial have taken the same course.

The height of these North Somerset peat moors, marshes, and actual fenlands hardly varies from an average seventeen feet above mean sea level from the sea to Somerton, Langport, and Taunton in one division, and to Glastonbury in the other. It is on record that the tide flowed in historic times up the Brue to Glastonbury, and at present its influence is felt at a point but a mile or two below. Up the Tone, it now reaches Creech St Michael, seven miles above Borough Bridge and just below Taunton, while it is still a practical aid to navigation up the Parrett from Bridgwater to Langport, which lies some six or seven miles beyond Borough Bridge. Barges of considerable size and draught when loaded are still taken up thither on every spring tide, and

the Danish "keels" of Alfred's time would therefore have had no difficulty in penetrating at least
so far inland. At these points of highest tide
influence the height of the marshes above mean
sea level is about twenty feet, while at different
places along the lower reaches of the rivers their
elevation may be as little as fourteen feet, or
even less.

These tracts of lower level evidently mark the
positions of ancient depressions which must have
held standing water until the days of modern
drainage and river embankment. To how late a
period some of these lakes actually remained is
proved by the fact that in Elizabethan times the
now drained lake at Meare on the course of the
Brue, just below Glastonbury, was still five miles
in circuit, as stated by Camden. Round Athelney
itself we find such names as Horlake, Eastlake,
Southlake, and Saltmoor, which no doubt in
Alfred's time, and almost certainly until as late
the corresponding depression at Meare, belonged
to actual lakes which, like the Norfolk Broads,
were connected with the main channel of the
river. That this was the fact is borne out by
Asser's description of Athelney at the time of the
founding by Alfred of the monastery there, as "a
spot so surrounded in all directions by waters
that save for one bridge there was no access to it
except by boat."

Between the islands and the Polden Hills similar
conditions of mere and morass are indicated by
the names of Greylake and Sedgmoor, the latter
having been finally reclaimed in quite recent
times.

The comparative depth of water in these meres
and the condition of the morasses in early days
must have been dependent to some extent on the
rise of the tides in the upper reaches of the rivers.
These tides are peculiar, and perhaps hardly to be
realised by those who are used to the equable rise
and fall which is the rule elsewhere, the duration
of flood and ebb being exceedingly short and the
current rapid.

The present very tortuous channel of the Parrett seems to have shifted little in historic times, though of course the embankments which now confine the rising waters to that channel may have caused some deepening, while at the same time they have greatly decreased the extent of periodically flooded foreshore in the lower reaches. Below Bridgwater, at about Downend, the river narrows suddenly, and at this point at spring tides the flood gathers itself into a head or "bore," which reaches Bridgwater about an hour and three-quarters before high water, and passing upwards thence is felt as far as Langport. Previous to the arrival of this tidal wave, the land water only has been passing down the deep, narrow channel, and consequently from the first of the flood to its turn the duration of the upward flow is barely two hours, in which short period the channel has filled by an additional 16 to 21 feet of water. The ebb tide lasts no longer, and for the remaining eight hours before the next flood is due the land water only occupies the channel.

The difference in rise at Bridwater between lowest neap and highest spring tides is some fifteen feet, the least rise being about four feet. During the neap tides, therefore, the fenlands, in the days when the land water had no free access to the rivers, must have dried appreciably by natural soakage into the channels. But at spring tides the expanses of mere and sodden morass would be immensely extended by the cessation of this outflow, and by actual inundation at high water. Even in the memory of man part of Sedgmoor has been practically impassable at these periods, and still when a heavy rainfall or melting snow increases the supply of land water from the hills, the effect of this temporary stoppage of the drainage by the tidal rise is severely felt, the marshes on either side of the Poldens remaining under water for periods of weeks before the accumulation can, even under modern conditions, be discharged.

The other lost feature of Saxon England which must be borne in mind is the far greater extent of forest and woodland beyond that at present remaining. Even in these marsh lands the higher ground must have been thickly covered with alder and willow, and possibly in places with the larger forest trees, whose remains are still preserved in the peat. Roger of Wendover tells us that Athelney was "girded in with fen on every side, and not to be come at, save by boat. Thereon is all dense alder brake, full of stags and goats and such creatures, and in the midst one bit of open ground, scarce two acres."

Inland the marshes extended to the great forest of Selwood, while the eastward slopes of the Quantock and Polden hills, which fall gradually to the level, were also densely wooded. The western faces of these two ranges are comparatively precipitous, and, except in the deep combes, may have been almost as open as at present. The actual ridge of the Poldens is indeed so narrow that in places the present high road, on the line of an ancient trackway, occupies its whole width, so that in Saxon times it ran between dense forest on the east, and an almost vertical fall on the west.

It is difficult to identify with any certainty the roads which existed in this district in Saxon times beyond the known Roman highways; but they must have been few. Of ancient roads, Roman or other, besides that along the Poldens just mentioned, running from Street and beyond to the estuaries, another way, possibly Romanised British, branched from this road to Taunton, *via* Bridgwater, along the fenward ridge of the Quantocks through North Petherton. The present name of Bridgwater does not however postulate a bridge there in early days. The name in pre-Norman times was simply "Burgh," which was amplified to Burgh-Walters when it came into the possession of Walter de Douay at the conquest, and the present local pronunciation "Burge-water," with the accent on the

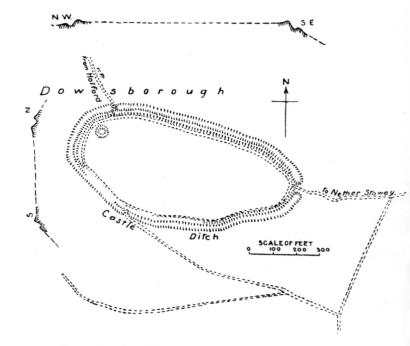

Plan and section of Dowsborough on the Quantocks.

From the existence of this trackway we may assume that some means of crossing the river at this point was available at this early date; but we do not overlook the possibility of changes in the river channel and the certainly greater width of the lower waters of the Parrett before it was embanked.

penultimate, preserves this derivation.

The well-known Roman Fosseway running through the district south of the Tone and Parrett fenland must also be mentioned as one of the certainly existing roads of Saxon times. The road along the Poldens was apparently a branch from this main highway to the port of Uxella.

An ancient British trackway can still be traced from the extremity of the Polden Hills to the tidal ford of the Parrett at Combwich, five miles in a direct line below Bridgwater, and thence to the great early camp of Danesborough, or Dowsborough on the Quantocks, and a few other unimportant subsidiary tracks are still known in the Quantock district.

It is possible that here and there the line of modern roads across the fenland may follow ancient trackways which led from point to point by way of the more solid patches of land, as in the case of the already mentioned road through the islands. The discovery of an ancient timbered or "corduroy" road in the Brue marshes, marked in the ordnance maps as "the Abbot's way" and presumably a Pilgrim's road to Glastonbury from a landing place on the Parrett, points to the difficulty which must have been found in making paths across the peat moors. Here and there also a raised causeway is known to be of very ancient date.

The main highway through Somerset from the east was the Fosseway, which enters the county at Bath, and crosses it to its extreme southern point near Chard, whence it passes on to Exeter and the further west. From Bath as far as the Mendips, which it crosses near Shepton Mallet, this road ran through comparatively open country; but thence its course westward lay between the outskirts of Selwood, and the fenlands of the lower levels. The passage of the road in this section would be dangerous if either the forest or the fen was held by a hostile force well acquainted with their intricacies.

Each of the main trackways leading from the marshlands westward is guarded on the high land of the Dumnonian side by specially strong camps, which should be specified. The Fosseway itself was commanded by the great Roman fortress of Hamdon Hill; and the important trade route inland from Watchet between the Quantock and Brendon Hills was guarded by the strong fortified position at Norton Fitzwarren. The westward road which crosses the Parrett at Combwich by the tidal ford is safeguarded by the ancient stone-walled fort in Cannington Park; and the difficult crossing further south at what is now Bridgwater had its Roman entrenchments. Both of these roads were further guarded by the Quantock camps at some point or other of their line.

Apparently the tidal ford is formed by a ledge of the lias rock which crosses the river from the hill above Combwich, and connects this high ground with the foot of the Poldens. The ancient trackway would follow this line, even in pre-embankment times, across the estuarine levels.

Dorset also is traversed by a great Roman highway, the "Via Iceniana" or "Icknield Street," which ran south-westward from Old Sarum to Badbury Rings, and thence turned westward to pass through Dorchester into Devon, joining the Fosseway not far from Axmouth. A lesser Roman road crossed the county in an almost north and south direction from Ilchester to Dorchester, and thence to Weymouth.

Icknield Street, the natural line of march by which invaders from the eastward would be looked for, is barred at its entrance into Dorset by the great earthwork known as Bokerly Dyke, which crosses it. The fosse of this work, the bottom of which is even now some fifty feet below the crest of the vallum, faces north. It is about four miles in length, and completely spans the gap between the northern and southern forest tracts of the frontier, through which line of open country the Romans as usual took their roadway. There is no doubt that the strength of this dyke had a marked influence in deflecting the line of Saxon advance.

However strong a frontier may be either by nature or art, or as in this case by both, it is obvious that its defences are useless without men to defend them. It is however certain that in early times the population of Somerset and Dorset was, even apart from the towns, dense in comparison to what it was at the beginning of the century. In Somerset the line of the Fosseway was set with Roman and Romano-British villas and villages between the military stations, and similar settlements are found even on the higher grounds of the marshes. The lead mines of the Mendips, and possibly the copper of the Quantocks, were actively worked, and there is hardly a district in Somerset, however remote, where Roman traces have not been found.

In Dorset there remain evidences of a rural population which was even more numerous. Every hillside bears the scars of ancient cultivation, and known British village sites are

Dr Colley March has suggested to us that Bokerly Dyke and other earthworks across the line of a road, or trackway, were probably barriers at which tolls were collected from cattle-drovers and other wayfarers. That this theory may account for some works of the kind is possible and it is possible that the reconstructed Bokerly Dyke may have replaced such a work. But as regards the dyke in its present form, its vast size and great extent, reaching as it does over a mile to the west and upwards of two miles to the east of the Roman road, are sufficient in our view to put any such theory out of court.

plentiful, while the number of tumuli is almost beyond reckoning. Dorchester itself, with its walls, and amphitheatre of the regular continental type, was the undoubted centre of a populous district in Roman and Romano-British times, as the older fortress of Maiden Castle, a mile or two further south-west, must have been in its day.

Putting all the evidence together it is clear that the south-west portion of England was at the time of the coming of the West Saxons one of the strongest and best organised districts opposed to them. The kingdom of Dyvnaint still occupied an important position two hundred years later than Cerdic, although after the battle of Deorham it had been cut off from communication by land with the Welsh kingdoms beyond the Severn. In spite of this comparative isolation Dyvnaint seems to have maintained close relations with South Wales, and even with the Britons of Armorica, who are stated by Welsh chroniclers to have sent contingents to aid during the struggle with the Saxons. At times Dyvnaint seems to have been able to claim some sort of overlordship among the Welsh kingdoms, if not to have actually exercised it. There was no serious attempt to conquer the district west of the frontier which we have described until the time of Kenwealh, 133 years after the battle of Deorham.

Chapter 4

It is doubtful whether the frontier between Wessex and Dyvnaint changed materially during the seventy-five years which followed the battle of Deorham, though in the long peace it is by no means impossible that some quiet creeping forward of Saxon settlers may have occurred here and there, without opposition, in unoccupied or forest land. South-east of Bath heathen burials or other remains of Anglo-Saxon heathendom have been recorded from the area between the line of the Avon and Wansdyke, and the Mendips, and no place-names reminiscent of heathenism are to be found there. It seems hardly possible that these could be entirely absent if the West Saxons had occupied the country for the seventy or eighty years which elapsed between the battle of Deorham and their conversion to Christianity. South-east of Bath the British frontier extended to the Avon, at least until the year 652, when the *Chronicle* says that Kenwealh fought at Bradford-on-Avon. From the position of the next recorded hostilities we infer that the result of this fighting was to push back the British from, roughly speaking, the line of the Avon to the Mendips. An ancient road, doubtfully Roman, ran from Old Sarum across the present Wiltshire boundary near Whitesheet Castle, and thence along the Mendips, and, for argument's sake, we assume that the frontier followed this line after leaving the natural boundary of the Mendip range.

Six years after the fight at Bradford-on-Avon we read in the *Chronicle* that Kenwealh fought with the Welsh at Peonna, and drove them to Pedridan (A.D. 658). Peonna is generally supposed to be in the neighbourhood of Penselwood (*Penna* in Domesday), where, beside the Pen Pits, we find the place-name Penridge still existing. Freeman says, in his *Old English History*, "Peonna is certainly one of our Pens in Somerset," and while not rejecting Penselwood, he suggests as alternatives Pen Hill, a point of Mendip, or Pen or Ben Knoll, close to Wells. The late Mr Kerslake, however, argued in favour of the identification of Peonna with Poyntington (D.B. *Ponditona*), near Sherborne, primarily on the ground that the Saxons would not have represented the short *e* in Pen by the dipthong *eo*. He pointed out that this position was well suited for the scene of an attempt by the Britons to check a Saxon force advancing from the direction of Gillingham, which he considered on philological grounds to represent an advanced Saxon post. He points in addition to the reported grant by Kenwealh of a hundred hides at Lanprobi to Sherborne Abbey as suggesting that he founded the abbey in commemoration of the victory, while there are some slight grounds for supposing that Lanprobi was also in the neighbourhood. He mentions traces of earthworks which might be the relics of the struggle, and says that the beaten force would naturally fly in the direction of the junction of the Ivel and Parrett at Langport.

It would rather seem that the Welsh, if beaten near Sherborne, would have fled along the Roman road leading to Dorchester, while Pedridan undoubtedly means the Parrett or some point upon its course; but the victory at either Peonna would leave the way open for an advance on the Dorset border, which might help to account for the delay of twelve years which elapsed between the battle and the date when Glastonbury appears to have first come under the rule of Kenwealh, though we give below other reasons which explain this delay.

On the whole, we see no reason for rejecting the general opinion in favour of Penselwood. The site lies at the point where the boundaries of modern Wilts, Dorset and Somerset meet, and where in those days Saxon Wilts drove in the point of its wedge between Somerset and Dorset. A Roman or pre-Roman way from Old Sarum to Ilchester ran past the spot, and an advance from the heart of Wessex across the line won by the fighting at Bradford-on-Avon must have taken

"The Welsh in Dorset," by T. Kerslake (Proceedings of the Dorset Field Club, *Vol. III, p. 81)* and *"The First West Saxon Penetration into Somerset"* (Proceedings of the Somerset Archaeological Society, *1876, Vol. XXII, pp. 61-70). See also "Camelot," by the late Rev. J. A. Bennett, F.S.A., in the* Proceedings *of the latter society, Vol. XXXVI, 1890, p. 16. Other suggested sites are Pen near Gillingham (*ib.*), and Pen Mill and Pen Hill near Yeovil (ib. Vol. XXX, p. 146).*

this direction; while the Welsh, if defeated by such an advance, would inevitably have been forced back towards the River Parrett. The acknowledged result of the defeat of the British at Peonna is the advance of the Wessex frontier from the line mentioned to Pedridan: but it is probable that the brief entry in the *Chronicle* sums up the results of a campaign rather than of a single battle.

Pedridan, as we have said, represents the river Parrett or some point on its course. The statement that Kenwealh drove the Welsh to Pedridan is usually, and loosely, taken to mean that the Saxons became masters of all the land lying between the Mendips and the river; but this view fails to recognise the fact that in the seventh century, and indeed, until far later, that country was covered by the vast estuary of the confluence of the rivers Parrett, Brue and Axe, which could hardly be named as a position on the Parrett itself.

There are three places whose names are based on that of the river—Puriton, North Petherton, and South Petherton—which must be considered. The second of these lies on the north of the Parrett, at a point where a Saxon crossing would be impossible, and may be dismissed as in the highest degree unlikely as the point meant. The first-named lies at the end of the Polden ridge, within sight of the present mouth of the Parrett, and not far from the old tidal crossing of the river at Combwich. An ancient track, probably made use of by the Romans, branched from the Fosseway, and ran down the length of the Poldens from Street to this crossing. Puriton, which according to Professor Boyd Dawkins preserves the old British form of the river-name "Peryddon," marks the point at which the river becomes estuarine.

That the beaten Welsh should have taken a line of flight which would bring them to a point where the tidal waters are still impassable except at one spot at the lowest spring-tides is almost

This and the road along the Mendips, already mentioned, are usually said to be Roman. Professor Haverfield, however, says that the evidence on the point is scanty (Victoria County History of Somerset, Vol. 1, pp. 206, 350).

inconceivable; their position would be as hopeless as that of the beaten Danes at the same point after Ethandun. Moreover, for reasons which we give below, it is almost certain that the Polden district was not won by the Saxons till after the time of Kenwealh.

A line of flight must needs be evident and easy, and should lead to some possible rallying-place. The evident line of retreat for the British, defeated at Penselwood, is along the road to Ilchester and thence along the Fosseway itself. Taking this route, the fugitives would skirt the marshlands until they came to Cadbury Castle, Ilchester and other rallying points, and would reach the Parrett at the point where the great road crossed it at South Petherton. Here the way was open for escape in various directions, either still along the Fosseway, covered by the Romano-British fortress on Hamdon Hill, in a south-westerly direction, or north-west to the British stronghold at Norton Fitzwarren, at the head of the valley which leads to the sea at Watchet between the Brendon and Quantock Hills. Westward also the way was open into the Blackdown Hills. At South Petherton (in Domesday, "Sut-Petret, Sut-Peretona") the great fenland of the Parrett practically reaches its farthest inland point, and the river-name of the place seems to mark the change from upland to fen waters, as the name of Puriton marks the head of the estuarine waters at its mouth.

We conclude therefore that the Parrett in the neighbourhood of South Petherton formed the limit of this advance of Wessex under Kenwealh. Whether he penetrated into Dorset to any extent is uncertain; but we may assume that the frontier of the new territory to the south-east followed the present county boundary, though it possibly included Sherborne. To the north-east the line of of the marshlands, roughly followed by the Fosseway itself, must have marked the limit to which the Wessex power extended. The frontier was literally carried forward "to the Parrett" on

As pointed out in the Antiquary of November, 1910, p. 437, in a review of The Story of the Battle of Edington, the theory of the Rev. W. Greswell, that Kenwealh drove the Welsh along the Poldens to the mouth of the Parrett, is founded on a mistaken reading of the Anglo-Saxon Chronicle. The entry under the year 658 does not mention "Pedridan Mupan," but only "Pedridan." Mr Greswell has apparently read in "Mupan" from the record of Bishop Ealhstan's victory over the Danes at "Pedridan Mupan" in 845.

In the same way the source of the Parrett on the Dorset border, near Crewkerne, is marked by the names of North and South Perrott. The persistence of these Celtic place names from its source to its mouth marks the long space of time during which the river was the frontier line between Saxon and West Welsh. It is worth notice that wherever the ancient Celtic "Avon" occurs as a river name, at least in Wessex, if not elsewhere, the line of "the water" has been the frontier for a long period.

its upper waters.

Here the advance of Wessex westward halted for a time. Kenwealh had made an attempt to recover the lost possessions of Wessex in the Severn valley from Mercia, weakened as she was by the death of Penda at the defeat at Winwidfield. At Easter in 661 he pushed as far as Shropshire, but met with what must have been a crushing defeat at Posentesbyrig (Pontesbury), at the hands of Wulfhere, Penda's son, a warrior no less redoubtable than his father, who followed up his victory. Wessex was ravaged as far south as Ashdown, Wulfhere eventually making himself master of Surrey, Sussex, and the Isle of Wight. This last, which was a Wessex possession, he gave to his ally, Ethelwalch of Sussex, as well as, according to Bede, the province of the Meonwaras, comprising a large part of Wessex east of Southampton Water. Both these districts, according to the same author, had been originally settled by Jutes. At this time Wulfhere was the undisputed lord of the Midlands from the Welsh border to the East Anglian shore, and of the whole south-east and part of the south of England, penning Wessex back into her earlier dominion. She could have had little left but the lands westward of a line from about Reading to Southampton Water. This disaster is fully sufficient to account for the slow progress which appears to have been made in the settlement of the newly won lands beyond the Mendips. It was apparently not until the year 670, twelve years after the battle of Peonna, that Glastonbury passed into the hands of Kenwealh, only two years before his death.

With regard to the events of this period and of the two succeeding reigns, a fresh source of information is available in the documents relating to the Abbey of Glastonbury, where records of gifts to the abbey by the earlier Saxon kings are frequent from this time forward. We believe that important details of the progress of Wessex westward may be recovered from certain entries

Professor Oman considers that the gift of the province of the Meonwaras included territory west of Southampton Water as well, but this is doubtful. England before the Norman Conquest, p. 287.

in early charters of the abbey, whose historical value has not hitherto been recognised, so far as we are aware, by any writer on the early history of Somerset before the Norman Conquest.

We ought to say at once that we quite recognise the doubts which have been thrown on the genuine nature of these early Glastonbury charters, especially as regards the famous one which William of Malmesbury professed to have seen, recording the grant of Inysvitryn to the "old church" by an unnamed King of Dumnonia in A.D. 601. Bishop Stubbs, while sharing in these doubts, says with regard to the early history of the abbey under the Saxon kings:

If we are right as to this, the view that Wessex was so weakened by the war with Wulfhere that no permanent advance westward was made before the time of Ine (see for instance England before the Norman Conquest, pp. 286, 8, 9) must undergo revision.

> Its existence as a monasterium is proved by an incontrovertible authority, the Letters of St Boniface, and the Life of the same great West Saxon saint, written by his countryman and disciple, St Willibald . . and the certainty of this much of the early history gives probability to many of the charters, the place of which in the Glastonbury Cartulary would afford by itself very little presumption of their credibility.

Memorials of St. Dunstan, *edited by W. Stubbs, Rolls Series, 1874, pp. lxxxii, lxxxiii.*

We ourselves have no hesitation in accepting the records of the grants made under Kings Kenwealh and Kentwine as at any rate embodying the trustworthy tradition of the abbey, even if they are not taken from authentic charters.

The historians of that abbey tell us that in the year 670, Kenwealh gave Ferramere, Westhei, and Godenei, also Beokerie, Martinseye, and Andreyseye, to Berhtwald, Abbot of Glastonbury. We are further told that this Berhtwald was the first Englishman who became Abbot of Glastonbury, and that the lands in question belonged to its ancient possessions in British times, but had been seized by the heathen Saxons, and were now restored after they were converted. This latter statement is probably not quite accurate. Kenwealh was converted, or reconverted, to Christianity while in exile in East Anglia, and was baptised in 646, six years before the victory at Bradford, and twelve years before the battle at Peonna. It seems, therefore,

Cf. William of Malmesbury, De Antiquitate Glastoniensis Ecclesia, ed. Hearne (Oxford 1727), and John of Glastonbury, Chronica sive Historia de Rebus Glastoniensibus, ed. Hearne (Oxford 1726).

The ruins of Glastonbury Abbey in Somerset.

doubtful whether the Saxon kings can have seized any of the abbey lands in their heathen days. There may have been, however, a gradual encroachment by independent settlers, in the course of which the abbey was despoiled of some of its possessions, reaching at length a point when British resentment culminated in the war which resulted in the disaster at Bradford.

This is highly probable, as William of Malmesbury says that the Britons were the aggressors at the battle of Peonna, six years later than that of Bradford. We have no details of the constant fighting which occurred between the West Saxons and the Welsh in and after the reign of Ceolwulf (597 to 611), but it may have taken place in this district and led up to the greater contests.

There is no reason to doubt that a religious foundation existed at Glastonbury in British times, and that this foundation, however much it may have suffered while the district in which it lay was a marchland between Briton and Saxon, maintained a practically unbroken existence into the Saxon period. We read these grants of Kenwealh to mean that, as soon as he became master of the site of Glastonbury, he confirmed the abbey in the possession of its ancient domains so far as they had passed under his rule, or restored them to it, where they had been lost by Saxon encroachment.

These grants to Abbot Berhtwald therefore indicate more or less exactly the limits of Kenwealh's dominion in the marshlands beyond the Mendips. The lands referred to lie in the immediate neighbourhood of the abbey, and within the boundary of the hundred known later as Glastonbury Twelve Hides. Ferramere is the present Meare, some two miles from Glastonbury, and Westhey and Godney lie on either side of it. Becary is close to Glastonbury, between it and the Brue, and had on it a chapel of St Bridget. Andreyseye is now known as Nyland Hill, an isolated rise between Wedmore and the Mendips.

The site of Martinseye alone seems doubtful, but it should probably be looked for under the Mendips, to the north of Andreyseye.

No possessions to the south of the Isle of Avalon are included in the grants made by Kenwealh, and it seems doubtful whether even the approaches from the direction of the Fosseway were secured in his reign. We have no evidence that they were Saxon until the time of Kentwine, the brother of Kentwine, the brother of Kenwealh, who succeeded him after a brief interval, and continued the war with the West Welsh. The island of Wedmore, however, lying north of Avalon, and directly between Andreyseye or Nyland and the grants at Meare, must certainly have been under the dominion of Kenwealh, though in this case also direct evidence of its being in Saxon hands is lacking until the reign of Kentwine, when Glastonbury documents record that Bishop Wilfrid gave to the abbey "the Island of Wedmore, 70 hides, which King Kentwine had given him." This may indicate that it was from the slopes of the Mendips to the north-east that Kenwealh reached Glastonbury, by way of Nyland and Wedmore, rather than from the side of the Fosseway.

The embankment and reclamation of the Brue and its marshes was commenced by Dunstan during his abbacy, but was not in any sense complete until the reign of Richard II.

But according to Glastonbury records, the domains of the abbey in British times had included Brent and its marshes, lying to the north-west between the mouths of the Axe and Brue, and Polden. It is clear from later evidence that this later term indicated the whole range of the Polden Hills, which separate the fens of the Brue from those of the Parrett. According to the story, these territories had been given to the abbey by King Arthur. Had Kenwealh's conquest extended over the whole of the marshlands down to the Parrett and the sea in this direction, it is reasonable to suppose that besides the territories named he would have given or restored to the abbey Brent and Polden also. They are not named, however, before the time of King Ine, when they appear in the charters in which the king, besides making fresh grants, confirmed the abbey in the possession of the gifts of previous kings.

We conclude, accordingly, that the conquest of the marshlands by Kenwealh was practically confined to Wedmore and the other island sites which he gave to Glastonbury, and we can make a fair approximation to the frontier between Wessex and West Wales which was the result of the battle at Peonna, the more certainly that in the seventh century a tract of fenland was a far more formidable barrier that it might seem at the present day.

The line followed the course of the Axe as far as Wedmore, whence it would follow the course of the Brue to Glastonbury, and thence to the Fosseway, which, with the adjacent fenlands, formed the new frontier as far as South Petherton, thence taking a line to the south-east which may have included Sherborne, either immediately after the battle or in the course of some years of steady advance. How far to the southward the frontier may have followed the Parrett we have no means of judging.

Chapter 5

Kenwealh died in 672, and was succeeded by his queen, Seaxburh. She held the throne for barely a year and was succeeded in 674 by Aescwine. The latter died in 676, but his brief reign was marked by another war with Mercia, resulting in a battle at Biedanheafod, probably Bedwin in Wilts, in which the advantage seems to have been on the side of Wulfhere, though, according to Henry of Huntingdon, the battle was indecisive. Wulfhere's death from disease in the same year relieved Wessex of immediate fear of Mercia, and under Kentwine, brother of Kenwealh, who succeeded Aescwine, the advance across Somerset was resumed in 682, when the *Anglo-Saxon Chronicle* records that Kentwine drove the Britons "to the sea." Florence of Worcester adds that the defeated Welsh were the "Britons of the West." It is not quite clear what this term "to the sea" is meant to convey, or indeed, what sea is meant; but the phrase is generally taken to imply a further advance across the Parrett to the line of the Quantocks or beyond. Freeman says:

In a paper on "King Ine" (Proceedings of the Somerset Archaeological Society, *1872, Vol. XVIII, p. 43), from which also the subsequent quotations are taken.*

I should infer from this that Kentwine's victory gained for the West Saxons the sea-coast west of the mouth of the Parrett, the coast of Watchet, which afterwards figures in the Danish invasions. In short, Kentwine's victory made the English masters of Quantock, as Ceawlin's victory a hundred years before had made them masters of Mendip. How far west toward Dunster, Porlock, and Linton, the frontier may have reached, I do not propose to say. We might expect that the hills of Exmoor would be one of the districts in which the Britons would hold longest, but the English may very well have made settlements on the coast long before the mountain tribes were wholly subdued or driven out. In this campaign, then, I conceive that the West Saxons won Bridgwater and Watchet, and we may, I think, venture to picture Kentwine as forcing the gate, the Lydiard . . . and driving the Welsh up the valley where in after-days Crowcombe was given for the soul of Godwine.

All this is confessedly conjecture, and is difficult to reconcile with the writer's subsequent statement, quoted hereafter, that the frontier was pushed forward to Taunton only in Ine's time; but Freeman goes on to argue as if by stating his inference he had proved an historical fact. Other writers have also put forward his conjectures as if they had been fully proved, and the evidence deserves a closer examination than it has hitherto received.

Here, again, the Glastonbury records contain entries whose importance has hardly been recognised. The first mention of Saxon possessions beyond the Parrett occurs when they state, in the words of William of Malmesbury, that King Kentwine gave to the abbey—

"MUNEKATONE, et juxta silvam, inquit, qua vocatur Cantucdun XXIII hidas, in Caric XX hidas, et in Crucam III hidas."

They further record that in the year 681 King Baldred gave Hengisl, Abbot of Glastonbury, "Penger VI hides, Logworesbeorh XVI hides, and the capture of fish in the Parrett with the consent and leave of Bishop Hedda, and the assent of King Kentwine," and that in the same year Bishop Hedda gave to Glastonbury "Lantocai VI hides, with the assent of Kentwine and Baldred."

John of Glastonbury, recording the same gifts, reads, "Baldredus rex Canciae," "Loggerisburh, quod nunc Mons Acutus dicitur," and "Lantocai, quod nunc Legh dicitur."

Hedda was Bishop of Winchester, and Lantocai or Legh is now known as Street. It lies about a mile and a half south-west of Glastonbury, on the edge of the Poldens, beyond the Brue, which with a stretch of marsh separates the Isle of Avalon from the Poldens and the mainland to the south. The modern name of Street is derived from the ancient road which crossed from Avalon to the hills at this point, and has already been mentioned as passing down the whole length of the Poldens to the sea at Puriton. The Brue must have been crossed by ford or ferry.

King Baldred occurs again as witnessing and assenting to grants to Glastonbury under Ine, and is then called "sub-regulus"—a term which explains his position with regard to Kentwine. If

The only actual road into the isle of Avalon was by a causeway from Pennard, which was defended by a strong dyke, still existing. Exploration of this dyke by Dr Bulleid in 1909 proved it to be of Early Iron Age construction. The Glastonbury Lake Village, by Arthur Bulleid and H. St George Gray, 1911, p. 37.

John of Glastonbury is right in calling him "rex Canciae," this Baldred may have been one of the Kentish royal family driven into exile at the Court of Wessex when Aethelred of Mercia ravaged Kent in 676. His gift, Penger, is now represented by East and West Pennard, some two miles or more to the south-east of Glastonbury, and covering the approach from the mainland to the island on that side, as Street covers it on the south-west. Logworesbeorh or Montacute lies about four miles east of South Petherton, and close to the strong Romano-British fortress on Hamdon Hill. From the position of King Baldred's grants, ranging from the Brue to the Parrett, we should infer that his charge as "sub-regulus" included the territory added by Kenwealh to the West Saxon domains.

We have left until last the grants made by Kentwine himself, as some of these have a very definite signification, though no special importance attaches to the Manor of Caric. It gave its name to Castle Cary, Babcary, and Cary Fitzpaine, on the line of the Fosseway, and within the territory won by Kenwealh. Later benefactors added to these possessions of the abbey, but we attach no special importance to this manor. As regards the others, it is not quite clear whether William of Malmesbury's "Munekatone and near the wood called Cantucdun" represents one grant or two. John of Glastonbury says: "He gave besides, near the wood of Cantucdune, the Manor of West Munkaton, XXIII hides," which seems to indicate a localised block manor.

"Munekatone" is identified with West Monkton, which lies at the southern end of the Quantocks, about four miles north-east of Taunton, and above the limit of tide-water on the River Tone. Bishop Hobhouse in his map of Somerset estates at the time of Domesday shows it as extending southward across the river, almost to Taunton. It is now included in the modern hundred of Whitley.

This grant may indicate that by this time the British had been driven from, or had abandoned, Hamdon Hill. Similarly, the grant of Street seems to prove that the way to the crossing of the Parrett at Bridgwater was now open along the Poldens.

Cantuc is the old form of Quantock, and the "wood called Cantucdun" represents the ancient forest of Quantock in some part of its extent or border. John of Glastonbury's description seems to imply that West Monkton lay on its edge, and there is a Quantock Farm near at hand. But the name "Quantock" is common as a place-name among the hills. We do find, however, the name "Cantucdun" localised 200 years later in the form of "Cantuctune," the name of a manor bequeathed by King Alfred to his son Edward. This manor appears in Domesday as part of the "vetus dominicum coronae" under the name "Candetona." Its modern name is Cannington, and the present village lies about three and a half miles north of Bridgwater, just under a spur of land running from the Quantocks to the Parrett marshes. The Abbey of Glastonbury certainly had property in this direction, though its only manor recorded near here in Domesday is at Durborough, in Stoke Courcy parish, where was a chapel, long since ruined, and a scion of the Holy Thorn. As this manor was not given until the time of Eadgar, Kentwine's grant is clearly not to be located here as separate from that of West Monkton. The mention of Cantucdun therefore seems merely explanatory of the position of Kentwine's Monkton, as distinguished from other places of like name.

The record of Kentwine's grant is the only evidence that the abbey held land in "Cruca," but as John of Glastonbury points out, many of the possessions which he records from the charters were subsequently alienated from various causes, and of these some were never restored to the abbey. He adds that he has omitted many doubtful grants, and only records those of which he has no doubt.

"Cruca" is not found as a present manor name. It appears, however, to survive in Domesday as "Cruce," a small possession held by Walter de Doway, for which Bates Harbin suggests the "Vill of Crosse juxta Bokeland in Durston,"

Victoria County History of Somerset, Vol. I, p. 497.

"Domesday Studies,"
Somerset, Vol. I, pp.
186-7; Vol. II, pp. 31-
2.

while Mr Eyton includes it in the hundred of North Petherton, on the ground that it is entered in Domesday between "Wallepille" (Walpole in Pawlett) and "Bur" (East Bower in Bridgwater). In the Exchequer Domesday the order is as follows: we quote from the *Victoria County History*. After "Wallepille,"

> Walter holds I virgate of land which is called Doneham. Algar held it T.R.E. This is that part of the land which the king gave him "inter duas acquas." It is worth 12 pence.
> Rademer holds of W(alter) Cruce (doubtful). Edward held it T.R.E. and paid geld for I virgate. There is land for I plough which is there in demesne with half a virgate and 4 bordars who have half a virgate. There are 3 beasts and 3 swine. It is worth 10 shillings.

Then follows "Bur" for which Bates Harbin suggests West Bower in Durleigh, Bridgwater. The position of the grant of "Cruce" in these entries would suggest a holding in the vicinity of Puriton or Bawdrip, which lie between Walpole and East Bower, on the east bank of the Parrett, or between the first two places and West Bower, on the western bank. As a matter of fact, there was a holding in Bawdrip called "Crook" of which a grant is on record dated 1470.

Referred to by the
Rev. W. Greswell in a
letter to the
Antiquary of Jan.
1912. Unfortunately
he does not give
references to the
authority for the
grant.

A reference to the map will show that precisely in the position indicated by these Domesday entries the Parrett makes a great bend, or crook, eastward from the high ground on its western bank at Cannington to Bridgwater, touching the extreme end of the Polden Hills on its eastern bank by Puriton, and thence recrossing the level to the town. Prior to 1677, in which year it was destroyed by leading the river into a straight channel, there was a small, almost circular bend within this great loop, running immediately under the Polden Hills between Dunball and Downend, where the ridge sinks to the marshes. The present course of the river has shifted away from the base of the hill within living memory, but in close proximity to the old lesser loop the field names "great and little Crook" occur in Bawdrip parish and lying alongside the old

See Collinson's
History of Somerset,
1791, Vol. II, p. 75;
also The Story of the
Battle of Edington,
by the Rev. W.
Greswell, 1910, p. 29.

causeway to Bridgwater. There cannot be the least doubt that these names are derived from the "crook" of the river, or that they represent the Domesday and later mediaeval holding of "Cruce," or "Crook."

The form of Kentwine's grant, "in Crucam III hidas," shows that in his day Cruca, like Caric, was a district within which the grant was situated, rather than a self-contained manor. The name, occurring so soon after the conquest of the district, may be derived with equal probability from the Welsh *crwg*, a crook, or bend, or the Saxon *cruc* of the same meaning, and obviously connects the grant, or rather the tract of land in which the three hides were situated, with the great bend of the river already described, close to which the later "Crook" names are found. It is evident, however, that the one virgate of the Domesday "Cruce" cannot represent the three hides of the original grant to the abbey, though it may preserve the name.

The river channel shifts unaccountably, and for lack of early records as to its course at any given date, it is impossible to assign lands to their position with regard to its actual course in the seventh century. The tendency of the channel has been to shift away from the base of the hill, and it is most likely that in early days it ran close under the Poldens as far as the old causeway, embracing the lands to which the name of "crook" is now applied, within its curve; but the mediaeval and modern names are of no actual value as determining ancient positions on the river bank. The only thing which is certain is that the general formation of the land always necessitated a great bend of the river, wherever the actual channel ran, from Cannington to Puriton, and thence to Bridgwater. The use of the accusative "in Crucam" of the grant is somewhat peculiar, and rather indicates a holding extending "into the bend," or stretching across the river, " on the bend." In close connection with the bend therefore, and partly at least on

Some early shift of the channel has transferred part of the parish of Huntspill, nearer the mouth of the river, from the eastern to the western bank.

the western bank, Cruca must be looked for. Except in the one small holding, the name has been covered and lost with the establishment of Saxon settlements, but the grant unmistakeably lay on the edge of Kentwine's new conquest, and covered the point where the trackway, already described, entered Saxon territory from Dyvnaint.

The exact date of the grants made by Kentwine himself is not given, but, as we have no reason to believe that the Wessex frontier was advanced across the Parrett until after the defeat of the Welsh, we must date them after 682. The grants by Baldred and Hedda, which all lie to the east of the Parrett, are assigned to the previous year. The grants in any case give us fixed points up to which, at least, the Saxons had advanced at the time of the donation; and so far as the manors beyond the Parrett are concerned, their position marks the limit of the Saxon progress. They prove that Kentwine undoubtedly advanced his frontier westward beyond that river, and north-ward across the Tone to the foothills of the Quantocks; but we fear that Freeman's sketch of the "forcing of the gate, the Lydiard," must be abandoned.

The thickly wooded range of the Quantocks some fifteen miles long, would in itself present a formidable barrier to an advancing force, while along its heights are four considerable earthworks, still in good condition, guarding the main passes, besides beacon-pits and other tokens of military activity in former days. They are in fact, evidence that here has been an ancient frontier line, and such Saxon names as the "Hare-path" and "Hare-knap" (A.-S. *Here-pao—knaep*), the path and ridge of the host, and "Will's Neck," the narrow connecting ridge between two of the highest points across which the old road led to and from the land of the "Waelas;" prove that these hills must have formed for a considerable time the border between Welsh and Saxon. Permanent names of this sort can only result

It will be understood that we do not necessarily refer the construction of these earthworks to this date. They are probably earlier, but only careful excavation can settle the point.

70

from an armed occupation extending over a protracted period.

There are strategic reasons against a line of advance down the Tone Valley to the south of the Quantocks. It was not until the further pushing forward of Wessex under Ine in 710 that the fortress of Taunton was considered as a necessity for the defence of the frontier, and up till that date the great Romano-British stronghold at Norton Fitzwarren barred the way down the valley to where the trade route from Wales across the sea began at Watchet. The late importance of this stronghold is even now recalled by the local rhyme which testifies that

> Norton was a market town
> When Taunton was a vuzzy down.

Excavations carried out on the earthworks, which lie about two miles and a half north-west of Taunton, by Mr H. St. George Gray for the Somerset Archaeological Society in 1908 have proved that, while the camp was of pre-Roman origin, it was occupied in Roman and Romano-British times. That no later occupation has been proved is fully compatible with the generally received theory that it was superseded by the Saxon fortress. While it remained in British hands, no Saxon advance between the Brendons and Quantocks could have been possible.

We fully agree with Freeman that in his advance Kentwine won Bridgwater, and we hold that thence he advanced into the Quantock country; but the positions of his grants to Glastonbury are significant as marking the limits of that advance. West Monkton lies between the Tone and the Quantock heights, as if interposed between the lands held indisputably by Briton to the north and west, and Saxon to its east. An advance beyond it, or across the Quantocks, must have incolved the reduction of the hill forts and the stronghold at Norton.

In the same way the advance northward from Bridgwater between the Parrett and the

The line of advance on Bridgwater must have been from Glastonbury along the Poldens. Bridgwater, though necessarily an important crossing-place, is apparently only "Burh" until Norman times.

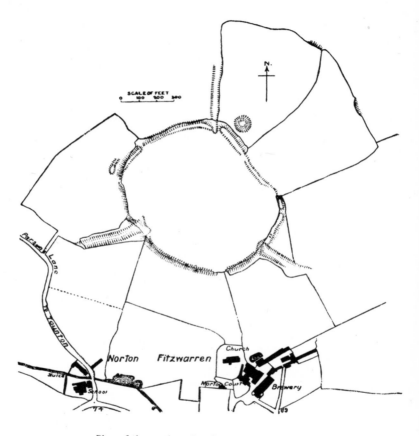

Plan of the earthworks of Norton Fitzwarren.

Quantocks would be checked on reaching the long tongue of hilly ground which runs between the Cannington Brook and the tidal inlet at Combwich, a mile or so farther northward, and stretches from the foot of the Quantocks to the Parrett itself. Both these streams were ancient tidal inlets of wide extent, and have only lately been reclaimed by floodgates from the salt water.

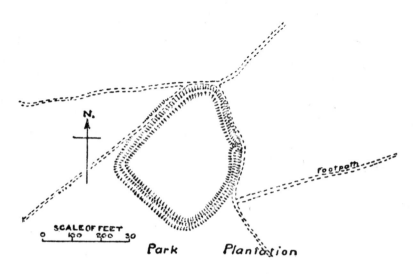

Plan of the earthworks in Over Stowey.

In the seventh century they must have been estuarine for many miles inland, the northern or Combwich inlet, which still forms a small haven at its mouth, being the more important and running farthest towards the hills.

The old trackway, which has been already referred to, leading from the tidal ford at Combwich to cross the Quantocks at Will's Neck, traverses this ridge of land between the streams from end to end, and its eastward end is guarded by a pre-Roman fortress of great strength, occupying an uncultivated area immediately above Cannington village, now known as Cannington Park. The crossing of these two inlets *See plan page 205* would be of great difficulty, and would involve the reduction of this fort before the second inlet could be negotiated. A line of march from Bridgwater would almost inevitably take the higher ground to the head of the inlets under the Quantocks, and here again the pass up which the trackway runs is guarded by a strong unnamed camp in Over Stowey parish above Aisholt which would have to be reduced.

That this was actually the line taken by some ancient invasion, which met with a determined opposition before the invading force could begin to breast the hills, seems to be certain from existing local tradition. A little below the spur of hill on which the Aisholt camp stands, and almost at the mouth of the pass, near the source of the Cannington Brook at Plainsfield, a field which is said to have been the scene of a terrible battle is still pointed out. The tradition runs "that it was the worst battle ever fought in these parts. The dead men were heaped as high as the top of the gates, and the blood ran as deep as the second gate bar." The statement is also added that "the old men could remember when the graves could be seen all over the field," and that spears and swords have often been dug up there. There is now no visible trace of graves of any sort, and no finds of weapons have been authenticated; but such traditions of what was once evident on an old battlefield may be handed on with the remembrance of the actual occurrence, for generations.

We had the tradition in the vernacular from an old Plainsfield man named Porter, who died in Stockland some few years since. The tradition however may be gathered from any old Aisholt or Stowey native. It is well known locally.

There is every reason to believe that this tradition is genuine. The locality, Plainsfield, has never been the subject of archaeological theory, and no suggestion that here was any historic battle has been mooted. Early theorists were very busy with the meaning of the names "Conquest" and "Grabburrowes" on the farther side of the hills, and their speculations seem to have passed into a sort of quasi-tradition, which nothing but the arbitrament of the spade will disperse. Here there has been no more than local notice of the folk-knowledge, and no antiquary could have invented the details. Nor is the battle confused with Sedgmoor, which is of course *the* battle of the neighbourhood.

It seems impossible to connect this battle with any historical epoch except that of Kentwine's campaign. With this it fits in exactly, and it seems entirely probable that Kentwine met with such stubborn resistance at the foot of the hills that, though able to hold the land already occupied, he did not care to push his advance farther, either across the hills or beyond the wide inlet of the Combwich Brook. This would leave the Welsh in possession of the narrow strip of land along the coast which lies to the northward of a line drawn from the foot of the hills below Will's Neck to the end of the tongue of land between the Combwich and Cannington inlet—a line which is practically that of the old trackway. To the south, or Saxon side of this line, lie the manors of Kentwine's grant.

The field-name "Welsh Grounds" is still found within this strip, near Stolford.

In this limitation of the Saxon advance, we have a full and natural explanation of the statement that Kentwine drove the British "to the sea." Most writers, Mr Freeman not excepted, have construed this phrase *"op sae"* as if it meant "into" or even "over" the sea. Professor Earle, however, gives the Latin equivalent "usque" for *"op"* and this no doubt expresses closely the meaning intended. Freeman's suggestion that Kentwine's conquest made the English masters of the coast at Watchet, and perhaps still farther west "toward Dunster, Porlock, and Linton," goes very far beyond the text. If the Saxon advance had been actually to these points on the shore, we should have found some term used in the *Chronicle* to intimate that the Welsh were driven into Exmoor. As it stands, the record exactly expresses the driving of the Welsh into some narrow strip of coast-line, such as that which we have indicated.

If Kentwine's northern frontier followed this line, the grant in Cruca would occupy a position with regard to the lands held by Saxon and Briton very similar to that of the grant at Monkton, which separated the two races on the south of the Quantocks. There seems to have been a deliberate policy which dictated the position of the grants of this date, as if it was

The arrangement of the Domesday Hundred of Williton seems to preserve a trace of this ancient strip of territory. It crosses the Quantocks and extends along the coast both to the east and west of them.

intended to place the lands of the church of Glastonbury, with its claims to unbroken existence from British times, as a mediator between Welsh and Saxon Christians. At the same time the abbey was given possessions which covered the main routes of pilgramage from the West to the Holy Island, at points where they passed from the kingdom of Dyvnaint into Wessex.

Cruca covered the landing-place at Downend, where the road to Avalon along the Poldens began. Monkton covered the main road from Norton, and Logworesbeorh is not far from the place where the great Fosseway crosses the Parrett. The contemporaneous grants at Street and Pennard gave the abbey command of the approaches from the south-west and the south-east. When we bear in mind that the great charter of King Ine records that Kentwine used to call Glastonbury "the mother of all saints, and liberated it from every secular and ecclesiastical service," it does not seem extravagant to credit him with the deliberate intention of placing under her control the avenues of approach to her shrines, where Welsh and Saxon would meet with equal feelings of veneration.

Chapter 6

Under Kentwine's successor, Ceadwalla, the line of Ceawlin regained the throne of Wessex in 686. He only reigned three years, but in that time Wessex began to reassert her power over the kingdoms south of the Thames which Wulfhere had torn from her. Kent was twice ravaged, the expeditions thither involving of course either the subjugation or co-operation of Sussex or Surrey, or both, and the Isle of Wight was recovered and forcibly converted to Christianity.

Ine succeeded to the throne in 688, and evidently continued the policy of asserting the supremacy of Wessex south of the Thames. In 694 Kent had to buy his friendship, and her king, Withred, remained as Ine's ally. Sussex must also have been made an under-kingdom, as Nun, or Nunna, a kinsman of Ine, appears in a charter as King of the South Saxons. In 710 the westward advance was resumed, the *Chronicle* stating that in this year Ine and Nun his kinsman fought against Gerent the Welsh king, one of the very few Welsh monarchs mentioned in the Anglo-Saxon accounts of the border wars. He was king of Dyvnaint, and probably the foremost among the British princes of the time, as there is reason to believe that the South Welsh kingdoms beyond the Severn, recognised his overlordship to some extent. His power was fully recognised by the Saxons, and there had been, previous to the outbreak of the war, some negotiation with him on the questions in dispute between the British and Saxon Churches. Aldhelm, Bishop of "the West of Selwood" in 705, while yet an abbot only, wrote him an epistle, still extant, addressing him as "Dominus gloriosissimus, occidentalis regni sceptri gubernator."

Aldhelm died in 709, and the war broke out next year. The *Chronicle* is absolutely silent as to the cause and eventual result of the struggle, but it is quite probable that the death of Aldhelm removed the man who had kept the peace, and that the Welsh were the aggressors in a sort of religious war which had as its object the regaining

Dyvnaint, the remains of the old Roman province of Dumnonia, at this time included Devon and Cornwall, and also all Somerset west of the Quantocks, and a strip of land to their eastward along the coast. See preceding chapter.

Bede, Eccles. Hist., Book v, c.18.

of Glastonbury for the British Church, of which it was the mother.

The war must have been a serious affair, as Ine called Nun, and presumably his Sussex levies, to his assistance. Apparently Gerent was worsted in its result, as Henry of Huntingdon states. The only evidence of the success of Wessex is in the founding of Taunton in advance of the frontier won by Kentwine. It is certain that Wessex made another step westward, but how far is not evident. At the same time the power of Dyvnaint was checked for a time, there seeming to be no more definite and open warfare with her until 755.

Compared with the effects of the campaigns under Kenwealh and Kentwine, Freeman says that the result of the victory of Ine over Gerent

> is less clearly marked, but a process of exhaustion would lead us to suppose that the land which was won by it was the south-western part of Somerset, Crewkerne, Ilminster, and that district. The Tone may not unlikely have been the frontier from 682 to 710. How far either conquest reached westward, whether either of them took in any part of Devonshire, we can only guess. In default of direct evidence either way, we may assume that the boundary of the shires, which must mean something, answers pretty well to the extent of the conquests of Centwine and Ine.

It is rather difficult to disentangle Mr Freeman's statements. If his previously-quoted theory is correct, the Tone was crossed and ceased to be a frontier line in 682, and as a matter of documentary record Kentwine had acquired Monkton beyond it, though he had not won so great an extent of country beyond the Quantocks as is involved in the "Lydiard" theory. As to the actual site of the battle with Gerent J. B. Davidson says:

> That the scene of the conflict of 710 between Ine and Gereint was on the northern slopes of the Blackdown Hills, just above Taunton, is a point on which all historians are agreed.

Transactions of the Devonshire Association, *Vol. IX*, p. 203.

Ine's conquests were no doubt in the south-west of the county, as Freeman thinks, but it is highly improbable that they extended on the west to the present border of Devon. In any case, he himself says:

> Taunton was founded by Ine at some time before 722; we can hardly doubt, therefore, that it was founded as a new border fortress for the defence of his conquests. Its almost certain date will be in, or soon after, the year 710, the year when these conquests were completed.

Whether the British fortress at Norton had by this time fallen or not is uncertain. The excavations in 1908 were confined to the outer fosse, and threw no light on the ultimate fate of the town. It seems likely that the name "Norton" was given to it while it still stood by the Saxons of Taunton, two miles to the south, and has persisted as the name of the Saxon village which took its place. The position of Taunton, on the opposite bank of the Tone, indicates that Ine erected his fortress as a check on his dangerous neighbour.

The establishment at this point of a border fortress is unintelligible if we imagine, with Freeman, that all North-Western Somerset was now added to Ine's kingdom; while as he himself has pointed out in the passage we first quoted, the wild forest lands of Brendon and Exmoor would be those in which the British would hold out the longest. That this was the case is evident from existing boundaries. Greswell says:

> Towards Exmoor the parishes are more scattered, the hundreds of far wider extent, and the place-names and language more reminiscent of the Celts or British. The Saxonization of West Somerset proceeded very slowly along the uplands of Brendon and Exmoor.

The Forests and Deer-Parks of Somerset, *p. 16. Taunton, 1905.*

Careful study of the question from every point only results in the conclusion that Freeman's opinion, that the county boundary between Somerset and Devon represents the limit of the conquest of Ine, is wrong. The victory over Gerent can only have advanced his frontier westward to a little beyond Taunton, certainly not across the twenty miles or more of waste moors, studded with camps, which stretch thence to the present county boundary, nor past Norton Fitzwarren stronghold and the strong line of the Quantocks. The linguistic peculiarities of the Quantock district and the persistence of names referring to the use of the tracks by the Welsh and as a military way, prove that until long after the days of Ine these hills were a march between the two nations. The thirty years between the advance of Kentwine and that of Ine is too short to account for these remains of Celtic independence.

Taunton itself is on a linguistic boundary. Elworthy, in his introduction to *The Dialect of West Somerset,* says:

> The people of the little village of Ruishton, only a mile and a half to the east of Taunton, speak the eastern dialect; while at Bishop's Hull, one mile to the west, they speak the western.

Such a linguistic division bears even stronger witness to the long existence at this point of a territorial boundary between folk speaking different tongues or dialects.

South of Taunton the line of frontier which must have been gained is far easier to trace. A Roman road running south from the Quantock foothills, through Taunton and Castle Neroche, to join the Fosseway near Chard, gave a well-marked line of demarcation, beyond which to the westward are the hills which reach to Dartmoor. The modern Devon boundary along the Blackdown hills is close to this frontier, and may have arisen from it.

The western, or Exmoor, boundary of modern Somerset, which Freeman would have us accept as the mark of Ine's conquest, is not Saxon at all. It is not a linguistic boundary, nor is it racial. It is nothing more than the boundary of the medieval royal forest of Exmoor, which was varied from time to time, and hardly fixed even so late as the fourteenth century. The factor which determined its line appears to have been the obvious convenience of grouping the royal domain west of the Parrett in the same county as the adjoining property of the King to the east of the river. By the time of Domesday we accordingly find the bulk of this property grouped under Somerset, though even at that date the boundary does not seem to have been strictly defined.

Greswell considers that the original boundary of Exmoor Forest was also the boundary of the land of the Sumorsaetas. This boundary was, however, variable and extremely indefinite until a late date. E. J. Rawle, states, with regard to the perambulations of Exmoor Forest in 1279 and 1298, that at that period no exact boundary between the counties had been fixed, and points out that several records and Acts of Parliament locate Exmoor Forest as being in the counties of Somerset and Devon. The charter of King John recorded in Greshwell's book frees the whole of Devon from all rules which belong to the forest and foresters up to the metes and bounds of the ancient regards of Dartmoor and Exmoor. Up to that date, therefore, the rules of Exmoor had covered part of Devon.

The fact is that the county boundary was fixed by the extent of the King's domain in the forest, but was not otherwise defined. The extent of

Annals of the Ancient Royal Forest of Exmoor, p. 5. Taunton 1893. He also draws attention to the fact that, while the eastward portions of Somerset are assessed in Domesday in the manner common to Wessex generally, the assessments in West Somerset approximate to the Devon methods.

Saxon glass from a burial.

land afforested varied from time to time, and was considerably added to in the days of the Norman kings. The one thing which is clear is that it is idle to base any arguments concerning the events of the time of Kentwine and Ine, or still later, of the time of Alfred, on a county boundary between Somerset and Devon which was undefined until the end of the thirteenth century.

The extent and position of the royal demesnes have a certain bearing on the progress of the Saxon conquests. Kenwealh's advance in 658 included the royal forest of Mendip, as well as Wedmore, where there was a royal residence. The victory of Kentwine added the Forest of Petherton south of Bridgwater with which went marsh and woodland tracts extending to the Somerton marshlands, and a tract of forest along the eastern foothills of the Quantocks. In connection with this demesne there was a royal house at Cannington eventually. Ine pushed the frontier westward, and won for himself the royal forest of Neroche, south of Taunton, and, according to tradition, set his palace at South Petherton.

When the remainder of the present county of Somerset came under the sway of Wessex we find almost the entire district from the Quantocks to the farthest limit of Exmoor added to this vast royal domain, which began at the Mendips, and stretched, roughly speaking, from the Severn Sea to the southern limits of the marshland which, later, sheltered Alfred. Practically, the only lands which were not royal in all this tract of country were those granted to Glastonbury, generous in extent, but hardly breaking the continuity of the "vetus dominicum coronae" of West Somerset.

The latest acquisitions from Dyvnaint were not at once included in the land of the Sumorsaetas, so far as that "Summurtunensis Paga" of the *Chronicles* had become a recognised political or administrative entity. As late as the year 894 we find the Parrett still forming an administrative boundary, the levies raised in that year being,

Old Burrow camp is just over the border on the Devon side, close to the sea-cliffs, but we do not attach any importance to its position with regard to the boundary. It was examined in 1911 by Mr W. M. Tapp, LL.D., F.S.A., and Mr H. St George Gray and showed very scanty signs of occupation. The finds pointed to its belonging to Romano-British times. Its position with an immense outlook over Exmoor and the Severn Sea suggests that it may have been an observation post, but it can have had little defensive value otherwise. "A survey of Old Burrow Camp, Exmoor," by H. St G. Gray, Transactions of the Devonshire Association, *1912.*

according to the *Chronicle,* drawn from "the east of Parrett and from the west as well as east of Selwood."

This district was chiefly royal forest, and Mr Eyton points out in his *Domesday Studies,* that the royal forests appear as a rule to have been excluded from the hundreds. The tract of royal property between the land of the Sumorsaetas and the newly-won Devon would be thus excluded, as must previously have been the case with the frontier marches between the Parrett and the Quantocks.

This royal domain would therefore form an administrative province of its own, cut off from Dyvnaint, yet not incorporated in Wessex proper.

This gives an explanation of an expression which occurs in the *Chronicle* under the year 876, when we are told that the brother of Ingwar and Healfdene came to "Wessex to Devonshire (on West-Seaxum on Defènascire)." The county of Devon seems never to have been regarded as a part of Wessex, and the phrase used by the chronicler evidently defines a portion of the county which had some special relation to the kingdom of Wessex. The natural conclusion in that case is that he meant the part of the ancient kingdom of Dyvnaint which the Kings of Wessex had added to their royal domain.

Whether the victory of Ine over Gerent enabled him to exert any wider authority than that which extended to the new frontier is not stated in so many words, but it is to this date that the recognition by Dorset of the overlordship of Wessex is best referred, if she was not actually incorporated in the kingdom on the defeat of Gerent. The war had carried the Somerset boundary southward to a point not ten miles from the English channel, cutting off Dorset almost entirely from Dyvnaint proper, and the inevitable result must have been the full establishment of Saxon dominion over the county.

There is no suggestion of conquest by force of

arms in this case, and it is rather a question of completion of what had already begun, so soon as the battle of Peonna had brought the territory of Wessex in closer contact with Dorset. Sherborne had certainly been a peaceful meeting-place before the war with Gerent, but the great barrier of the camp-crested downs of North Dorset had never been forced, and there is no record of any attempt to force the frontier which had limited the realm of Cerdic. Within those lines there are no Saxon heathen burials, or names which seem to date from heathen Saxon times, to show that Dorset was entered much before the conversion of the Wessex folk. Early settlement of peaceful origin there may most likely have been, but only on the coast in the way of trade, in the way which is common to every country with coterminous shores.

The monastery at Wareham, destroyed by the Danes in 871, is said to be the oldest religious foundation in the county, but according to William of Malmesbury, a trustworthy authority as regards this district, it was founded by Aldhelm. This however, does not negative the existence of an early Saxon settlement on Poole haven, if it does not rather imply that there was one. Both the abbey of Sherborne and the nunnery at Wimborne were in existence in 705, the former a foundation of Aldhelm's, and the latter belonging to St Cuthberga, a sister of King Ine. But there may have been an earlier foundation at Sherborne, which received grants from Kenwealh. The frontier of independent Dorset in his days was no doubt the line of the north downs.

It is certain that there was a large Welsh population under the care of Aldhelm as bishop of "the west of Selwood," in 705, as in the letter to Gerent, already referred to, he attempted to arrange for the conformity of British Christians to Saxon ecclesiastical rules. That such action was taken by the great bishop proves that there was a growing friendship between the Britons of

Victoria County History of Dorset. *William of Malmesbury also records a tradition that Cerne Abbey was founded by St Augustine, but there is no evidence to date it before the time of Eadgar (A.D. 950). Of course Cerne may have been in existence in the time of Augustine as a British foundation, and there is no reason to suppose that it was ever disturbed by heathen Saxons. Cerne may well have had an unbroken existence from British times onward. The vast figure of the Giant on the hillside above the town seems to prove that the place was a pre-Christian sanctuary of some sort: and a place once held sacred seems always to have been respected and adopted by the earliest Christian missionaries.*

Saxon glass vessels from burials.

the south and their Saxon neighbours, and it is
extremely probable that he anticipated the time
when Dorset as a whole would be united to
Wessex. At all events, it is certain that while we
have no authentic proofs of actual Saxon
possession of Dorset before the days of Ine, we
have equal certainty that from his time forward
that county is an unquestioned part of Wessex.
The establishment of the royal nunnery at
Wimborne, almost under the shadow of the great
British fortress of Badbury, proves that the line
of cramps and forest which had been impassable
to Cerdic and his successors had been crossed,
probably peaceably.

The well-known Laws of Ine, in which he
legislates for the Welsh on equal terms with the
Saxons, show that in his days there was a great
accession to his realm of undisturbed Britons
who were not in the position of conquered and
enslaved enemies, and for whom treatment as
mere thralls would not suffice. There is
documentary evidence to show who these
Britons were, which incidentally helps to define
the new frontier on the west of Dorset.

King Alfred in his will bequeathes all his lands
"among the Welsh kin" (on Wealcynne) to his
youngest son, specifying manors which lie within

the never forced encircling line of Dorset camps, as well as some just over the modern Dorset boundary on the line of the river Axe, which may most likely define the new frontier south of Chard to the English Channel. They are Down, Sturminster, Whitchurch and Litton in Dorset; Milbourne, Somerset or Dorset; Crewkerne in Somerset on the Dorset border in the later won territory; and Gidley, Axminster, Axmouth, Branscombe and Columbton in the Devon of to-day. Gidley and Columbton belong to later acquisitions, and Branscombe is on the coast close to Axmouth.

To sum up, the advance of Ine after the victory over Gerent set the Wessex frontier practically to a line from the mouth of the Devon Axe to Chard, thence by the line of the Blackdown hills to the Fosseway, and so by the Roman road to the foot of the Quantocks, with Taunton as the border stronghold, and thence by the line won by Kentwine across the Quantock foothills to Combwich on the Parrett.

West of this line we cannot find that Ine made any of the usual grants to Glastonbury which seem to have followed the Saxon advances. In a charter recorded by William of Malmesbury he confirms that grants already noted and commented on, but he makes no fresh additions which are proof of westward extension. What he does give "of his own royal demesne" are the ten hides of Brent, one hide of the adjacent Bleadon, and ten hides of "Sowy": with other lands in the Mendip districts. The "Sowy" ten hides are important, however, as they represent the chain of islands, Othery, Middlezoy, Weston-Zoyland, and Chedzoy, between the Poldens and the Parrett, and the gift indicates that the possession of the great fenland was considered secure after the defeat of Gerent.

It remained for Wessex to conquer the lands westward of this new frontier. Beyond it there is no sharp, defensible line of country in any way comparable to the physical boundaries which marked the first stages of the conquest of Dyvnaint. The Saxons had reached the wild approaches to the great moorlands of Exmoor and Dartmoor, and nothing short of a series of campaigns would reduce them. If Wessex were still to expand westward, the West Welsh as a nation must be overcome.

Until that was accomplished, the moors remained as a constant menace. They were the natural stronghold of the Welsh, and the refuge of every outlaw who fled from Wessex justice. Border warfare must have been perpetual and harassing along the new line, and it is by no means certain that Ine's victory had, at least in the north-west, any long-felt effects. Taunton itself was too far advanced, and was deliberately burnt by Saxon hands after not more than twelve years' existence. With the destruction of Taunton a new phase of the war with Dyvnaint seems to begin.

Chapter 7

Five years after the defeat of Gerent there was war with Mercia, the reason of its outbreak not being evident, though as Ine met Ceolred at the old battle-ground, Woddesbeorg, in Wessex, it would seem that the Mercians were the aggressors. The battle was indecisive, and both forces suffered heavily, the quarrel apparently leading to no advance on either side.

The next trouble with which Ine had to deal arose at his fortress of Taunton, and was serious. An atheling of the name of Cynewulf rose in revolt and was slain in 721, and in the next year, 722, another atheling, Ealdbriht, "the exile," rose and seized Taunton. There were some strange points about this affair which are worth discussion, but at the present moment it is enough to say the Queen Aethelburh, who seems to have been on the spot—probably at South Petherton—stormed the fortress and drove Ealdbriht to take refuge in Sussex. She then razed Taunton.

This action is perfectly intelligible if the fortress was on the extreme frontier. Unless it were held in force it was worse than useless, for the moment it passed into disloyal or hostile hands it was an actual danger. As we have said, it was too far advanced.

Aethelburh's action proves that Taunton lay on the actual frontier, and incidentally corroborates the line which we have indicated as marking Ine's advance. The fortress was isolated to a great extent, lying beyond the great fenland as a whole, and with the river between it and the small strip of Quantock foothills in which Monkton had been gained. It was close to the Brendon and Blackdown fastnesses, against which it was supposed to be a defence; and it is almost certain that its dangerous neighbour, the fortress at Norton Fitzwarren, was still in existence. Even if that were weakened, or at this time almost deserted, Taunton lay open to attack from the Quantock-Brendon valley and the hills on either side, to say nothing of the likelihood of a landing

"Ealdbriht wrecca," A.-S. Chronicle.

88

of Welsh from across the Severn at Watchet, if Gerent called them.

Under those conditions the destruction of Taunton was justified when once Aethelburh had seen that she had not force sufficient to hold it, while Ealdbriht had escaped. She must have foreseen that it might take long to end his revolt, and as a matter of fact, there was trouble with him on the eastern border for the next three years.

It is possible, as Freeman thinks, that Ealdbriht was in league with the Welsh. It is certain that he had the inhabitants of Taunton on his side. It is almost a matter of certainty that the garrison of Taunton was composed of South Saxons, and that Ealdbriht "the exile" was a South Saxon atheling of the royal line who was either a hostage with Ine, or taking refuge with him.

The settlement of the Taunton district by South Saxons is well known, owing to the sporadic occurence of distinctive Sussex customs in the Manor of Taunton Deane. T. W. Shore says, in his *Origin of the Anglo-Saxon Race,* that here "the customs which prevailed were almost identical with those of the Rape of Lewes. This great Liberty in Somerset resembled in its constitution a Sussex Rape in containing hundreds within it." There are other points also which he notes, and these have been fully recognised by other writers. But so far as we know, the origin of the connection between Sussex and Taunton has not been pointed out.

Sussex was reduced to dependence on Wessex by Ceolwulf in 607, and from that time forward was probably held by an under-king, whether he was of the line of Cissa, or of Cerdic.

This state of dependence was ended by the wars of Wulfhere, who deprived Kenwealh of his possessions eastward of the Hampshire boundary in or about 661. Ethelwalch, who now became king of Sussex, remained as a close friend of Mercia during his reign of thirty-eight years.

The first result of a sudden change of this sort, coming after forty years of close connection with Wessex, must have been the flight of many sympathisers with Wessex from their own land to Kenwealh. That king must have had a numerous following of "exiles" from Sussex, and from the ravaged Isle of Wight, who were more than willing to follow him in his wars, and most ready to find new lands in the course of his conquests.

Ceadwalla, the successor of Kenwealh, recovered Sussex for Wessex and in 686 it was again held by an under-king, probably Nun, or Nunna, who was king of Sussex under Ine, whose kinsman he was. There is some reason to believe that he was a son of Ceadwalla.

See the genealogy of the kings of Wessex in Britannia Saxonica, *by J. W. Collen. Unfortunately Mr Collen does not give his authorities, an ommission which seriously impairs the value of his work.*

Nun, as we have seen, took part in the victory over Gerent, and with him would be a South Saxon contingent. With Ine would also be sons of the nobles who had fled to Wessex on the Mercian annexation of Sussex. That these should be rewarded by gifts of lands in the newly won country is to be expected, and the Taunton manor was no doubt a block grant to the Sussex contingent, with the condition of holding Taunton for the king. Nun almost certainly died, or was slain in some border fight, near Taunton, as the first Ordnance maps show a tumulus known as "Noon's Barrow" on the eastern slope of the Blackdown hills, which has since disappeared.

It may have been on the death of Nun that Ealdbriht the exile rose against Ine. It is quite likely. He eventually found help in Sussex, and might have planned for it. That he is called an exile at this date seems to indicate that he was not a voluntary follower of Ine, but was one of the old royal family of Sussex, who was, after the fashion of the times, held as a hostage at the court of Ine; and the trouble caused by the rising of Cynewulf seemed to give him his chance of escape, if not of successful civil war. He had the South Saxon colony on the Welsh border at his back, and if the Welsh helped him, so much the better. They could not harm Sussex, and they would certainly embarrass Ine.

Aethelburh's prompt action saved that complication. The great fenland took its place again as the impassable frontier, and we hear nothing of the Welsh. Certainly the land won on the north-west Somerset border must have reverted for a time to Welsh hands, for we do not so much as know when Taunton was rebuilt.

Ealdbriht made his way by Surrey to Sussex, and there found supporters enough, and it was not until 725 that he was finally overcome and slain. It is perhaps to this period that the strange story of Aethelburh's dismantling of the palace at South Petherton may belong. It was an advanced position, though an old Wessex possession. Ine was evidently more fond of it than she thought fit, for some reason, and she took the way of working on his deep religious feelings to induce him to abandon it. That the queen was far-sighted, and had a well founded fear of the Welsh is evident enough in her prompt slighting of Taunton. We have literally no evidence that Gerent was not still to be feared.

South Petherton is the traditional site of Ine's palace (vide Collinson's Somerset), but we do not attach any great importance to its identification.

Ine abdicated in 728, going to Rome, where like others of the English princes who sought that centre of civilisation, religion, and fever, he died shortly. His abdication seems to have been the work of Aethelburh, and saved him from troubles which she no doubt foresaw.

He was succeeded by a son of his predecessor Aescwine of the line of Ceolwulf, one Aethelheard, who had to dispute the throne with Oswald, a prince of the house of Ceawlin. The internal troubles of Wessex opened the way to Mercia, and in 733 Aethelbald, the Mercian king, fell on Wessex and penetrated to the heart of the land, laying siege to Somerton itself and capturing it. Wessex after this was reduced to the position of a mere dependent on Mercia, even to the extent of being obliged to send contigents to the assistance of Aethelbald, the two kings fighting together against the North Welsh in 743.

It seems to have been the policy of Mercia at this time to foment internal troubles between the king and his nobles in Wessex. There was in 750 a war between Cuthred, who succeeded Aethelheard in 741, and the ealdorman Aethelhun; but two years later Cuthred and Aethelhun were fighting side by side against Mercia. The war ended in the desperate battle of Burford in Oxfordshire, near the Gloucestershire border. According to Henry of Huntingdon the two kings met in single combat, but Aethelbald the Mercian was seized with panic, and led the flight of his forces. The result of the battle was decisive, and Wessex regained her independence.

During this period of Mercian overlordship and intrigue it is not possible that any westward advance on Dyvnaint can have been made. As we have pointed out, it is far more likely that an actual loss of territory gained by Kentwine and Ine took place. It is certain that no sooner had Wessex regained her independence after the battle of Burford, than Cuthred was at war with the Welsh, and this must mark either a new advance on Dyvnaint, or else a check to Welsh aggression.

We have no precise information to guide us in following the remaining stages by which Dyvnaint as a whole was won for Wessex. The probability is that the Welsh gave way slowly during the reign of Cynewulf (755–784), as he is said to have fought often in great battles against the Brito-Welsh. No Welsh leaders are mentioned, and the places where the battles were fought are not known. It may be taken that this is a record of thirty years of warfare, in which the steadily growing power of Wessex set her border still westward.

In all probability the Quantock strip of Dyvnaint was absorbed early in these wars, Watchet and perhaps Porlock falling into Saxon hands in the second half of the eighth century accordingly. Westward of the Quantock-Brendon valley, among the wild hills that stretch to the

Taw and Torridge, the Saxon dominion must have extended more slowly, and not as a matter of conquest, but rather as a gradual acquisition by influence. In the same way the Dartmoor district would have held out longer than the rest of Devon, as Freeman thinks, even if there were any special attempt to reduce it, beyond such as would suffice for keeping raiders in check.

There is no doubt that the conquest of Devon proceeded more rapidly from the side of Dorset and along the shores of the English Channel than from across the moorlands. The Fosseway itself gave a ready line of approach into the heart of Gerent's kingdom. There is a tradition of a great battle at Axminster, which Leland managed to confound with Brunanburh, which might be the memory of one of Cynewulf's fights, but is much more likely the tradition of the battle with the Danes who landed at Charmouth in 833. Axminster was certainly a Saxon possession at the end of Cynewulf's reign, as the atheling who slew him was taken there for burial.

The position of Exeter itself as connected with Wessex is somewhat exceptional, some writers being inclined to think that the city had become Saxon during or before the last quarter of the seventh century; but all the evidence goes to show that at so early a date this cannot have been a Saxon conquest. The supposed early possession of the city by the Saxons is deduced from the statement in the contemporary life of Wynfrith, better known as St. Boniface, that the saint was educated at the monastery at a place called "Adescancestre" (Exeter). A further tradition recorded in a fourteenth century MS states that he was born at Crediton.

It would be a fair deduction from the bringing up of a Saxon within the lands of the hated British Church that the parents of the saint were fugitives who had sought shelter from the raids of Ceadwalla with the prince of Dyvnaint; but it is far more likely that there was actually a very early Saxon trading settlement at Exeter, dating

"The birthplace of Wynfrith," by Mr J. R. King, Proc. Som. Arch. Society, Vol. XX, 1875.

from the time when Wessex was not yet feared by Dyvnaint as a powerful and encroaching enemy. Such trading settlements were by no means uncommon, and they no more involve conquest of the surrounding country than, say, the existence of the powerful German (Hanse) trading settlement at Bergen presupposes conquest of the south of Norway before it could be established.

According to William of Malmesbury the city was divided between an English and Welsh population up to the time of Athelstan, and such a division would entirely agree with an old priviliged settlement. The church dedications as traced by Kerslake prove this division of the city, and according to him show that the Saxons approached the place from the south and east. This of course is quite our view, but the natural explanation of the position of the different dedications is that they mark the Saxon and Welsh quarters. Conquest does not stop short at a street line as does settlement in concord. Such a settlement was possible, and we may say, probable, in the last quarter of the seventh century. It would not have been carried out in the days of perpetual warfare in the last half of the eighth. Neither if Devon had been already conquered by that time would that warfare have taken place. The position of Exeter therefore is exceptional, and of consequently exceptional interest, but it does not help us to date the actual conquest of South Devon.

"The Celt and the Teuton in Exeter," Journal of the Arch. Institute.

Cf. the contemporary Scandinavian settlements in S. Wales and N. Somerset, Book II, chap. II.

Towards the end of Cynewulf's reign there was renewed strife with Mercia, which under the great Offa had gradually been regaining the position it held under Penda and Wulfhere. In 774 Offa won a victory over Kent at Otford and this was followed in 777 by a crushing defeat of Cynewulf at Bensington (Benson in Oxfordshire). As a result of this defeat Wessex had again to acknowledge the Mercian supremacy, besides apparently losing all her possessions north of the Thames.

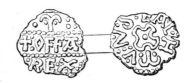

Coin of Offa.

There is no Welsh war recorded in the days of Beorhtric, Cynewulf's successor. He was a son in law of Offa and it was about the time of his accession to the throne, or shortly after, that the Mercian king threw up Offa's Dyke as a line of demarcation between Mercia and Wales. This, though did not entirely put an end to warfare between those states, seems to have marked a definite abandonment by Mercia of the policy of conquest. Possibly Beorhtric's attitude was influenced by that of his father-in-law, but it is almost a commonplace to say that Wessex trouble with Mercia was the opportunity of Dyvnaint, and the close alliance that now existed between the two kingdoms gave the Britons no opening for aggression. His reign marked only by the coming of the first ships of the Northmen to Dorset. Beorhtric died in 800, and Ecgberht took the throne.

It is worth noticing that with Ecgberht continental methods of warfare came into England. Being of the line of Ceawlin he had fled from the court of Offa on the accession of Beorhtric of the line of Cuthwulf, and the marriage of the latter with Offa's daughter. There is no doubt that he had a strong party in Wessex who looked for his return; but for some reason, which may well have been the wish to save his country from civil war, he chose to remain with Charlemagne. With that great captain he learnt all that was to be learnt of successful warfare, and there is no doubt that his extraordinary and rapid conquest of the whole of England was due to his personality and methods.

It would seem that in the first twelve years of his reign he was content to reorganise his kingdom, no action on his part being recorded until 813, when he attacked the West Welsh, harrying from east to west, but effecting no lasting conquest. In 823 the *Chronicle* records a fight between the "Wala and Defna" at "Gafulford" which is generally supposed to be Camelford. This is the   first mention of the

Galford in the parish of Lew in West Devon has also been suggested.

English inhabitants of Dyvnaint, and worth notice as such. The place of the fight is rather far west for anything but an expedition, and the term "Defna" as applied to Saxons would mean also the men of the old Dyvnaint, west of Ine's line at this date, the "Devon in Wessex" of the time of Alfred.

This year, 822, saw the beginning of the supremacy of Ecgberht and of Wessex with the great defeat of Mercia at Ellandun, which won back Surrey, Sussex, Kent and Essex, and after which all East Anglia hailed Ecgberht as their protector against the Mercian oppression, which had begun with the murder of King Aethelberht by Offa. In 827 he was the master of all England south of the Humber, and the Northumbrians offered him homage. In the next year he reduced the North Welsh to "humble obedience" and was master of all England.

Professor Oman considers that this was in Wiltshire, probably Allington near Amesbury, and suggests that King Beornwulf of Mercia had invaded Wessex during Ecgberht's absence in Devon or Cornwall.

The ready subjection of Northumbria was probably due to internal dissensions, and to a growing fear of the Danes, whose attacks in the north had become formidable. In a few years they found their way to the southern shores of Wessex, where a new foe was to be met.

In 832 and 833 the Danes ravaged Sheppey, and defeated Ecgberht in a landing at Charmouth in Dorset. In 835 they combined with the West Welsh against him, and were defeated at "Hengestesdun" which is generally supposed to be Hingston Down, near Plymouth. Florence of Worcester says that this battle was on the borders of Ecgberht's dominion, so that we can say with some certainty that by the end of the reign of Ecgberht the whole of Devon, as at present bounded, must have been within his realm, if not yet definitely marked off from Cornwall.

What trouble there was between Wessex and the remains of Dyvnaint in the years to come seems to have arisen from the tendency of the Britons to favour the Danes, which may be traced in the wars of Alfred, and resulted in the final expulsion of the Welsh from Exeter by Athelstan, and the definite establishment in 936 of the line of the Tamar as the Cornish boundary. The fortification of Exeter, and the building of the fortress at Barnstaple are of this date, when the actual inclusion of modern Devon in the Wessex dominion seems to have been at last complete. The long wars with the Danes no doubt retarded the progress of settlement, for the coming of the great hosts marks a new stage in the history of Wessex and of England.

The known close alliance of these newcomers with the Welsh of Cornwall seriously retarded the pacification of the far west, and enabled Cornwall, the last cantle of Dyvnaint, to retain some sort of independence for nearly a century after Devon had passed into Saxon hands. It is quite likely that during the troubled reign of Alfred fear of western attack was added to the anxiety consequent on the advance of the Danes on Wessex under Guthrum, and that only personal and diplomatic action on the part of the king kept the far west quiet. It is known that he rode into Cornwall to speak with his kinsman, St Neot, during the Athelney period, and returned from him with renewed hopes of victory, which, though claimed as due to some prophecy on the part of the saint, may have been the result of successful negotiations with Dungarth, the Cornish king, whom Alfred is said to have visited as a friend at another time.

Whether this was the case or not, it is somewhat remarkable that in the great gathering at Ecgbryht's Stone previous to the victory at Ethandun, neither the Devon nor Dorset levies are mentioned, although the gathering-place is actually on the border of the latter county. The inference is inevitable that while the Dorset levies had to watch the coast and the line of the North Dorset downs in order to prevent any flanking attack by the Danes, the Devon men had to guard against a possible rising of the far west in concert with the invaders, the precaution being in both cases successful.

Coin of Alfred.

Alfred seems to have considered some part at least of Cornwall as in his dominions, as he speaks of "Trigonshire" in his will. The term has been lost, and it is not certain whether he can mean the whole of the present county, or some isolated part of it where he had personal possessions.

The actual conquest of Cornwall is due to Athelstan. According to Borlase and other authorities on the history of the county, he defeated in 936 the Welsh, under Howel, their last king, at Haldon (Howel Down?) near Teignmouth, and again near the Land's End. There must have been a Welsh advance into Devon to account for this former battle, and a complete rout and pursuit with the final crushing of the Welsh forces "in the last ditch" as a result, after which Athelstan is said to have conquered the Scilly Isles. The county must however have been still allowed a certain independence, as it was subjected to a yearly tribute, which was payable in gold and silver, with the service of a few men. Athelstan also established Saxon religious houses in Cornwall here and there, the predominance of the old British Church in Cornwall apparently ending at this time. At the same time the Danish influence in the west came to an end, and with the Saxon rule, Cornwall was exposed to the attacks of her former allies, Bodmin and the southern towns being burnt at one time or another, and the country wasted by the Danes in a thorough way from which it has never recovered.

While the setting of the Devon-Cornish boundary at the line of the Tamar by Ecgberht and Athelstan is definite and permanent, we have no similar certainty with regard to the final delimitation of the lands of the "Sumorsaeta" and "Defna," owing no doubt to the absence of so well-marked a frontier as that afforded by the western river. To the west of Taunton the Exmoor line remained undecided, as we have seen, until a very late date. Immediately south of

See A Compendium of the History of Cornwall, *Rev. J. J. Daniell, Truro, 1880.*

Taunton again is a gap with no natural frontier line, where the boundary must have depended on the varying extent of the great royal forest of Neroche from time to time. The crest of the Blackdown hills, which the modern county boundary follows from this gap to near Chard, no doubt is the ancient frontier of the kingdom of Gerent. The Dorset-Devon boundary thence follows a branch of the Fosseway south until the road crosses the river Axe, after which it takes a less well-defined course which is probably due to some administrative arrangements between the shrievalties of Lyme and Axminster, in days when coast defence was a serious local responsibility. We can therefore only claim for the central or Blackdown section of the boundary between Wessex and Dyvnaint that it represents Gerent's frontier. His wars with Ine settled some sort of "march" between the two kingdoms, but the sharp line which we find on our maps to-day is the result of later centuries. Even in the time of Edward the Confessor, the old Dyvnaint seems to have been considered as one administrative district, the earldoms of Devonshire, Somersetshire and Dorsetshire being granted by him to one Odda, according to Henry of Huntingdon. It is noteworthy that an Odda was earl of Devon in the time of Alfred, name and title being in this case perhaps alike hereditary.

Alfred's jewel, found at Athelney. Now in the Ashmolean Museum, Oxford.

Chapter 8

In any endeavour to reconstruct a picture of the
warfare through which the south-western
counties of England became Saxon, and of the
later campaigns in which Wessex checked the
Danes and paved the way for the eventual union
of the English and Northmen in one kingdom,
many of the details must be conjectural, and no
more than a broad outline is possible. The
historical records prior to the date of Alfred are
meagre in the extreme, and documentary
evidences from other sources are almost non-
existent. The outlines we can trace must be filled
in by an appeal to the evidences of physical
geography, archaeology, and perhaps of folk-lore,
difficult to decipher, and liable to be misread.
The utmost that can be done is to seek the best
evidence available from whatever source it can be
gathered, and to read it into something like a
consistent whole without trying to twist any fact
to fit in with preconceived theories.

Rebuilt in this way these dim struggles of a
half-forgotten and long neglected past have an
interest which is not purely local. They take a
rank higher than the "battle of kites and crows"
with which Milton classed them, for they were
the means of shaping the destiny of the Saxon
kingdom to which belongs the honour of saving
England for her own folk from the almost
victorious Danish invaders.

It is one of the curiosities of our early history
that in the struggle for supremacy between
Northumbria, Mercia, and Wessex the last should
have emerged as pre-eminent. The indications
seem all to have pointed toward the victory of
one of the other two powers. From the time when
they first came into collision Wessex never won a
decisive victory over either of the other
kingdoms, until the defeat of Mercia at the battle
of Burford 752. Even after that defeat, Mercia
had completely recovered her power, and in 777
defeated Wessex afresh at Bensington, and
stripped her of her possessions north of the
Thames. Yet it was only fifty years later that

Mercia succumbed entirely, and the greater part of England and Wales accepted Ecgberht of Wessex as overlord almost without a blow.

In the course of the succeeding century Wessex alone was able to oppose any steady resistance to the Danes. Northumbria fell early, and the history of Mercia is nothing but a record of defeat and misery. The reason for the failure of the kingdoms north of the Thames is fairly evident, and has been pointed out by other writers. Green, for instance has noted that Northumbria suffered from the initial drawback of being formed by the union of two co-equal provinces, which were never really welded into one, the result being constant disunion and the anarchy which finally wrecked her. Mercia, in much the same way, was never a homogeneous kingdom, but an agglomeration of states whose only bond of unity was geographic proximity and a powerful overlord. The absence of a commanding personality at once let to internal strife.

Wessex cannot claim that she was free from this last trouble, for the rivalry between the houses of Ceawlin and Cutha was frequent. But in her case the quarrels were more purely personal and dynastic than in the other kingdoms, and, though while they lasted they were a source of weakness, these disputes left the kingdom united in the face of the common enemy.

But it was the fact that, from the beginning of her history, Wessex had to face a determined enemy, which was the most important factor in her steady rise to power. In the case of the other kingdoms there was nothing quite like the long struggle in which, by slow degrees, the old British kingdom of Dyvnaint was conquered, and absorbed into the kingdom of Wessex. The Welsh states which they had to encounter were, singly, less powerful and less able to offer a sustained resistance to encroachment than Dyvnaint, and their internal jealousies rendered it impossible for them to act in concert. From the first, Dyvnaint suffered from no disunion, and was slowly forced into closer cohesion still.

The difficulty of the task that tried the strength of Wessex to the utmost is seen in the length of time that it took to reduce the Britons of the west, and the sharp lines which mark the limits of the Saxon advance. To a certain extent these lines were due to the nature of the country, as we have tried to show, but the natural strength of a frontier must needs be taken full advantage of, if it is to be of any avail. Dyvnaint was strong enough to use her advantages in this way to the full, though at the last she had no such impenetrable fastnesses on which to fall back as confronted Mercia in Wales, and Northumbria in the mountains of the Picts and Scots.

From the date of the capture of Old Sarum in 552 the advance of Wessex was rapid until after the battle of Fethanleag in 584, when the dynastic quarrel first broke out within her borders, and she met the southward advance of the other English kingdoms. The battle of Deorham brought Wessex to the borders of Dumnonia in earnest, and from that time forward we may be certain that desultory warfare was incessant between Saxon and Welsh from the shores of the Channel to the Severn Sea—warfare which was not of sufficient moment for chronicle by the Saxon writers, but rather a matter of course, as the first settlers made their way into what were still Welsh lands, in East Somerset.

If we chose to take extreme dates, therefore, we might reckon the war with Dyvnaint, as a kingdom, as lasting from the battle of Deorham in 577 to the final conquest of Cornwall, which was not actually complete until the time of Athelstan, who subjugated Howel, the last independent prince of the West Welsh in the tenth century, a period of some three hundred and fifty years.

Reckoning however from the first recorded pitched battle between Wessex and Dyvnaint, when Kenwealh won the victory at Bradford on Avon in 652, it might perhaps be fair to omit from the count the period when Wessex was distracted from all thought of aggrandizement by the Danish peril at the end of the ninth century, and consider the conquest of Dyvnaint as ending with the battle of Gafulford in 822, when Ecgberht completed the conquest of Devon, and may have established some sort of overlordship over Cornwall. Within these dates the time required for the conquest is fully one hundred and seventy years. In that long period the territory won is comparatively small, and the final stages of the occupation of Devon long drawn out.

Until Wessex lost her acquisitions in the Severn valley to Penda of Mercia, seventy-five years after the battle of Deorham, and was unable to expand further in that direction, her leaders would seem to have shrunk from war with Dyvnaint. Yet Wessex must expand in some direction, and this necessity seems to have led to the advance under Kenwealh, probably, as we have said, with constant border bickerings as the immediate excuse.

Before this new advance occurred an event had taken place which must have had a profound influence on the conditions of the struggle. Wessex had accepted Christianity, and though the British Christians of the old Western Church hated the Saxon followers of Augustine almost as bitterly as they had hated them as heathen, the profession of a common Faith must at least have put an end to the internecine methods of heathen Saxondom; and this new feature of the relations between the two races must be taken into account in considering the slowness of the advance of the Saxons into Dyvnaint.

In one respect however this new acceptance of Christianity may have actually prompted the fresh advance. The lavish generosity of the early Saxon conquerors to Glastonbury suggests that they had set their hearts on winning a shrine which both Briton and Saxon held sacred. The motives of the Crusades are natural and will show themselves in the wish to acquire the ancient holy sites in any age, or in any land, and the new convert is even more enthusiastic than the man who has held the Faith from his birth. It is possible, too, that motives of policy led Kentwine to value the possession of the Isle of Avalon, for we find evidence that he endeavoured to make the Abbey the mediator between the two races who were drawn to worship at their holy spot. On the other hand, the fact that Glastonbury had passed into Saxon power must have had its full influence in the prosecution of the war by Dyvnaint, so long as that ancient kingdom retained its independence. It is hardly conceivable that the hope of regaining Glastonbury did not animate the West Welsh at least in the early days of the long warfare, while from their frontier outposts on the Blackdown hills they could still look undisturbed across the fenlands and the Polden hills to where the Tor marked the lost shrines. Year after year, moreover, the dispute between the two Churches was brought home to the pilgrims from the west and from across the Severn, as they found their Easter disregarded, and reached the shrines either too late for the Saxon festival, or too early. Those were great matters, and worth fighting for, in those days of simple faith. They must not be forgotten. The struggle between the two Churches had their full influence in the war between Ine and Gerent. Aldhelm had kept the peace with his wise counsel, but his death let loose what was from all evidence a religious war.

Excepting during the disastrous period of the subjection of Wessex to Mercia, thirty years is the longest period which goes by without a record in the *Chronicle* of a war with the West Welsh. The intervals are generally much shorter, and no doubt during these intervals there was much unrecorded fighting on the border, and many raids and forays from either side which were looked upon as ordinary incidents. There may have been British victories, and transient periods of British success, but we have no reliable British records, and the Saxon writers record little beyond important actions and the main stages of their advance, though with a fine impartiality they will set down as a calamity a defeat inflicted on their own people, if it had any serious result. We are really gainers by the fact that the chroniclers recognised that a border fight, whether won or lost, was but a matter of course, as the accumulation of small details is most apt to obscure the broad outline of actual progress.

The fighting with the West Welsh was incessant. The battle at Bradford in 652 is follwed six years later by the battle of Peonna, and twenty-four years after that, Kentwine drives the Welsh to the sea. Twenty-eight years later Ine and Gerent fought, and Taunton was built. Then Wessex strove with Mercia, and Dyvnaint was at rest for forty years, unless she regained some of her lost ground. Probably that was the case, for with the end of the Mercian trouble in 753, Cuthred of Wessex had to fight Dyvnaint afresh, and the battles of Cynewulf are apparently too many to record. One may suppose that Wessex was successful in curbing the Welsh, for until Ecgberht was well established on his throne, and was ready to make a bid for the overlordship of all England, he had no need to trouble about Dyvnaint. Cynewulf's battles against her had exhausted the Welsh for the time. Yet, driven as she was into narrower bounds, the resistance of Dyvnaint had grown more fierce, and even the great captain, Ecgberht had to fight for ten years, from 813 to 822, before he won his decisive victory at Gafulford.

How materially this long struggle had trained Wessex for war can be best realised from the events of the years following. Once the fear of Welsh action on his frontier had been relieved, in

Coin of Ecgberht.

the same year as that of Gafulford, Ecgberht broke the power of Mercia at Ellandun, and brought into subjection the whole of southern England. Within six years he had extended his sway over Mercia and Northumbria, and was lord of North Wales, at least in name. The Wessex levies were composed of veterans of the Welsh wars, and Ecgberht had learnt the art of war with the greatest leader in Europe—Charlemagne.

The western Wessex frontier was for two centuries practically the school of arms for England. In the days when a standing army was unknown the thanes in such a district, which was never really at peace, must have kept the men-at-arms of their own households and manors ready for instant service. At any moment the beacon fires might signal a Welsh raid which, unless checked at once might flare into a war which would devastate the whole countryside. The courts of such local princes as Baldred at Somerton, or of Ealdbriht the exile at Taunton later, must have been full of the sons of Wessex thanes who were eager to learn something of the art of war against the West Welsh.

The result of this long training of the men of Somerset, who had of necessity borne the heaviest part of the watching of the frontier, until the fight at Gafulford proved that the Devon men were able to keep back the Cornish, is seen as soon as a new enemy was to be met. It speaks well also for the readiness of western Wessex that, on the landing of the viking fleet in 845 at the Parrett mouth, the Dorset levies were marched across the country, from sea to sea, to take part in the victory won by Bishop Ealhstan with his Somerset levies. There seems to be a note of compactness and organisation in the record, which one looks for in vain in the feeble resistance to Danish landings in Mercia. It cannot be doubted that the same conditions rendered possible the sudden and swift rally of apparently beaten Wessex to the call of Alfred, which gained the great victory of Ethandun. Somerset after this date was only attacked at long intervals by passing fleets, for she was known to be well prepared.

Wessex was still in the state of growth and expansion when the peril of the Danes fell upon England. Northumbria had relapsed into anarchy, and had long ceased to attempt progress northward in the lands of the Picts and Scots. Mercia, safe behind the line of Offa's Dyke, had reached her culminating point with the completion of that work under her greatest king, and had begun a period of slow decay. Her relapse into sloth and luxury is lamented by the old mediaeval chroniclers as accounting for her easy subjugation by the invaders. Wessex alone had not yet grown to her full strength. She was still in arms against the desperate Welsh of the far west, with Devon barely won, and Cornwall yet unconquered. Her levies knew the need for instant response to the gathering summons, and her thanes had little to learn of how to lead them. The wars with the Welsh merged into the wars with the Danes, and Wessex could hold her own with either foe.

Cf. Lappenberg's England under the Anglo-Saxon Kings, *Vol. I, p. 251.*

BOOK 2

Chapter 1

Evidence has of late been accumulating which tends to prove that intercourse between the Scandinavian countries and Britian was much closer, and dates back to earlier times than has been supposed. At the same time it is growing more clear that the wave of migration southward was not confined to the eastern coasts of our islands, but must have found its way slowly but steadily down the coasts bordering the Irish sea also, reaching the great inlet of the Severn long before historic times. It is possible to regard the great historic inroads of "the Danes" on the southern shores of the Severn as events in a sequence which began even as early as the Bronze Age.

Professor Oscar Montelius, the Royal Antiquary of Sweden, is of the opinion that trade between Great Britain and the Scandinavian Peninsula began as far back as the Stone Age. As evidence of this he points to the fact that in the country round Gothenburg there have been found twenty-five burial cists, built of stone slabs, of a type which is only met with, elsewhere, in England. According to his reckoning these burials date from at least 2000 BC. The connection seems conclusive, as there is nothing more distinctive than national, or even tribal, burial customs.

"Trade in Ancient Days" (Nordisk Tidsskrift *for 1908, Nos. V and VI).*

The later occurrence in Sweden of a certain type of shield and other objects of bronze, which otherwise appear to be peculiar to England, the Professor considers as proof that the connection continued into the Bronze Age.

It is more than interesting to find this conclusion confirmed by an unexpected discovery in West Somerset. The very remarkable circular wall discovered in the centre of the Wick Mound excavated in 1907 by the Somerset Archaeological Society and the Viking Club has few resembling examples in these islands, only some half-dozen having been found, one of which is in Somerset, and two in Gloucestershire. A fifth example, which more closely resembles

Excavations at Wick Barrow, *by H. St George Gray. Taunton, 1908.*

that at Wick than the others is the wall found in the "Horned cairn" of Ormiegill, in Caithness.

Grave mounds containing similar walls are however not uncommon in Denmark, and a tumulus examined in 1879 in Norway by Mr A. Lorange of the Bergen Museum, showed a similar structure. These northern examples and the Wick mound alike belong to the Late Stone or Early Bronze Age, and the conclusion is obvious. Graves of an unusual and specialised type in the days of the earliest "Folk-wanderings" have their own meaning. There must needs have been a connection between the northern continental bronze-using folk and the western shores of England, of which the evidence from Somerset is early, but cannot be the less important. Possibly as one tries to trace the wave of migration or trade south, the cairn in Caithness may serve as a connecting link between the far north and the Severn shore.

This growing evidence of early Teuto-Gothic intercourse with our islands strengthens the opinion that even before the accepted date for the Anglo-Saxon invasion of Britain the northern influence must be looked for, if only along the coasts. Probably the earliest settlements were made by traders who came on peaceful errands, and died and were laid to rest after the manner of their own people. We have also to reckon with the auxiliaries of Gothic stock who were brought over by the Romans to hold the land, and remained, as it were perforce, to colonise here and there. Lastly came the sea-rovers who began to harry the coasts for many recorded years before they finally came to conquer.

The attacks from the Scandinavian north in historic times were not confined to the south-eastern corner of England, though the more pressing danger of invasions in that quarter has brought them into greater prominence. It is now almost a commonplace to say that what was known as "Saxon shore" on the east coast of England was already more or less colonised by

The types of crania found at Wick prove that the mound was made by the mixed race resulting from the meeting of Stone and Bronze Age races.

Dr Fridtjof Nansen considers that as early as the time of the explorer Pytheas, three hundred or more years B.C., there was communication between Shetland and Norway, and that Pytheas himself probably made a voyage to Norway on information gained either in Shetland or the north of Scotland (In Northern Mists, Vol. I, p. 60, London, 1911).

Stone carving of a ship from Gotland, Sweden.

Saxons when the Romans came, and that point need not be gone into. But as regards the western coast we may recall the fact that when the Romans reached it two legions were stationed at Chester, one to guard the land against the Celts of North Wales, and the other to watch against pirates from the western sea. The Roman historian, Ammianus Marcellinus, tells us that in the year 364 the Saxons joined with the Picts and Scots to attack the Britons, and it is therefore clear that even at that early date the inroads from the north had begun. It is to about this time also that the inscription on the well-known "Cat-stane" near Edinburgh belongs. This reads as "In oc tumulo jacit Vetta F. Victi," a reading which if correct, as there seems no reason to doubt, shows that the stone was the monument of the grandfather of Hengist and Horsa, named in the pedigree of those chiefs. The coincidence of name can hardly be accidental, and the finding of it on the shores of the Firth of Forth is another link with the dimmer past and evidence of the historic existence of chieftans who have been regarded as half legendary.

The Cat-Stane, Edinburghshire, by J. Y. Simpson, M.D., F.R.S., Edinburgh, 1862. See also Haigh's Anglo-Saxon Conquest, p. 142, and Stephens' Old Northern Runic Monuments, Vol. I, pp. 59-71. The Latin annalist Prosper says that by the year 425 Britain was under the power of the Saxons. They were fighting as allies of the Picts at the "Alleluia Victory" in 429, according to Bede (B.I. CXX).

Nordisk Aandsliv i
Vikingetid og tidlig
Middelalder, *pp. 10,
11.*

King Alfred's Orosius.
*The statement in the
Icelandic*
Heimskringla *that Ivar
Vidfadme, an early
Swedish king,
subdued "a fifth part
of England" seems to
point to these early
Saxon people and
their first colonies*
(Heimskringla, *S.I, C.
XLV).*

*See "Two
Derivations," by
Professor Erik
Bjorkman,* Saga-Book
of the Viking Club,
Vol. VII, pp. 138-40.

Vesterlandenes
Indflydelse paa
Nordboerne, *by Dr.
Alexander Bugge, pp.
11, 317.*

See a paper on The
Sculptured Stones of
Norway and their
relation to some
British Monuments,
*by Dr Haakon
Schetelig, read before
the British
Association in 1908;
also* Norges Historie,
*by Dr A. Bugge, Vol.
I, Part I, pp. 119-23,
Christiania 1912.*

One is somewhat accustomed to think of the Anglo-Saxons and Danes of our early history as two entirely different races, but it is beginning to be recognised that the former people stood in much closer relationship to the Scandinavian than to the Low-German folk. Professor Axel Olrik draws a sharp line, linguistic in the main, between the Jutish Anglo-Saxon and the Low-German races, and it is too often overlooked that besides Sleswick, Jutland, and the Danish islands, the Angles actually occupied part of south Sweden before their migration. It is hard in fact to disentangle Dane from Anglo-Saxon in these early stages of the northern folk-wanderings. The great epic of *Beowulf* belongs equally to either race, for after the conquest of England Hygelac, the "Chochilaicus" of the Frankish annalists, made his famous raid on the Netherlands (circa 520 A.D.) from the same lands whence the Angles had sailed, as the saga and history alike bear witness.

The early invasions of England by the Anglo-Saxons were in all essentials like those of the later Danes, and it is noteworthy that the word "Viking" (Wicinga) is found in use in Anglo-Saxon literature before the Danish period, though it is nowhere applied to the invaders of the fifth and sixth centuries.

The first traces of very early occupation of our islands by adventurers from the far north would naturally be looked for in the Scottish islands. Here are Norse place-names of forms dating back to times earlier than 700 A.D.: permanent names of this sort of course involving long settlement, though this is not always recognised.

Here are also found certain well-recognised types of sculptured memorial stones, the Christian symbolism of which is repeated on similar stones in the south of Norway, and finds affinities in the south of Sweden. The best authorities assign these stones to the end of the seventh century. Still earlier occupation of these northern Scottish islands may be inferred, if we

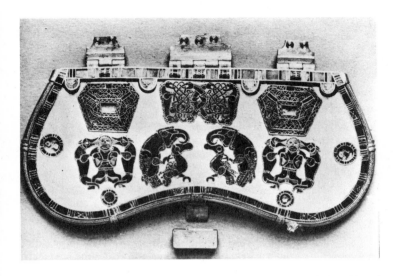

7th Century purse-lid with gold plaques inset with garnets and glass. Found
at Sutton Hoo, Suffolk.

accept Dr Alexander Bugge's proposed
identification of *Straumeyjarnes,* where
according to the "Haleygiatal" of Eyvind
Skaldaspillir a king of Halogaland was put to
death by two Swedish kings about the middle of
the sixth century, with *Straumsey,* now Stronsay,
in Orkney.

Heimskringla, *S. I, c.
XXVI.*

The view that adventurers from the west coast
of Norway had reached the Shetlands between
the years 590 and 644 seems therefore likely to
be correct. The devastation of Tory Island off
the Irish coast, recorded by "the Four Masters"
in 612, and the burning of the monastery on the
island of Eigg on April 17, 617, by a fleet coming
from the ocean, may be referred to the same
source, unless it is to be considered a matter of
local warfare between the Celts themselves.

Vikingerne, *Vol. II, p.
40, Christiania, 1906.*

The question of the development period of
Irish decorative art and its influence on Norse
design is still in debate, and though it has some
bearing on the date of the earlier settlements
from the north along the Irish coasts, it cannot
outweigh the linguistic and generally cumulative
result of the evidence which points to those

Prof. H. Zimmer,
Ueber die fruhesten
Beruhrungen der Iren
mit der Nord-
Germanen, *p. 21. Dr
Nansen dates the
establishment of
Norwegian
settlements in
Shetland and their
raids to Ireland and
the Hebrides as
occurring in 612.*

settlements being in existence by the end of the sixth and beginning of the seventh centuries.

Historic records are concerned in the main with warfare and its results. It is a commonplace of history to say that trade and the trading settlement precede the raider and conquest, and it is safe to infer in any case that, even if the once peaceful trader did not occasionally return as an armed invader, the natural line of raid would be directed to districts where trade had ascertained that the most profit could be looked for. The visits of traders, or even the permission given to outlanders to establish trading posts, are too insignificant to find a place in the chronicles. They may be inferred, but it would be unusual to find them recorded. Such settlements of traders have however left their traces, and it is not impossible that closer study of local peculiarities might disclose still further evidence of their existence.

The first definitely historic attacks on the Irish coast made by the Norsemen are recorded in 795, and the first warfare with them on the mainland in 807. Attempts at settlement by conquest did not begin until some fifteen years later, yet at least as early as 857 we find a mixed Norse and Irish race, the Gall-Gael, joined with denationalised Irish, playing an important part in the history of that time, which cannot be accounted for by considering this mixed race as the result of one generation only. Of these Gall-Gael, Eleanor Hull writes:

"The Gall and the Gael. Notes on the social condition of Ireland during the Norse Period." Saga-Book of the Viking Club, *Vol. V, pp. 375 et seq.*

They seem from early times to have formed a considerable population in some districts. They had their own fleets, and were formed into bodies of fighting troups who warred sometimes on their own account and sometimes on behalf of the Northmen.

She then quotes MacFirbis, *Fragments of Annals,* where we read under the year 852,

A battle was fought by Aedh, king of Aileach, and the fleet of the Gall-Gael. These were Irish who had been foster-children to the Northmen, and at one time they used to be called Northmen.

On the question of fosterage she says,

This system of fosterage among people who were their country's enemies must have begun very early, if the mixed race had become a distinct body with their own troops and fleet so early as the year 854-5. It suggests that even during the earlier period of the Norse incursions, before the kingdom of Dublin had been formed, or what we usually consider the period of settlement had begun, a good deal has to be taken into account that is not covered by the theory of perpetual feuds and enmity. A parent would not place out his young child to be brought up during the whole of his or her youth . . . unless a feeling of confidence and friendship had already been established between the races . . . I am led by this fact alone, if we had no other, to believe that the Norse races had penetrated into Ireland and had established a not entirely unfriendly footing there along before the period at which the annalistic records notice their advent. It does not appear to me that the space of 50 or 60 years was sufficient to breed up this race of semi-Northmanised Gaels . . . It was not among the ravages of his home and village that the Irish father would choose to place out his children: it was among a people more or less settled among themselves, and on friendly and familiar terms with his tribe and people that he would desire to foster his family. We are led thus to conceive of the peaceful and gradual settlement of considerable bodies of Northmen long before and quite independent of the organised coast attacks of the unfriendly invaders.

Geoffrey of Monmouth makes in his *British History* (Book XI, c. 8) a curious statement which is usually considered as sheer romance. He says that a body of Africans, under one Gormund, came from Ireland to assist the Saxons, and captured Cirencester. No date is given, but the context shows that these events were supposed to have taken place some years before the landing of Augustine in 596. Of course Africans from Ireland are impossible, but if Geoffrey took materials for his history from Irish chronicles, he would find mention of the "Black Heathen"—the "Dubh-genti"—under which name the Danish invaders and settlers in Ireland are designated. The only "Black Heathen" known to Geoffrey would of course be Africans, and his statement may be more valuable than it

115

Professor Alexander Bugge has pointed out the obvious explanation of "African" in this passage as "Black Heathen," e.g. Dane. But following his method of trying to refer all such legendary statements to some known historical character, he considers that Geoffrey has transferred the Guthrum of King Alfred's time to an earlier period. There is however, nothing but the name, not an uncommon one, to connect the two. "Havelock and Olaf Tryggvason," Saga Book of the Viking Club, Vol. VI, p. 292.

"Brut y Tywysogion." "Gwentian Chronicle." "Annals of Ulster."

seems at first sight. Gormund certainly represents a Scandinavian name (Gorm, Guthorm, Guthrum), and is used by Gaimar for Guthrum. It is, therefore, quite possible that behind the tradition recorded by Geoffrey there may lurk the fact that a Danish contingent from Ireland did co-operate with the West Saxons in 577, the date of the battle of Deorham and capture of Cirencester.

The conclusion is irresistible that, as Miss Hull considers, there were well-established settlements of Northmen in Ireland preceding the chronicled raids, and therefore earlier than 795. Another point with regard to fosterage may be noticed, as defining the position of these early settlements to some extent. Among the Norsemen, to foster the child of another was regarded as a sort of tacit admission of the superior position of the parent of the child. The Norse trader, established by sufferance in the midst of aliens, would be ready to cultivate friendly relationships by taking children of Irish chieftains to foster. The quasi-relationship of foster-parents in those days was almost sacred, and the rough common-sense of the Norseman would accept the implied inferiority of himself to the chief on whose lands he had made a home without any loss of self-respect.

If these peaceful settlements were possible in Ireland, they would be even more so in Saxon England, and there is no reason to suppose that they did not take place. In the more exclusively Anglo-Saxon districts it might be impossible to distinguish them from settlements of Northmen in the Viking Age, or from those of Northmen who originally came with the English conquerors of the island; but in the districts which remained Celtic in the main, their place nomenclature may be recovered, even if documentary evidence of settlements is almost necessarily lacking for the reason that the trading settler was not worth notice. The expulsion of the Danes from South Wales is given in Welsh Annals as occurring in

795, which is the same date as that of the first recorded warlike raids on Ireland, but the names of northern settlements prove that here is recorded but the end of a long occupation.

Chapter 2

The stream of migration from the north which we have traced to its permanent resting-place in Ireland naturally travelled down the opposite coast at the same time. The midway-lying Isle of Man was occupied early, and the settlements of the migrants can be traced in the Cheshire Wirral, and in the flat lands to the north of the Mersey estuary, where the place-names are of the same type as those of Danish East Anglia. South again the northern names reappear along the Welsh coast, and notably in the well-known and recognised "Danish" settlements on the Severn shores of South Wales.

How long before 795, the recorded year of the expulsion of the Danes, the trading settlements had existed is uncertain, but it is not unreasonable to suppose that they were founded not much, if any, later than those in Ireland, which we date back at least to the seventh century. The same conditions which produced the Gall-Gael in Ireland would naturally obtain in Wales, and it is not likely that the expulsion of the Danes was so sweeping and complete that those related to the Cymro by fosterage and intermarriage were involved. Certainly there was still at a much later date a close connection between Norse colonies in Wales and Ireland, as sculptured stone in the churchyard of Llanrhidian in the Gower peninsula is recognised by Professor Collingwood as a "hog-back" tombstone of typical Celto-Scandinavian type, similar to those found in the north of England.

It is almost impossible to suppose that the far richer shores and inlets of the coast across the Severn were not exploited by the migrants who found the way to South Wales. Even the northwest wind of the Severn estuary was in itself an incentive to hold on toward the southern shore, when once the narrow waters were entered, and there was as yet no reason for the Celt to dread the coming of outlanders who wished only to trade. There was tin to be had from the farthest west by known trade routes, and the Quantock copper and the Mendip lead to tempt the newcomers—the first two metals being indispensable in days when bronze was still the universally used material of every day. Possibly it will be at some time realised what the search for bronze-making metals meant in the early days of trade and of the founding of havens. It must have been almost as important as the present search for gold.

In the eighth and ninth centuries the "Danes" appear as the allies of Dyvnaint. The Britons of the west knew them as friends from the first, and looked to them for help as the growing power of Wessex pressed on Devon and Cornwall. It was only after the whole western peninsula had become Saxon that the Danes marauded in the lands of their old allies. The presumption that the friendship, and friendly settlement on the coasts, was of ancient standing, and that here also was a mixed race as in Ireland, is very strong.

We cannot expect documentary evidence of the coming of the northern traders to North Somerset. As we have said, the trader finds no place in the chronicles until his success brings the raider. Yet he leaves his traces, and they are still plain in the place-names and traditions, and in the actual racial characteristics, of the shores to the eastward of the Quantocks, where the coast lends itself to settlement by a seafaring race. The strips of fertile land along the coast are for the most part backed by marshes or moorland and forest that would render them difficult to attack and would afford safe retreat in case of need. There are two definite trade routes also, one into the interior of the ancient Dyvnaint, and the other into Wessex, which would render trading posts at their coastward ends almost certain. They may of course have been there from time immemorial, but there is no doubt that they were occupied, and perhaps revived after disuse since the departure of the Romans, by the traders from the north.

The first of these small ports was Watchet, the

Worsaae, The Danes and Norwegians in England, Scotland, and Ireland, *London 1852, pp. 339-40. This king was more than once driven into exile, and as he used this mint as well as others in England, must have made Watchet his port of refuge.*

ancient *Weced,* or as in Domesday, *Wecet.* The
derivation of the name is doubtful, but the oldest
form, Weced, may perhaps have the same root as
the Scandinavian settlement of Wexford. The
little haven stands at the mouth of the great
valley running between the western slopes of the
Quantocks and the broken forest country of the
wilds of Brendon and Exmoor, which stretch for
thirty miles or more westward behind a coast
which is for the most part cliff-bound and
harbourless. Up this valley was practically the
only road from the Severn sea into Dyvnaint, and
the haven of Watchet must always have been of
some importance, the close connection between
the British kingdoms on either side of the Severn
sea being well known. At the head of the valley
was the strongly fortified British position at
Norton Fitzwarren, which was superseded on
Ine's advance westward by the Saxon fortress at
Taunton.

The present harbour at Watchet is small and
artificial, owing to the steady gain of land on sea,
but in early times the tide ran inland thence up a
narrow valley as far as Washford, not more than
two miles from its mouth, where the name is
evidence that the head of the inlet could be
crossed by a tidal ford. Watchet then stood on a
natural haven, well sheltered from the prevailing
north-west winds. Only a short distance to the
eastward, toward the foot of the Quantocks, was
another inlet, wider and shallower, and between
these two ran the road from the haven up the
great valley to Norton and the rest of Dyvnaint.
Two miles or so from Watchet and across this
road, lies the village of Williton.

The name of this village is usually, and no
doubt correctly, held to mean "the town of the
Welshmen," and both the name and position of
the place seem to have definite meaning in
connection with the port. The village is in such a
position as to bar the passage inland by the road,
and as a matter of fact has been the scene of
some severe battles, the burial mounds resulting

from which still remain and are the subject of more or less vague traditions and theories. These are almost as a matter of course concerned with the Danes, but no reliance can be placed on them until the mounds have been scientifically examined.

The sharp racial definition implied by the name renders it almost certain that here at Williton was the guarded point at which the British traders from Dyvnaint met the outland sea-faring merchants from the haven which they occupied. The distinction of this village as the "Welsh town" specially, rather than any other or others on the borders of Dyvnaint, can only have to do with its position in reference to the town at the haven, and the name must have been given by the occupants of Watchet itself. It can hardly have arisen after the conquest of this portion of Dyvnaint by the Saxons, for there is no reason why the Saxons should have distinguished any particular town in Dyvnaint as "the Welshmen's town" rather than another. The existence of a Saxon trading post in this district before that time is not indeed impossible, but any such settlement is far less likely here than in South Dyvnaint, owing to the natural jealousy caused by the steady encroachment of Wessex on the Somerset border. The only other outland traders who would consider and call the British "Wealas" were the northern adventurers from across the channel, they using the same term for the Celtic races with which they came in contact. They would be welcome in the days when Dyvnaint was a powerful and independent British kingdom in the end of the seventh and beginning of the eighth century, and the conclusion that Watchet and Williton were practically founded at that time and dependent on one another seems inevitable and altogether reasonable. When the district became Saxon the kindred Danes would amalgamate with the conquerors even more easily than their Welsh neighbours and the use of the names would continue.

Watchet at all events lost neither its importance nor its connection with the Danes of Ireland in Saxon times. At the end of the tenth century it had a mint, where not only coins of the Saxon kings were struck, but also those of Sigtrygg Silkbeard, king of Dublin. It is only the natural and historic sequence of events that the port was raided by the Danes in the Viking period as a known trade depot over and over again. The marauding viking had no objection to falling on men of his own race when "acquiring property" as the phrase went. Even Harold Godwinsson raided Watchet on his way from Wales in the early eleventh century. Possibly it was still a known Danish settlement.

The second trade route from the Severn sea which we have mentioned is from the mouth of the Parrett into Wessex, and the traces of occupation by "the Danes" is even more definite here than at Watchet, the strip of coast between the marshes and the sea to the west of the estuary giving more scope for settlement than the narrow space between the two sea inlets at Watchet, while the Quantock camps were sufficient safeguard against undue encroachment by the northern strangers.

The haven is now represented by the little Combwich "pill," or tidal creek, which is all that remains of a considerable tidal inlet which at no very distant date ran for some miles inland toward the Quantocks. A well-known ancient trackway, still traceable on the Ordnance maps, crosses to the tidal ford at Combwich from Dyvnaint by way of the pass known as "Will's Neck" on the Quantocks, and continues on the east of the river to the Poldens, where it joins the ancient, and possibly Roman road through Street to the Fosseway. A haven at Combwich therefore had the same advantage of direct routes to Wessex as that at Watchet possessed with regard to Dyvnaint.

Combwich was superseded, probably after the foundation of Taunton and the consequent

This track is mentioned in Phelp's Somerset. For further local information as to the trackways of the district, the Rev. W. Greswell's Land of Quantock *may be consulted, with a warning that the course of the trackways in the neighbourhood of Combwich is not shown correctly in the sketch maps in the last-named book and in* The Story of the Battle of Edington *by the same writer.*

diversion of trade routes, by the port at Bridgwater with its subsidiary at Downend, where the Polden road reaches the river. The result has been that the neglected Parrett haven has retained characteristics which have been obscured at Watchet. At the same time the formation of the country has allowed undisturbed settlement by the haven makers to a greater extent, every inlet seeming to have been made use of by them. The name of Combwich itself is undoubtedly British, but there are several small inlets on the actual Severn shore which have names which are of evident northern origin.

West of the actual Parrett mouth were inlets at Whitewick, Wick and Lilstock, which are even now only protected with difficulty from the tides by a sea wall against which the pebble ridge (known here, as in Dorset, as the "chesil") seems to form an unbroken foreshore. Each of these inlets may have formed a small haven, and the Wick channel certainly did so up to quite a late date, old maps marking the westward point at its mouth as "Botestall." Between Whitewick and the higher land toward Wick is Catford, and on the edge of the Wick inlet, which is now called Wick moor, is the fishing village of Stolford. There can be no doubt that these inlets derive their name from the Old Norse "vik," a bay, and the adjacent place-names of Stolford and Catford on their shores are from the Old Norse "fjord," the former being a compound with "stall," which occurs in "botestall" already mentioned, and the latter having perhaps some affinity with the name of the "Cattegat" between Denmark and Norway. The occurrence of these forms in conjunction proves that they are rather of northern than of Anglo-Saxon origin.

The fisherfolk along this strip of coast are of a racial type differing markedly from the generality of the population of the Quantock district, which shows a strong Celtic admixture with the Saxon population, the black-haired brachycephalic type being very common, and the dialect belonging to the Devon group, which has noticeable peculiarities not found to the east of the Parrett. The fishing population of Stolford, Stert (at the Parrett mouth) and Combwich, and to some extent at Burnham across the Parrett mouth, are of the fair-haired, blue-eyed Scandinavian type, and would pass for natives of Norway anywhere along the coast from Christiania to Bergen. They have intermarried for ages, and still hold themselves somewhat apart from the neighbouring population, and preserve family traditions which are significant.

The fishing methods and customs peculiar to this district are perhaps due to local necessities, but the boats in use are of a type not found elsewhere, and are of a three-strake, flat-floored, double-ended build, with a marked "flare" at bows and stern which is strongly reminiscent of the Norse longship. The smaller boats are quite usually without thwarts, and are steered with an oar astern. They are very swift and extremely handy. The rowers in the boats without thwarts sit on three-legged stools, and the baler in use is of the exact pattern of those found with buried ships of the Viking age, carved out of a single block of wood. The centre-board was introduced by a returned emigrant to America some twenty years ago, or less, and was immediately adapted to these boats, with good results, otherwise the type has been unchanged from time immemorial. The boats are built by traditional "rule of thumb," which is marvellously accurate, and unfortunately likely to be lost with the death of the last hereditary boat-builders. The fishing is losing its profitable nature, and the demand for boats is ceasing.

The family traditions among the fishermen are not given away to the first comer, and are not to be drawn by leading questions. There has been no theorising by local antiquaries on the spot, which by dint of repetition has grown to be the matter of "they say" among the villagers, the bane of the tradition hunter of to-day, and

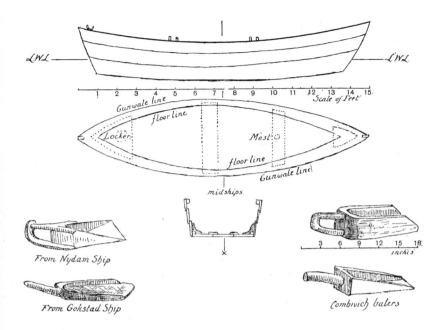

Combwich sailing boat and balers.

nowhere to a greater extent than in districts sacred to King Alfred. What is said of the Danes on the shores from Wick to Combwich is genuine tradition of a kind which cannot have been invented.

We may pass over the Quantock tradition that there was a great slaughter of the Danes at the camp of Dowsborough on the Quantocks. It is repeated with regard to the battle-burials under the walls of Cannington Park camp, and was known to Wordsworth, who based a poem on it. The local tradition records that "some of the Danes had married our women," and tells how that on a prearranged night these women slew their husbands. But this is hardly a tradition of peaceful settlement, but of Sabine tactics — possibly relating to some unrecorded wintering of a small Danish force in the havens of the district.

But one coast family has a definite claim to Danish origin, from actual settlers. Some twenty-five years ago a member of this family organised

The modern name "Danesborough" given to this camp is probably due to the tradition. The local name is always "Dowsborough."

and trained the local band at Combwich. He seems to have been self taught, but then "he came from the old Danes, and they were the most musical people that ever were. When they were about here some of them stopped and settled down, and he came from them. So that is where he got his music from." Two traditions are involved here, one being of the difference between the northern and Welsh music, and the other of actual settlement.

Another Stolford family of the fair type (Rawlins, locally pronounced "Hrollins," and probably derived from the Norse "Hrolfing") has a definite tradition that they were driven out of Wales and came to Stolford, but at what date they do not know. It seems impossible to refer this tradition to the end of the eighth century, unless the extraordinary persistence of personal tradition among an isolated population is taken into full account, but in any case the family is evidently connected with the Danes of South Wales.

That any connection with the Danes at all is claimed here is the more significant when the known dislike to "red-headed Danes," common through Somerset, is remembered. Probably those shore folk are the only individuals of their class who would not indignantly resent the suggestion that they were of that origin.

More personal names of Scandinavian form occur among the Quantock district tenants of de Briewer at the time of Domesday than anywhere else in Somerset.

The records of inroads in historic times refer to short instances, such as defeated landings only, and it seems impossible to refer settlement traditions to a date later than the eighth century. It would hardly be likely that the survival of occasional individuals from these later raids would be remembered.

The existence of a very marked series of quite local traditions, or rather, folk-tales, of a heathen and northern type has also to be accounted for, occurring as they do in a district which was not acquired by the Saxons until they had been for some time Christian. They are associated with the country from Combwich along the line of the old trade route across the Quantocks, and the only heathen from whom they can be derived are men settled at and near the haven itself.

The belief that the Danes of the already mentioned massacre are still living within the crest of the hills on which Dowsborough camp stands, and that their songs and revelry can occasionally be heard at midnight there is of Scandinavian type, and also the statement that the most beautiful music was to be heard from the large tumulus on Wick moor. The name of Wayland the smith (Volundr) occurs at "Wayland's pool" a shallow, peaty, but never dried up, pool at the intersection of four ancient boundaries at the base of Dowsborough. Also at Keenthorne, the point of intersection of the main road with the old track, halfway between the hills and Combwich, where a smithy has stood from time immemorial, there is a legend of an unusually skilful smith who boasted that he would shoe the devil's own horse if needed, and had to do so accordingly, recalling again the smith of the Asir.

The "wild hunt" is still said to pass from Cannington Park camp to the Quantocks, and is still feared. The hill known as the "Park" is itself an outcrop of mountain limestone through the red sandstone, and its occurrence is said to be due to diabolic origin, it being a basketful of material brough across the Parrett by the fiend when he cut Cheddar gorge. The footprints he made in his leap over the river are still to be seen at the foot of the camp, one being a hoof-mark, and the other that of a vast foot.

The Wild Huntsman is met here in three forms, one of which is most unusual. He is seen as a headless horseman in black, riding a great black horse: as a man following great black hounds with fiery tongues, and riding a horse which is headless: and as the rider of a vast pig which passes overhead. The legend tells further how the last named of these three riders once halted to speak with a belated wayfarer, who was only saved by the accidental use of the Holy Name. The belief in these apparitions is so real that within the last ten years it has been impossible to retain the tenant in the shepherd's cottage on the edge of the park, close to which the old track runs, owing to "the devil" continually looking into the windows and barring the man's way home in the dark.

These three appearances of the fiend, occurring together thus, are decidedly significant. The headless horseman occurs elsewhere in England, but in any district represents the hooded Odin of the old belief. The headless horse also occurs occasionally, we believe, but much less frequently. The horse was the favourite sacrifice to the Asir among the Scandinavians, and the method of sacrifice was usually by beheading. The third appearance is extremely unusual, and is practically that of Frey, the rider of the golden bristled boar "Gullinbursti." We have here accordingly the tradition of the three leading Asir with their special characteristics—Odin who rides with hooded and hidden head, Thor to whom the horse sacrifice, forbidden to Christians was made, and Frey.

The road from Combwich to Cannington passes over what is known as "Rodway hill," and the local statement is that it is so called from the Rood erected there to prevent the wild hunt from passing across to the latter village. Cannington Park has certainly for some reason been invested with supernatural associations which are most easily to be accounted for by the existence at one time of a sanctuary of the old Gods within its walls. It is rather remarkable that only on this outcrop of the limestone do the ash trees, sacred to the Asir, grow within a radius of many miles, and their exceptional presence might be connected with such a spot.

The legends of Scandinavian type connected with Wick mound are worth notice, the field, "Pixies' patch," in which it is situated being close to Stolford. One legend is associated with the

These legends have been recorded in detail in Folk Lore, *Vol. XIX, No. I, March, 1908.*

Horses thus sacrificed by beheading were found with the Oseberg ship-burial (Saga-Book of the Viking Club, *Vol. IV, p. 64).*

It is not suggested that the walls or camp are Scandinavian. They were used in the Early Iron Age, and are probably far older.

Rawlins family already mentioned. The pixies who lived in the mound were disturbed by "Mr Rawlins' uncle," when threshing in his barn. The legend is repeated with reference to an old barn at Cannington but without the traditional name. The other legend tells how a ploughman found the broken baker's "peel" of a lamenting pixie on the mound, mended it, and was rewarded by finding on his way home a cake baked for him by the grateful owner. Craigie gives an almost identical story in his *Scandinavian Folk Lore*.

Certainly if these converging lines of place-names, tradition, and folklore were found grouped thus in Lincolnshire or Holderness they would be at once claimed and recognised as Scandinavian, and it is doubtful if anyone would be found bold enough to question that conclusion. We think that there is not the least reason to question the existence of a pre-Saxon, heathen settlement of Scandinavian origin on the coast from Combwich to Stolford, with the small haven at the foot of Cannington Park as its head-quarters, and as a possibility, a sanctuary of the Asir within the camp walls, which the Saxon conqueror of the district, probably Kentwine, found already in existence.

The records and date of the Saxon advance on West Somerset preclude the idea that the Odinic traditions can be due to Wessex men, who did not come into touch with this part of the country until they had long accepted Christianity. Of course occasional references to the Asir as "the Devil" can be found scattered through England, but that the heathen associations which are grouped round Cannington Park could have originated and taken firm root there after the conquest of the district by Christian Wessex is impossible.

A pre-conquest settlement of heathen Saxons in what was then independent Dyvnaint is for political and other reasons as unlikely here as at Watchet, and the place-names compounded with "wick" and "fjord" are against any such theory of the settlement. There was no possible settlement of the Danes made in historic times, the records being entirely of passing raids. It requires long and peaceful occupation of a district to account for permanent and deeply rooted traditions.

The only possible conclusion is that toward the close of the seventh century there were settlements of Scandinavian traders, contemporary with those in South Wales, established at the Parrett mouth and at Watchet, at the least tolerated by the princes of independent Dyvnaint, as useful to them, and probably profitable.

It may have been one of the reasons which induced Kentwine on his conquest of this district to leave untouched a strip of land along the coast from Parrett mouth to the Quantocks, that it was occupied by men of kindred race who would be useful as allies and dangerous as enemies. It was on the borders of this strip that he placed lands in the hands of Glastonbury, and it may have been the monks of that establishment who raised the Rood on Rodway hill against the "diabolic" gods of the heathen men of the haven.

Chapter 3

In reading the *Chronicles* which recount the
successes of the Norse and Danish hosts in
England, there are one or two points which are
not always recognised, but should be borne in
mind. At first sight it would seem extraordinary
that an invading host should be able to do much
what it would in the face of what should be an
overwhelming rising of the folk of the raided
country, even if the landing had been made but
from a few ships. It may seem incomprehensible
again, that after a solemn pact had been made
with a Danish host, there should be the very next
year perhaps a record of the return of a fleet and
yet more terrible raidings, as if the word of a
northern leader were worth nothing, or the
Danes were habitual oath-breakers. But both
these difficulties vanish to a great extent with
some further consideration of the conditions of
the case.

As regards the almost unchecked landings of
the earlier invaders, it should be noticed that the
successes were temporary, the invaders sooner or
later being driven off by the local levies. But they
seem almost invariably to have carried their
booty with them, and that they lost their ships is
never recorded, except where a sea force had
some success against them, or there were wrecks.

The earlier landings were entirely for plunder.
The ships were beached, or berthed in some
haven, and a strong shipguard left with them.
The remainder of the crews went inland and
raided without opposition while the beacon fires
were lighted, and the fugitives sought the sheriff.
By the time he was found, and the men of the
shire had word where they were to gather, the
vikings were on their way back to the ships with
as much plunder as they could carry, and
probably reached them without a fight. They
would then pass on to the next haven, and repeat
the progress through the country within reach.
Even supposing the slow levies came up with
them, or by some luck intercepted them, on the
way to the sea from inland, the advantage was

entirely on the side of the invaders, "whose trade was war," as one of the old chroniclers says in accounting for a Saxon defeat. The Viking had come to fight, while the Saxon levies came up unwillingly, with nothing more than a dull fury at the disturbance of their peace, and the burning of their homesteads, to inspire them. They fell on their enemies, outnumbering them utterly, and the enemy fell back, as he had intended to do. There was no reason for him to stay longer, and, above all, he had not the least objection to fighting his way back. To fall fighting against odds, if so it must be, was part of his religion.

But the arms of the Viking were immensely superior to those of the Saxon levies, among whom was little or no mail, and whose usual weapon was the long spear. Missile weapons on both sides were probably much alike, but the Norse and Danish sword and axe were far better weapons than those of even the Saxon thanes.

There was little actual discipline in the Saxon forces. Each thane had his few housecarles round him, and after them was a mass whose only idea of cohesion was to stick together, parish by parish, and farm by farm, following the few thanes whom they knew by sight. On the side of the Vikings was the stern discipline of the trained crews of the ships, each man of which had learned in the hard necessities of the sea the need for instant obedience, and knowledge of his own place and leader. They had been told off from the first to the oar banks, three men to each oar, one to row, one to shield, and one to fight, each knowing the place which he was to fill when one of his two comrades fell. Each man knew where he was to be posted when the rowing stopped, and the foredeck, and after deck, and amidships were manned as they ran alongside another vessel and grappled for close-quarter contest; and each leader knew his place, and his men, who knew the one whom they were to follow. The crews held together ashore in the same way. The terrible "wedge formation" of the Norsemen

Reconstruction of a Scandinavian ship found at Oseberg.

reproduced the form of the ship, with her best
men in the bows, and the three-deep lines of
rowers, sword, shield, and reserve man, along its
sides, and the rear guard closing all in with the
men of•the after deck. Even the shield-holding
was a matter of science as carefully learned as the
sword-wielding, and it was the part of the second
in a "holmgang" duel to shield his principal.
There is no wonder that the raiders took their
booty with them, and regained their ships. The
men of the wedge would make short work of the
crowding mass of spearmen round them, whose
long weapons and very numbers hindered them.

It was the same on a greater scale with the later
hosts. The very fact that they were in hostile
country kept the Danes together, and while the
crews of the ships were always a rallying point
for any force, the men learned to know their
leaders by sight and to follow them implicitly.
The Saxon levies melted away to their homes
after a victory or after defeat, and the loss of a
known leader was fatal.

In the earlier days of the Viking landings, as distinct from the coming of the hosts of Ingvar and Guthrum, or of Sweyn and Cnut, the numbers of the invaders were very small. To set the crew of a ship at about 100 is probably nearly correct on the average, but the whole of the crew was not available for a march inland, as a strong shipguard must be accounted for. It will be overstating the strength of a force to multiply the number of ships by 100 to give the numbers of the actual enemy to be met by the local levies. Their success was a matter of discipline and of weapon craft, combined with good leadership. Long experience had given the chiefs full knowledge of the best way in which to proceed in any sort of country which might lie beyond the shore.

Of the numbers of the greater hosts we can form little estimate. We read of fleets whose vessels were counted by the hundred, and these must have ranged in size from the best longship with her crew of six score or so, to the smallest craft which could cross the open sea in summer weather and in company. No doubt there were constant, unnoticed arrivals of later detachments all through the months of the more terrible raidings, while each fleet left a proportion of its men in England, at least in the eastern counties, to join again in the next raid. It was rather the compactness and the swiftness of the later Danish hosts which demoralised the English resistance, than their actual numbers. The pitched battle, where each host deliberately sought the other and fought the matter out, as at Ethandun, or at Penselwood and Sherston, was the exception. The interception of a host on its way to the sea was the rule, and such a host expected attack and was not to be caught unprepared.

Against such trained forces England had no men available except in Wessex, where the long wars with Dyvnaint had kept alive the knowledge of the value of discipline; had produced a line of veterans who knew the leaders of the counties; and whose thanes must of necessity have kept their housecarles ready for instant battle with the Welsh raiders from across the border. Looking back on the records of Wessex warfare it is hard to point to any time when it could be said, as it might be said of the midland kingdom, that there was hardly a man in the land who knew what warfare was. The tales of the last fighting were still being told by the men who had fought, when the next need for the levies came.

With regard to the pacts made with the Danish hosts, it should be remembered that, until the eleventh century, practically every fresh host which came to England was independent and acting entirely on its own initiative, from the day when the chiefs agreed to sail together with what ships they could gather until they set sail with their plunder on the homeward voyage. They were as independent as, or more so than, the "gallants of Fowey," their descendants, who made war on France without leave of the king, or the "Gentlemen adventurers" who, like the vikings, "sought to gather property" in the Spanish main, in the days of Elizabeth.

One chief and his men might make terms with the Saxons, and if he did so, he would keep his word—but that word by no means bound any other host under another chief, or even the men who chose to leave the peacemaker and join another leader. The oath sworn "on the Holy Ring" at Wareham is a case in point. The sea-borne host made peace, but the mounted force which had ridden from Cambridge would not be so bound, and rode through Alfred's lines accordingly. The king learnt his lesson, and after Ethandun he had all the chiefs of note before him, and bound them. That frith was well kept. Later, when both Denmark and Norway were under one king, the oath of the king was enough, as in the case of Olaf Tryggvason. But in the earlier days the independence of the several hosts must not be overlooked. There is also the

See Book III, Chapter I.

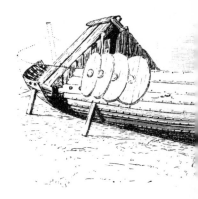

Viking ship unearthed at Gokstad,
Sweden.

question as to whether the hosts were in any way
connected.

It is not always easy to recognise from the
accounts of the *Chronicles* whether the raiding
fleets whose comings are recorded are Norse or
Danish, as the old writers make little distinction
between the two nations. In Ireland indeed,
where the Norse and Danish hosts were in actual
rivalry, some racial distinction, whether from
peculiarity of arms or from physique, was

Viking ship unearthed at Tune,
South Norway.

recognised between the "White" Norse, and
"Black" Danish heathen; but to the Saxon the
two were much alike. They both spoke the easily
understandable Dansk tongue, came in the same
remarkable type of ship, on the same errand of
plunder in the earlier days, and were alike armed
in a way which was far superior to that of the
Saxons. It is due to the greater importance and
definite intention of conquest on the part of the
swarming hosts of the Danes in the later stages of

137

*Coins of the eighth
and ninth centuries
brought from England
are rare in the north,
though there are more
coins of Aethelred the
Unredy found in
Scandinavia than in
England. Of the nine
earlier English coins
eight were found in
graves in Norway, and
only one in Denmark.
This is some
indication that the
earlier Viking raids
were mostly carried
out by Norse fleets.
Four of the coins
found in Norway are
Mercian, three
Northumbrian, and
one Kentish. The
single specimen from
Denmark is a penny
of Alfred (Dr A. W.
Brogger,
Angelsaksiske Mynter
fra VII-IX
Aarhundrede i
Norden, Norsk
historisk tidsskrift,
1912).*

*Asser no doubt uses
"pirate" as the
equivalent of the
Anglo-Saxon wicinga,
a word which is first
used in the* Chronicle
*for the army that
occupied Fulham in
879.*

the invasions that the name of the Norseman has been almost lost in that of his northern neighbours.

In the latest phases of the invasions the Norse hosts are more clearly recognised, as in the tenth century the rivalry between Norway and Denmark was marked, and the Norsemen appear as allies of the Saxons against the Danes in England. Even as early as the days of Alfred tradition has it that he asked for help from Rolf Granger, the conqueror of Normandy, to show that he may at some time or another have actually had Norse mercenaries fighting for him, and it is almost certain that the "pirates" with whom he manned his first ships must have been Norsemen, of whom the channel was full at the time. There was a strong Norse contingent with Athelstan at Brunanburh, and later still Olaf the Saint was the best ally of Aethelred and Eadmund Ironside.

The greatest Danish hosts landed in the east of England, long after the shores of western Wessex had learnt to dread the coming of the fleets. The western peninsula lay open both on the shores of the English Channel and of the Severn Sea to attack by the Viking fleets from the Danish and Norse settlements in Ireland and in the Scottish isles. The first wave of invasion passed from the north down the Irish Sea, leaving the settlements which we have traced; and at last, finding peaceful lodgement of the South Welsh and North Somerset shores which are still traceable, opened the way to the more desperate expeditions which came in the last years of the eighth century. It is quite likely that beside those settlements which we have noted there may have been more in Devon and in Cornwall which a little research would locate with some certainty. Danish settlements in Cornwall are traditional, at all events. Exeter seems to have been a known haven where Danes would find some sort of welcome, but this may have been owing to its late Welsh population. Trade and the settlement of the trader, as we have said, preceded the raiding host, and Exeter may have had its Danish quarter from an early date.

It is hardly surprising therefore that the first hostile landing of Viking crews recorded occurred in Wessex. One is so much used to the records of the coming of the Danish fleets that the east coast of England might have seemed the more likely shore, but it was as yet too early for the gathering of the great Danish hosts. Next in likelihood might have seemed the Severn coast; but here were peaceful settlements in friendly Dyvnaint which would not be meddled with. To land at Watchet or in the Parrett would be to jeopardise the traders there; and it was not until the expulsion of the Danes from South Wales, which was apparently the result of just such a raiding landing which recoiled on the traders, that Somerset was attacked. The first landing was just beyond the borders of Dyvnaint, in Dorset within a ride of Dorchester, in 787.

The entry in the *Anglo-Saxon Chronicle* is remarkable in several points and is as follows:

A.D. 787. Here King Beorhtric wedded Eadburga, Offa's daughter. And in his days first came three ships of Northmen of Hereoa-land. And then the reeve rode to the place and would have driven them to the king's town, because he knew not who they were. And they there slew him. These were the first ships of Danish men which sought the land of the "Angelcynne."

According to Ethelwerd the reeve was the sheriff of Dorchester, whose name he preserves (one Beaduheard, the first Englishman of all slain by the "Danes"). This officer took the Vikings for traders, and fell in trying to enforce his authority on them. The Viking paid his harbour dues by the sword after his fashion. It must be owing to the cross-questioning of the Norsemen by this sheriff that we actually know the district in Norway whence the ships came—Hordaland; and the passage is remarkable as one of the few where the Northman is specified and the confusion with the "Dane" is made also.

The actual haven in question is not known, but may be either Weymouth, Poole, or Charmouth. For some reason the Northmen knew that haven, little used as it is at the present time.

As the sheriff had reason to think that these ships were traders, the very distinct type of Norse vessel must have been favourably known to him as frequenting the neighbouring coasts of Dyvnaint, in the land of the "Weal-cynne," which they did seek, the racial distinction made by the unusual use of the term "Angel-cynne" in speaking of Wessex being thus quite explainable. There is no reason to suppose that, as the *Chronicle* says, this was not actually the first appearance of Norse ships on the shores which were definitely Saxon at this date. The raiding fleets from the north had reached Ireland only two years before, so that we may consider this appearance of raiders in the Channel as early and adventurous; and we shall not be far wrong if we take it that these three ships were stragglers, or even explorers, from the greater fleets beyond the Land's End. It is quite possible that they were storm-driven, or making a passage, and put in for food and water, as both Ethelwerd and Huntingdon imply that the fighting was due to the high-handed action of the sheriff, and, at all events, no ships followed these for a generation.

The next recorded appearance of the Danes in the west of England was in 833, when 35 ships came to Charmouth in Dorset, and there defeated Ecgberht. Two years later the men of a large fleet joined forces with the West Welsh, and were defeated by Ecgberht at Hengestesdune on the Cornish border. In 837 a fleet of 33 ships made an unsuccessful descent on Southampton, and in 840 a victorious landing was again made at Charmouth from 35 ships.

As the recorded number of vessels remains practically the same is is quite likely that the same fleet is responsible for these consecutive landings, and the alliance with Dyvnaint. The short intervals between the attacks is about sufficient for recruiting in the north. Southern Wessex was left in peace after this, but now the troubles of Somerset were to begin. The record of the landing is as follows, in the *Anglo-Saxon Chronicle.*

> A.D. 845. In this year Ealdorman Eanulf with the men of Somerset, and Bishop Ealhstan and Ealdorman Osric with the men of Dorset, fought at the mouth of the Parrett with the Danish army and there made great slaughter and had the victory.

Presumably, as the levies engaged came from the Somerton and Sherborne districts, the landing was made on the east bank of the Parrett, and therefore in what was definitely Somerset territory. The surviving local traditions of a great battle under Brent Knoll most probably refer to this engagement.

This victory must have been crushing to the invaders, as there was no further attack from the Severn for a generation—while the memory of the defeat lasted, that is. As a Norse fleet was defeated at Ith, in Ireland, in this same year, it is quite probable that the ships which were beaten off by the Irish sought plunder in the Severn before turning homeward. It is noticeable that they seem to have left Dyvnaint unharried still.

By this time the Danes were active in the eastern counties, where the first landing had been made in 838, fifty years after the first attack on the west. In that year and the next the whole coast from the Humber to Kent was ravaged, and from this time the records of the Danish landings to the eastward are incessant, but as yet the landings were temporary, the fleets returning to Denmark for the winter until the year 851, when they wintered for the first time in England, taking up their quarters in Thanet.

In 851 Ceorl the ealdorman and the Devon men fought against the heathen men at Wicganbeorh, and had the victory. This battle was probably at Wembury at the mouth of the Yealm, near Plymouth, and the invaders would be men of some of the fleets which we know from various

The identification
with Wembury is
questioned by Mr
Stevenson (Asser's
Life of King Alfred,
p. 176) and
Wigborough near
South Petherton, is
suggested as a possible
site. Professor Oman
(England before the
Norman Conquest,
425) points out that
this place might have
been reached either
by a raid up the Axe
or up the Parrett. The
possibility that this
may have been
another raid into
Somerset from the
Severn Sea is
interesting, but there
is no evidence on
which any such
speculation can be
based.

Mardon near Devizes,
Marden near
Hungerford and
Bedwyn, Merton near
Bicester, and Merton
in Surrey have each
been suggested. "So
generic a name is a
poor geographical
guide" (Earle, Two of
the Saxon Chronicles.
Note on year 871).

chronicles were infesting the channel in that year. Athelstan the under-king of Kent himself had a naval engagement with one of them off Sandwich, taking nine ships, and this year also saw the coming of the terrible fleet into the Thames, whose men stormed London and Canterbury, and were crushed by king Aethelwulf at the great battle of Ockley.

In 860 there was a landing, presumably at Southampton, and Winchester was stormed. The men of Berks and Hants, however, drove out the invaders eventually.

After 860 the war with the Danes was to the eastward of Wessex until the coming of the great invading host, under the sons of Lodbrok and their associates, with the definite intention of settlement. Wessex was fallen upon in the course of conquest in 871, the year of the nine battles in the kingdom south of the Thames fought by Alfred and his brother. The last two of these battles were at Meretone and Wilton on the road to the sea at Wareham.

King Aethelred died a month after the battle of Merton, and was buried at Wimborne. John of Brompton says he was mortally wounded in battle with the Danes and died after great agony, and the inscription on his tomb is also said to have recorded that he met his death at the hands of the Danes. Bishop Heahmund of Sherborne was slain in the same battle, which is likely to have taken place in the neighbourhood of Wimborne, though, as a matter of course in the case of a common place-name, the site of the battle-field is disputed. Warne in his *Ancient Dorset* suggests that it was the present village of Martin in south Wilts (the earlier forms of which name are Merton and Mertone), lying a mile north of Bokerly Dyke, which forms the boundary between Wilts and Dorset, and fourteen miles from Wimborne. He has preserved a tradition of the death of a king in battle on Hanham Hill in the neighbourhood, and another that King Aethelred died at Wichampton, which is on the Roman road some ten miles south of Martin and five north-west of Wimborne.

Ancient Dorset, by Charles Warne, F.S.A., 1872, pp. 267-74.

In the absence of documentary evidence to the contrary, or in favour of any other Merton, Warne's identification may be considered as correct, the traditions not being of modern fabrication. The position on the ancient bulwark of Bokerly Dyke points in the same direction, the next battle, fought only a month after Alfred's accession, being fought at Wilton, eight or ten miles further north.

It would seem that the Danes were making an attempt to cut their way across Wessex to the sea at Wareham, and that the old barrier across the Roman road and between the forests was held against them by the Saxons with as good effect as when it was held against the early comers by the Britons. The endeavour to reach Wareham was to be made again later, under different conditions, and with complete success.

Neither of these battles seems to have been a Saxon victory, as though in both cases the Danes gave way at one time during the day, they eventually retained possession of the battle-field. The loss on both sides is recorded as very heavy, and the Danes probably found the forcing of Bokerly Dyke a task beyond their strength. At any rate, the result was the conclusion of peace with "the army," which retired from Reading to London, and thence to East Anglia, leaving Wessex alone until 876, while they completed the conquest of Northumbria and Mercia.

The campaign which began in 876 is that which ended with the decisive battle of Ethandun, and the delimitation of the Danelagh. This campaign is dealt with in its own chapters, and we pass it over for the time. The sixteen years' peace which it ensured was only broken, as far as the west country was concerned, by what was evidently a strategic landing in Devon in 894, planned in order to create a diversion and divide the Saxon forces, which were operating in the eastern counties against new hosts.

This was effected by means of a fleet gathered in Northumbria and East Anglia. Apparently the eastern ships to the number of about 100 sailed south into the Channel while 40 northern vessels entered the Severn. The former fleet besieged Exeter, and the latter an unnamed Devon fortress on the Severn shore. King Alfred was thereupon forced to march westward, and eventually raised the siege of Exeter. Meanwhile the eastern Danes had received reinforcements, and now marched up the Thames valley until they came to the Severn, when the western levies were called out "from every town east of the Parrett, and as well west as east of Selwood, and also north of the Thames, and west of the Severn and also some part of the North Welsh people." This detailed account of the Saxon gathering is important, as it gives not only the names of administrative districts, but is also the first record of Welsh assistance against invaders.

It is possible to recognise in the *Chronicle* accounts of this year the origin of the mistake which has placed the landing of Hubba at Appledore in Devon. The entry runs, "some forty ships besieged a fortress in Devon by the north sea, and those who went about to the south besieged Exeter. When the king heard that he turned westward toward Exter. . .Hasten was then come with his band (to Bamfleet), and the great army was also come thereto which before that had sat at Appledore near Limenemouth." Confusion with Appledore and *Lynmouth* in Devon is very easy. Most probably any actual tradition of a Danish defeat near Bideford and the adjacent Appledore referred to this western landing of the men of Hasten. But it is now hopelessly ruined, and beyond reference with any certainty, even if it has not become a mere matter of romance.

In the end, the Danes were penned into some fort at Buttington on Severn, where they were defeated after a sort, but regained their ships in Essex, whence they marched in what was

Appledore and the river Limene (Rother) in Kent.

apparently a most remarkable retreat right across England to the Wirral in Cheshire, "at one stretch day and night." Here they wintered, but again passed unchecked through Northumbria back to East Anglia in the next year, effecting a junction with the sea force driven from Exeter, which had been beaten off from Chichester with heavy loss on the way. It is on record in the *Chronicle* that these marches were so swift that the Saxon levies could not overtake the retreating hosts.

Chapter 4

In 897 the Danish hosts broke up, as if they had come to the conclusion that further conquest in England was impossible. "Some went to East Anglia, some to Northumbria, and they who were moneyless procured themselves ships there, and went southward over sea to the Seine." This moneyless acquisition of ships seems curious at first sight, but is elucidated in a following sentence. "That same year the armies from among the East Anglians and Northumbrians harassed the land of the West Saxons, chiefly on the south coast, by predatory bands, most of all by their "aescs" which they had built many years before."

Evidently the "moneyless" repaired and launched afresh some locally built vessels which had been laid up in the eastern estuaries since the Danelagh was handed over to Guthrum. The term used, "aesc," is a Saxon general name for a ship, derived from the ash timber of which it was made, according to the dictionaries; but more likely, in this case, it is chosen as representing the northern "skuta," which appears in Old French as "escute," and still survives in the Dutch "schuyt." The existence of an English name so closely approximating in sound to a northern term would be quite enough to prompt its use. The "skuta" was a light vessel of shallow draught, fitted for sail and oar, pulling from ten to fifteen oars a side, and adapted for use in tidal and inland waters. No doubt these English-built "(e)scuta" had been made for use in the many waterways of the eastern counties, and even for the expeditions up the Thames, where the more valuable sea-going longships were not available owing to their size and draught, or where it was inadvisable to risk them. The size of the "aescs" is roughly given by the statement that Alfred's new ships, built on purpose to cope with them, were of twice their length, with sixty or more oars—thirty a side that is—and this answers precisely to the usual dimensions of the northern "skuta," which would be quite fit for summer

The dictionary explanation of "aesc" is probably deduced from this passage.

See "Notes on ship-building in the North," by Eirikr Magnusson, Saga-Book of the Viking Club, Vol. IV, Pt. I, 1905.

Map showing area (shaded) under Danish control in A.D. 880.

use in the Channel.

The ships planned at this time to meet the raids of the "aescs" were not the first English fleet. Alfred's predecessor, Aethelwulf, had, as already noted, ships which gave a good account of themselves off the Kentish coast; and Alfred himself won a fight or two at sea in 885-6 with a fleet manned by "wicingas," who at that date would be Norse. The present ships were built to meet an emergency, planned on special lines which were neither altogether Danish nor Frisian, and seem to have been manned in part by Frisians, who would almost certainly have built them.

The first engagement in which these new ships took part was not altogether a success, the enemy which they had to meet not being the small "skuta," but the far more formidable sea-going ships from the westward. Six of these had harried in Devon in 897, and were encountered in the Solent by nine of the new vessels. There was a good deal of mishandling on both sides, probably owing to ignorance of the double tides of the Solent, and three ships from each fleet ran aground, and their crews fought at low water, both Saxons and Danes losing heavily. Three Danish ships escaped for the time, but were subsequently driven ashore, only one reaching East Anglia in the end.

The new ships answered their purpose, however, as there is no record of more depredation by the "aescs," and what trouble arose with Danes for the next twenty years was mainly with those who were settled in the Danelagh, who occasionally rose and marauded after the ancient fashion of the Saxons themselves in the first centuries of their settlement. The likeness between the Saxon conquest of Britian and the Danish conquest of the Danelagh is very close.

The year 898 has an entry which is significant as regards the position of Dyvnaint. The death of one Wulfric, the king's "horse-thane" (master of the horse, one would suppose, unless he was a known cavalry leader), is recorded and the chronicler adds: "He was also Wealhgerefa."

There is no doubt that this Wulfric was a high official whose duties were concerned with the Welsh frontier. Kemble supposes that he was master of Alfred's Welsh serfs, but they would be sufficiently well overseen on each estate where they were in existence by the local foremen, and the term must be of a wider scope. Professor Earle thinks he was "a Margrave commissioned to watch the Welsh border," and quotes evidence, dated in 855 and in 1053, to show that such an officer was needed on the Mercian Welsh borders. It may however be a question whether the line of Offa's Dyke was very much in Saxon hands during the Danish occupation of Mercia, but is is quite certain that an officer in charge of the Dyvnaint border was needed. The duties of Wulfric may have been mainly military, but his position must have been political also, and the "Welsh-reeve," whose death is worth recording amid what might seem more important matters, would be the probable forerunner of our own political officers in quasi-independent parts of our later empire among other "Weal-cynne."

In 910 a fleet came from Brittany and ravaged in the Severn. This would be a Norse fleet, unconnected with the Danish hosts, and probably the expedition was nothing more than a viking raid. The record is that "they afterward almost all perished there."

The next actually recorded landing is in 918, when a Danish force under Ottar and Hroald was defeated, probably in Herefordshire, and beset near the mouth of the Severn. This fleet also came from Brittany.

Two of the Saxon Chronicles, note to year 898. The quotations from Kemble is there given also. A variant 'gefera'' also occurs in one or two MSS of the Chronicle; and the meaning "steward" or "agent" is rather confirmation of the political position of the officer.

And the king had arranged so that his force sat opposite to them on the south side of the Severn mouth west from the (Welsh) shore, as far as the mouth of the Avon east, so that they durst not anywhere seek the land on that side. Then nevertheless they stole away by night on some two occasions, once up to the east of Watchet, and on another occasion to Porlock. Then they were beaten on both occasions, so that few of them came away save only those who there swam out to the ships. And these seated themselves out on the island of Flatholme ("Bradanrelice" in one MS., "Steapanreolice" in another—the two islands are close together, and both were no doubt occupied) until the time when they were greatly destitute of food, and many perished from hunger, because they could not obtain any food. They then went to South Wales and then out to Ireland: and this was in the autumn.

This raiding is probably responsible for the tradition given at pp. 214, 215, where the ships were cut loose. This detail corresponds with the chronicled statement that only those who swam out to the ships escaped. Unless the vessels were lying off shore they must have been set adrift.

After these two raids, which were disastrous to the invaders, we read of no more attacks upon the western shores for upwards of sixty years. The north had for the time exhausted her resources, and the record of the *Chronicles* becomes one of the gradual reconquest by the English of the north-eastern portions of their own land which had been left as the "Danelagh" after the Frith of Wedmore.

In 980 the Danish attacks on the west recommenced, and Hampshire was ravaged, the fleet passing northward to Chester. The raid seems to have been noted as one in which slaves were taken, as the record is that in Southampton

"Most part of the townsmen were slain and taken captive." In the next year, 981, Padstow was ravaged and there was harm done in Devon as well. In the year following, a landing from three ships was effected in Portland.

"A.D. 988. In this year Watchet was ravaged, and Goda the Devonshire thane slain, and with him great slaughter made." Henry of Huntingdon adds that the Danes advanced from Watchet and so fell in with the English forces, slaying Goda their leader, and crushing that part of the army. Florence of Worcester adds the name of another thane, Strenwald, who was slain among others, and says that the English remained masters of the field. The tradition of the battle at Williton probably belongs to this event.

The fatal mistake of buying off the fleets was first made in 994, but the same year saw the truce made at Southampton with Olaf Tryggvason of Norway, which was loyally kept during his life. William of Malmesbury says that of £26,000 paid to the hosts he and his men received £16,000. Olaf sealed his peacemaking by becoming a Christian, and the conversion of Norway practically dates from his return from England.

The years 997-8 saw a terrible renewal of Danish inroads in the west which coincides with some significance with united action by the Irish kings, Brian Boroimhe and Mailsechlainn II against the invaders, who suffered a severe defeat, and the subsequent loss of Dublin for a time. There need be no hesitation in assigning the expeditions to England of these years to fleets beaten off from Ireland, or deterred by the unexpected alliance of the princes from landing there. The Severn was naturally their next objective. The record runs:

997. In this year the army went about Devonshire into the mouth of the Severn and there harried, as well in Cornwall as in North Wales, and in Devon. And then they went up to Watchet, and there wrought great evil in burning and man-slayings. And after that went round the Land's End to the south side, and into the mouth of the Tamar: and then up until they came to Lydford, and burnt and slew all that they met with. And they burnt Ordulf's minster at Tavistock, and brought unspeakable booty to their ships.

Apparently they wintered in the Tamar, unopposed until the spring when they left for a landing further to the eastward, and fell on Dorset. They landed "In the mouth of the Frome, and everywhere they went up as far as they would into Dorsetshire. And oft was the levy gathered against them, but as soon as they should have given battle, then was there ever flight ordered, and in the end they ever had the victory." The record seems to be one of the incompetence of the men whom Aethelred "the Unredy" chose for leaders, rather than of panic in the levies themselves. This fleet wintered in Wight, levying supplies from the Hampshire and Sussex coasts. Thence they passed on to the Thames, and at last to Normandy, to return thence on Wessex in 1001, raiding Hampshire first, and defeating the levies there, though with heavier losses than they inflicted. The leaders did well here, as six high officers are recorded to have fallen, with 180 men, on the Saxon side.

It would seem that at this time Aethelred's ships were manned by mercenaries under one Pallig, of whom we hear but this once, as he renounced his agreement with the king to join the new invasion. He and his men would of course be Norse, and a new position of affairs in the north may have been the reason for his action rather than treachery. Olaf Tryggvason had fallen in the previous year, and the frith which he had made with the English was at an end. At the same time Norway had passed into Danish hands. Pallig and his men may therefore have considered themselves bound to leave Aethelred, or else, as a fleet which came from Normandy would certainly be largely Norse, had no mind to fight against their own countrymen. His defection seems to have left the English sea force almost useless, as the record of the two next years proves.

From Hampshire in 1001 the fleet from Normandy sailed westward

until they came to Devonshire, and there came Pallig to meet them with the ships which he could gather, because he had deserted from King Aethelred against all the troth which he had plighted to him, the king moreover having well gifted him with lands (hamon) and gold and silver. And they burned Teignton and many other goods vills which we cannot name, and peace was afterward made with them. And then they went to the mouth of the Exe, and up to the fortress (Exeter) and stoutly fought there, but were very firmly and boldly withstood. Then they went through·

ꝼ ealle þa boclanꝺ þe ic on ænᴢ hæbbe�

Cnut and Emma making a donation to New
Minster.

the land and did after their wont, slaying and burning.
Then was gathered against them an immense host of
the Devonshire and Somersetshire folk, and they met
(the Danes) at Peonnhoe. And as soon as they came to
grips (togaedere fengon) there the English levy was
worsted, and there was great slaughter, and then they
(the Danes) rode over the land and burnt the town at
Penhoe, and at Clist, and many good vills which we
cannot name, and their later deeds were ever worse
than what they had wrought before. And they brought
with them a mighty spoil to the ships.

Coin of Cnut.

From the Exe, apparently not having taken Exeter, they went "to Wight, and there fared just as they would. No fleet by sea, dare meet them, nor land force either, however far they went up."

In the next year peace was made on payment by Aethelréd of £24,000. Taking into account the ghastly ravages of this host, it is perhaps not surprising that the desperation of the weak king, if not of the people, resulted in the terrible massacre of St Brice's day in this year (1002) which, like other similar historic massacres, was ineffectual, and brought immediate and terrible retribution. Sweyn of Denmark himself took command, and from this time forward the Danes aimed definitely at an actual conquest, not only of the lost Danelagh, but of the whole of England. Wessex again was the one hope of Saxon England, and held out until the last. Indeed, it was only by the death of Eadmund Ironside that she passed under the Danish yoke in the time of Cnut, by peaceful agreement rather than by conquest, when at last the resources of Denmark were exhausted, and England was worn out.

In the year 1003 Exeter was taken by storm, the fault being that of the Frenchman, Hugo, whom Emma, the Norman queen, had appointed as Reeve. There seems to be a distinct hint of some treacherous action on his part, and certainly Exeter had held out well against previous attacks. The enemy then totally ruined the town, and carried off great booty, afterward passing on into Wiltshire where the Wilts and Hants levies were gathered to meet them. The Saxon leader, Aelfric, like others of Aethelred's men, failed "through his old devices" in face of the enemy, and Sweyn, who was in command personally, led his army unhindered to Wilton, which he plundered and burnt, afterwards raiding Sarum, and going thence to "the sea, where he knew that his wave-horses were," probably at the old rendezvous, Wareham. The fleet went eastward to Norwich, and the west had peace for a few years.

In 1006 the ravages of the "great fleet" seem to have been too widely extended for detailed description, the Isle of Wight being one of the headquarters.

They went through Hampshire, lighting their war-beacons as they went. . .and there might the Winchester men see an army, daring and fearless, as they went by their gates to the sea and fetched themselves food and treasure from over fifty miles inland. . .they had every shire in Wessex sadly marked by burning and by plunder.

Truce was made by payment of £36,000.

This truce was utilised for a great shipbuilding throughout the kingdom, at Aethelred's orders, "one ship for each 310 hides, with a helm and a coat of mail from every ten hides." There was in fact to be a general re-armament with the hope of meeting the Danes on some terms of equality of fleet and weapons. The ships were ready in the next year, and were at once used by the southern thanes for their private feuds. It was the greatest English fleet which had ever been gathered, and was thus rendered useless. Part was mishandled and wrecked, part burned in private feud by Wulfnoth of Sussex, and the remnant abandoned: "and they left the toil of the nation thus lightly pass away, and no better was that victory on which the whole English nation had fixed their hopes."

In 1010, after a terrrible inroad on the whole of England from Ispwich to the Thames in Buckinghamshire, the Danes crossed into Wessex, "and so by Canigan mersc and burned all that." Where this was is not quite certain; Prof. Earle in his edition of the *Anglo-Saxon Chronicle* suggests "in West Somerset," meaning Cannington marsh, without doubt. Thorpe's suggestion is "All Cannings near Devizes, Wilts." Forester in his translation of Florence of Worcester thinks the place was Keynsham, which is on the borders Gloucestershire and Somerset, at the junction of the Avon and Chew rivers. Florence however says that the burning was of "Caninga-mersce and the greater part of Wiltshire." In the contemporary record in the *Chronicle* of next year there is given a list of the districts overrrun by the great hosts up to that date, and there is no mention of ravage further west than "much of Wiltshire." West Somerset is not spoken of.

In 1013 Sweyn and his host wintered in Bath, and there received the submission of the western thanes, led by ealdorman Aethelmar of Devon. Wessex had given up the struggle at last, and after her submission, "all the nation then considered Sweyn as full king." Aethelred fled to his brother-in-law, the Duke of Normandy, in hopes of finding help thence.

Sweyn died in the next year, 1014, and Aethelred backed by Olaf of Norway and his ships, returned to London, where he was hailed joyfully. The unquiet end of his reign was marked by perpetual treachery among his thanes, with Edric Streone as their leader, and desultory warfare with Cnut and the great Jarls who were his guardians. The tactics of Cnut for a time seem to have been based on a swift sea passage and landing beyond reach of the slow land forces of the king, and in 1015 he left Kent, and sailed into the mouth of the Frome, "and then he ravaged in Dorset and in Wiltshire and in Somerset." Treachery on the part of Streone prevented any fighting, though the Saxon levies were gathered, and at last Streone "enticed forty ships from the king, and went over to Cnut. And then the men of Wessex submitted, and delivered hostages, and horsed the army: and there it was until midwinter."

This seems to have been the most complete subjection of Wessex on record, but it did not last long. Aethelred the Unredy died, and Eadmund Ironside was king in the spring of 1016, and the first act of Eadmund was to secure the allegiance of Wessex, which ralliied to him afresh and heartily, winning a battle on the old frontier line of Dyvnaint at Penselwood, and passing forward to fight the drawn battle of Sceorstan followed by the disastrous defeat at Assandun, again due to Edric Streone's treachery, which ended the long struggle.

The resulting frith made at Olney left the kingdom parted between Saxon and Dane much as in the time of Alfred, Eadmund keeping the southern half of the realm, and Cnut the Danelagh. Eadmund was slain by the treachery of Edric Streone, whom as the northern Sagas say, "he trusted as he would his own father," and Cnut took the whole realm. Shortly after this, he divided it into four provinces, keeping Wessex for himself, and setting earls over Northumbria, Mercia and East Anglia.

Apparently Wessex made one more bid for freedom, for though no fighting is recorded, "Norman, son of Leofwin the ealdorman, Ethelward, son of Ethelmar the great, and Brihtric son of Elphege," were slain in Devon. Aethelmar was that Devon ealdorman who was the first to submit to Sweyn, and Leofwin was the high steward, who fell in battle in Hampshire in 1001. Another son of his fell later fighting against Sweyn. As Cnut banished and slew Edwy the atheling, and another Edwy, known as "king of the churls" at the same time, it is likely that there had been at least a plot in Wessex in favour of the old line.

After the time of Alfred and his final defeat of the Danes at Ethandun, it should be noted that during all the Danish wars the western counties suffered little, until the very last, from more than temporary raids carried out by the fleets. The ancient strategic frontier formed by the line of the Mendips and Selwood, which had kept back the West Saxon advance on Dyvnaint for so long, again served as a barrier, and though Wilts was penetrated several times from across the Thames, and the hosts marched across it to Wareham by way of Wilton and Sarum, no attempt was made to pass the old line until Cnut made his unsuccessful march against Eadmund.

See also as to Danish influence in Wessex a paper by Dr H. Colley March, F.S.A., on "Scando-Gothic Art in Wessex," Proc. Dorset N. H. and Antiquarian Field Club, Vol. XXXIV.

BOOK 3

Chapter 1

In our review of the Danish invasions of Wessex we have so far omitted all details of the campaign of 876-878. Most writers have dealt with the warfare of these years as a series of unconnected episodes, purposeless raids in Dorset and South Devon, followed by a surprise attack which drove King Alfred into hiding in the Somerset marshlands. Thence after prolonged skirmishing he emerges and in some unexplained way gathers an army and defeats the Danes in a pitched battle close to their original base in Wilts, sixty miles from his place of refuge. Incidentally, between the first and last operations an independent Danish landing takes place somewhere on the Devon coast with no particular object and is crushingly defeated, but with no result of any consequence.

It is possible on the other hand to regard all the movements of the Danes during this period as part of a definite campaign, steadily pursued with the one object of breaking down the power of Wessex, the last unconquered kingdom left in England, an attempt foiled when within an ace of succeeding by the king's determined resistance and his rally of the Wessex levies for another fight in the ancient cock-pit of the war with Dyvnaint. These two theories involve such radically different opinions as to the course of events which led to the supremacy of Alfred, and incidentally require such different readings of the chronicles, that we have purposely left them for close and exhaustive study in order if possible to decide this vexed question, which is important, as the year marks a new stage in the position of the Danes in England.

After the first recorded descents on the coasts in the latter half of the eighth century, which were of the nature of inroads for the sake of plunder only, there was a lull until the year 832, when heathen men ravaged Sheppey. Thenceforward the raids became incessant, some of them being most formidable. None, however, threatened the safety of the English kingdoms until 866, the first year of the reign of Aethelred, Alfred's brother. In that year a fresh army landed in East Anglia, more formidable than any before it on account of the definite intention of conquest which appears to have animated its leaders. From this date the presence of the Danish host is permanent in England, and the names of the leaders take their places alongside those of the Saxon kings in our history.

Prof. Allen Mawer has shown that whatever mythical elements may have found their way into the story of Ragnar Lodbrok, there is no doubt that these three were actually his sons (Saga-Book of the Viking Club, *Vol. VI, 1909, pp. 68-89).*

Of these leaders the chief were the three "sons of Lodbrok," Ivar, who is the Ingvar of the English writers, Halfdan, and Hubba. The master mind of these invaders seems to have been that of Ivar, though after a time he was not so prominent in England as his brothers.

Prof. W. G. Collingwood, Scandinavian Britain, *pp. 83-7. Cf. "Ingwar stood first in craft, Hubba in valour";* Henry of Huntingdon, *Book V, Sect. 9.*

Under these chiefs East Anglia and Northumbria were first subdued, and the conquest of Mercia was commenced. But after the death of St Eadmund of East Anglia, in 870, at the hands of the heathen, the name of Ivar entirely disappears from the English Chronicles, and that of his brother Hubba is not again mentioned in our records until 878. These two chiefs had taken their men westward, and according to the *Annals of Ulster* they had joined the Northmen of Dublin, and took part in the siege of Alcluith (Dumbarton). Ivar died in 872 or 873. Hubba was with his men in Wales in 877.

Chronicle of Crowland.

Under the remaining leaders, of whom Halfdan was certainly one, and Guthrum, who later appears as sole leader, another, the army made a desperate attack on Wessex in 871, fighting nine battles south of the Thames in that year against Aethelred and his brother Alfred, who succeeded to the throne during the struggle. As a result of these battles the Danes withdrew from Wessex, and completed the subjugation of Mercia. By the year 875 they had so far established themselves that they proceeded to apportion their conquests, Halfdan taking Northumbria, while Guthrum became king of East Anglia and probably part of Mercia, where an English under-king was allowed to remain as nominal ruler. By this time Alfred had a fleet at sea, and in the same year (875) fought a battle with seven Danish ships, the Chronicles not stating whence they came, or where the fight took place.

Guthrum had made his headquarters in Cambridge, and thence he made a sudden and unexpected move on Wessex in 876, marching across the land and occupying Wareham, where he met with a strong fleet which had come from the westward. The details given in the Chronicles are few, but may be noted.

A.-S. Chronicle, 876. "Here the army stole away to Wareham from the West Saxon levy. And afterward the king made peace with the army, and they sware oaths to him on the Holy Ring, the which they would never before do to any nation, that they would speedily depart from his kingdom. And nevertheless their mounted force stole away from the levies by night, and went to Exeter."

Asser adds, "Leaving Grantabridge by night, they entered a castle called Wareham."

Ethelwerd supplements these accounts with a statement which explains the presence of the ships at Wareham, and also the apparent oath-breaking. "The army which had been at Cambridge made a junction with the western army, a thing which they had not done before, at the town which is called Wareham, and ravaged the greater part of that province." Asser also says that the mounted host cut their way through Alfred's horsemen when they rode to Exeter.

As a matter of fact, in the subsequent events it is clear that Alfred had to deal with two separate forces—one a strong mounted land host, and the other a sea-borne army which was still to be reckoned with after losing 100-120 ships. The strength of the mounted contingent accounts fully for the swift and apparently unopposed march of Guthrum from Mercia. The "western host" can only have been the men who followed Ivar and Hubba in Ireland, as Professor Collingwood has suggested. There is no record of

Prof. Earle in his edition of the Anglo-Saxon Chronicle (Preface, p. 59) considers this passage in Ethelwerd as entirely imaginary and deduced from the somewhat difficult form of the Chronicle Saxon, as there was no "Western army." Ethelwerd is, however, quite correct. The Professor has overlooked the western fleets from Ireland, and the fact that a junction was actually effected at Wareham, as the context in the Chronicle proves.

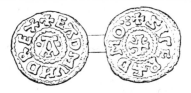

Coin of Eadmund of East Anglia.

any Danish host to the west other than this.

Here is the first evidence of a concerted movement on Wessex from east and west which resulted in the decisive campaign of 878. That this was a planned combination was first suggested by Lappenberg, who saw that the arrival of the fleet at Wareham must have been arranged in concert with the movement from Cambridge; and now that the Danes had definitely embarked on a policy of conquest such a course of action is only what might be expected. Halfdan was, as we have said, securely established in Northumbria. Guthrum held East Anglia and probably that part of Mercia which was afterwards known as the Danelagh, while the rest was under his puppet king, the "unwise" Ceolwulf. Wessex alone remained unconquered, and so long as that kingdom remained unsubdued and independent, was a focus of Saxon resistance and a constant menace to Danish power.

The descent on Wareham must have been made by one of those terrible rides of a mounted force of which we read so frequently, and which show how fully the Danes had mastered the secret and learned the value of a mobile striking force.

The name of the leader who accomplished this remarkable march is not given. The similarity of the descent to that on Chippenham in the next winter suggests that he was Guthrum, who was at this time in command in the eastern counties. The enterprise was one which no timid leader would undertake, while it was certainly planned at headquarters to meet the sea-borne host at Wareham.

The ride from Cambridge is worth tracing, as it was to be repeated, in a measure, later. The road taken can be followed with tolerable certainty, and is one which was well adapted for the swift passage of the mounted infantry of the period, and could be taken without exciting any suspicion in Wessex until too late. The passage of a Danish force through the midlands as they harried and subdued the country north of the

Thames was to be expected, and might have any objective, within what was afterwards known as the Danelagh. Some ten miles south of Cambridge the Icknield Street ran along the borders of Hertfordshire, and across Bedfordshire following the slopes of the Chilterns to the Thames at Streatley, the whole distance to this point being about sixty miles. From the river crossing, a track, the Ridgeway, climbed the hills that on the southern side close in the Vale of White Horse, and thence ran along their crest. There seems also to have been a lower Roman road, running nearly parallel with the Ridgeway, to join it where it bent southward on reaching the Wiltshire border, after its westerly course through Berkshire. Hence it runs between Marlborough and Avebury, due south across the Wansdyke, and down to Salisbury Plain.

Its exact course across the plain is not perhaps traceable, but no doubt it joined the roads to Old Sarum and to Wilton, and ultimately joined the Ackling Ditch, the Via Iceniana of the Romans, which runs from Old Sarum to Badbury. Thence, this road turned westward, but a branch road continued south to the shore of Poole Harbour at Hamworthy, only some five miles from Wareham. There was therefore a clear, well-defined, and easily rideable road from the Thames to Salisbury Plain and across it to Wareham, the whole distance from Streatley to the sea being by this route under 100 miles. It was country which was well known to the Danes moreover, as they had fought over it in 871, the year of the nine battles, as far south as Martin and Wilton, where the last of the recorded fights took place, when they doubtless learned what a formidable barrier Bokerly Dyke presented if the Saxons had time to man it against them.

As far as Treatley, where the Wessex boundary, so far as it was definable at the time, was crossed, the Danes would have taken their time. They may have gathered men on the way, but as their horses came from the eastern counties as a rule, the host was probably mustered, almost entirely, at Cambridge, as indeed is intimated. The hundred miles across Wessex would require haste, and probably it is to this part of the expedition that the night work is to be assigned. There is no evident reason why the departure from their own post in Cambridge should have been secret, but even if the construction of the sentence will not allow the transposition of "by night" to its end, night marches through Wessex would be enough to lead the chroniclers to assume them all through the march.

After leaving Streatley the road passes near no towns until toward its end, when it approaches Old Sarum, Wilton and Wimborne. A Danish army riding this road and passing the towns by night, carrying their provisions and lying quietly by day, must have outridden all news of its approach, or if that was known, of the direction in which it was making. Until it had passed the Roman road from Marlborough to Bath its intention to make for the far south could not have been guessed, and it would have been absolutely impossible for the slow Wessex levies to have been gathered in time to intercept its swift march at any point, even at the old barrier of Bokerly Dyke.

Even if we allow a long halt among the folds of the Chilterns to rest the horses before the forced march across Wessex, the ride from Cambridge to Wareham should have been possible in five days. Once across the border the second night should have seen the host in Wareham, two stages of less than fifty miles each being quite possible, the first halt being in the solitude of Salisbury Plain.

Taken by surprise as he was, Alfred was yet able to hold his own against this new attack. He had now a fleet, and was able to blockade the Danes in Wareham so closely that they made terms with him, swearing to leave the kingdom. The subsequent event is hard to understand unless there was a definite understanding between the eastern and western forces that the conquest of Wessex was not yet to be given up as hopeless.

One matter of supreme importance in negotiations with the Danes Alfred had to learn at Wareham, where for the first time he had to deal with two independent hosts. One leader and his men would not be bound by an agreement made by another unless he chose. If the men of the western fleet chose to swear to leave the land, that was nothing to the men of Guthrum, who had their own homes in East Anglia, and could not do so. No doubt the oath sworn on the "Holy Ring" (which was the great silver armlet kept, at home, in the "Ve" of the Asir, and carried now and again on great expeditions if one of the leaders was the "Godi," who was its custodian) was kept by the sea-borne host. The mounted force from Cambridge would not take any oath at all.

Consequently the mounted Cambridge force cut its way through Alfred's lines, and made for the open. The way by which they had come was by this time barred to them, and they rode west down the Roman road through Dorchester to Exeter—the last road they might have been expected to take, but with friendly, half-Welsh Exeter at the end of it.

But though there was, properly speaking, no oath-breaking, there must have been an understanding that the fleet was to pass round to Exeter as soon as might be, there to meet the men who had fled, and who had to find some way home to Mercia and the east. It may well have been that they considered Exeter as in Dyvnaint, and outside Alfred's dominions, for the purpose of a wartime arrangement.

However that may have been, in that fortress they were blockaded by Alfred, until, some time in 877, the fleet from Wareham, or rather what was left of it after rough handling by Alfred's ships, and a storm off Swanage which destroyed over 100 of the vessels, joined them. Probably this heavy loss saved Wessex for the time, for the

The "Stalla-Hring" or Temple ring, was only worn by the Godi, who was to have it on his arm at any meeting where an oath might be needed. It is quite likely that the omission of this formality on previous occasions was simply due to the absence of any Godi with the host. The oath on the ring was quite usual, and nothing to be objected to.

result of the siege of Exeter was that the Danes again swore to leave the kingdom, and this time kept their oath, withdrawing to Mercia. The chroniclers do not state how this withdrawal was effected. It seems clear, however, that the fleet passed from Exeter westward round the Land's End into the Bristol Channel, some part finding refuge in South Wales, and others apparently passing up to Gloucester. At all events, the next appearance of Danish ships is from Demetia, under the brother of Halfdan and Ingvar, whom we need have no hesitation in identifying with Hubba, as he is named by one or two of the later chroniclers, while according to Ethelwerd Gloucester was occupied by the Danes at this time.

It is of course possible that the whole of the eastern Danish host was shipped to Gloucester and so passed into Mercia, rather that that it was allowed to march through the length of Wessex. But this is immaterial. The end of the campaign of 876-7 was that Wessex was cleared once more of the Danes.

But it was for the time only. It is plain that when the Danes left Exeter in 877 they had no intention of keeping the peace they had made for any length of time. Their unwillingness to withdraw was probably due to the very heavy losses of the fleet, and if Henry of Huntingdon is right in stating that after this retreat they received immense reinforcements from Denmark, it is not surprising that they commenced a new campaign early in the following year, 878.

The ride across Wessex had been well planned and carried out, and was to be repeated. It had failed for the time, and its result was defeat in the end, but rather by misadventure than by force, and there is no doubt that it prepared the way for the descent on Chippenham which did for a time make the Danes masters of Wessex.

Chapter 2

The events of the year 878 need careful study, and we give them in a consecutive narrative made up of the story as told by the *Anglo-Saxon Chronicle* and, in brackets, Asser, the two contemporary authorities. In a parallel column we have added details from other writers which seem to supplement their records. The amount of such additional material available seems to show that there was much tradition, if not other written records, known to us and made use of the the later writers quoted on this important campaign. This we give for what it is worth, where it does not clash with the *Chronicle* and Asser, and is not on the face of it unreasonable.

CATENA OF THE CHRONICLES

A.D. 877.

At harvest time (in August) the army went into the Mercians' land*, and some part of it they divided, and some part they gave to Ceolwulf (an unwise servant of the king).

A.D. 878.

(In this year of the Incarnation of our Lord, which was the 30th of the birth of King Alfred), during midwinter after Twelfth night, the army† stole away to Chippenham, and over-rode the West Saxons' land, and there settled*. And many of the folk they drove (by force of arms and through need and fear) over the sea †, and of the remainder the greater part they brought under their sway, except King Alfred, and he with a small band with difficulty fared through the woods* and moorfastnesses. (And at that time King Alfred, with a few of his nobles and some warriors and vassals besides, led an unquiet life in great tribulation in the woodland and marshy parts of Somerset †. For he had nothing on which to live except what he could win by frequent sallies, either openly or by stealth, from the pagans, or from the Christians who had submitted to the pagans' rule.) In the same winter the brother of Inwaer and Halfdene* with

*The erect their huts in the town of Gloucester. (Ethelwerd).

†With a wonderful multitude of men who had lately come from Denmark. (Hen. Huntingdon).

*They take up their winter quarters at Chippenham. (Ethelwerd).

†Over the sea into Gaul. (Ethelwerd).

*("Per sylvestra." Earle, note to loc. cit.)

†And he long lay hidden with a certain herdsman of his. (Vit. S. Neot).

*Hubba, the brother of Hinguar. (John of Brompton.)
A brother of Iware and Halfdene. . .his name was Ubbe. (Gaimar).

23 ships (sailed from the region of Demetia where he had wintered after many slaughters of the Christians made there, to Domnonia) to Wessex, to Devonshire. And there he was slain and with him 840 (1200) men of his army (by the king's servants, with a wretched ending while acting rashly before the stronghold of Cynuit. For in that stronghold many of the king's servants had shut themselves† with their men for safety. But when the pagans saw that the stronghold was unprepared and altogether unfortified, except only that it had walls constructed in our fashion, they would not assault it, because the place is by the nature of the ground very secure on every side except the east, as we ourselves have seen, but began to besiege it, thinking that those men within would soon be compelled to surrender by hunger and thirst, and by blockade, since there is no water adjoining that stronghold. But it did not turn out as they thought. For the Christians, before they at all submitted to suffer such misery, inspired by heaven, thinking it far better to earn either death or victory, unexpectedly sally out on the pagans at dawn, and from the first onset overthrow the enemy, slaying them, together with their king, for the most part, though a few fled and escaped to their ships)*. And there was taken the flag which is called the Raven†. And thereupon at Easter King Alfred* with a little band wrought a work at Athelney, and from that work, with the part of the Somerset men which was nighest thereto (nobles and vassels), waged war untiringly† against the army.

Then in the seventh week after Easter, he rode to Ecgbryht's Stone, (which is in the eastern part of the wood which is called Selwood, but in Latin Sylva magna, and in Welsh Coit maur). And thither came to meet him all Somerset and Wiltshire and of Hampshire* that part which was on this side of the sea (who had not sailed beyond the sea for fear of the pagans) and they were fain of him. (And when the king was seen,

†He besieged Odda, Duke of Devon, in a certain castle. (Ethelwerd).

*(Alfred) slew a brother of Iware and Halfdene whose name was Ubbe—in the Forest of Pene.

†"woven by the sisters of Hinguar and Hubba." (Ann. S. Neot).

*King Alfred then, comforted by this victory. (Hen. Hunt.)

†Fought daily battles against the barbarians. (Ethelwerd).

*Summurtunensis, Wiltunensis Hamtunensis pagae accolae. (Asser.) Somerton, Wilton, and Hampton. (S. Dunelm).

receiving him as was right as one returned from the dead after such tribulation, they were filled with boundless joy, and there they camped for one night.) Thence from that camp (in the early morn dawn following, the king came to the place which is called Aecglea and there camped for one night. Thence†, as it dawned on the following morning) after one night he came to Ethandun*, and there fought against all the army (fiercly in a dense shield-locked array, and long maintaining a stubborn fight, at length by the Divine will he gained the victory†, and overthrew the pagans with the greatest slaughter, and striking down the fugitives) followed them as far as their stronghold*. (And all that he found outside the stronghold he seized, whether men, horses, or cattle, slaying the men at once. And before the gates of the pagan stronghold he with all his army manfully pitched his camp). And there he sat for 14 nights. And then the army gave him hostages and mighty oaths that they would leave his kingdom†. (And when he had tarried there for 14 days, the pagans, worn out with hunger, fear and cold at last in despair sought peace on this condition, that the king should receive from them as many hostages as he chose to name, while he himself should give them none, these being such terms of peace as they had never before concluded with anyone. After hearing their embassy, the king, after his wont, being moved with pity, received from them the hostages he had named, as many as he would. Which being accepted, the pagans further took oath that they would depart as swiftly as possible from his kingdom. And moreover Guthrum their king promised to submit to Christianity and receive baptism at the hand of King Alfred. And all that he and his men had promised they fulfilled.) And three weeks thereafter came Guthrum the king and thirty of the worthiest men in his army to him at Aller, which is opposite Athelney, and the king there received him at baptism* (as the son of his adoption.) and

†Learning the position of the barbarians exactly from scouts whom he had sent out for the purpose, he suddenly attacked them. (Wm. Malmesbury.)

*To Edderandun, with an immense army, and there found equally immense bodies of pagans ready for battle. (S. Dunelm.)

†Forming in line of battle, they previously took the nearest promontory, whence they watched the movements of the enemy. (Vit. S. Neot).

*A castle which was in the neighbourhood. (Matt. West.)

†With the terms that they would leave the land by a certain day, or become Christian. (Liviere de Reis de Brittanie et de Engleterre).

*Alfred became his godfather. (Hen. Hunt.) And gave him the name of Athelstan. (Flor. Worcest.)

169

†Duke Ethelnoth also purified the same at Wedmore (Ethelwerd).

*After a year from the time of the pagan army leaving Gloucester, they marched to Cirencester, and there wintered. (Ethelwerd).

†Such of the Danes as had refused to become Christians went over the sea with Hasting. (Wm. Malmesbury.)

This seems to be the only passage in any English chronicler pointing to the presence in England of the famous Hasting before the campaign of 892-896. In those latter years the operations in which he took part were mainly conducted in the south-eastern counties.

his chrism-loosing was at Wedmore† (a royal Vill on the eighth day). After he was baptised he remained with the king for twelve nights, and the king greatly honoured him and his comrades with gifts.

A.D. 879.

In this year the army fared from Chippenham to Cirencester*, and there sat for one year.

A.D. 880.

In this year the army fared from Cirencester to East Anglia, and settled in and shared that land†.

The foregoing account is remarkably full, and is practically enough. We fully believe that anyone who read the story of Ethandun as given in the *Chronicles,* for the first time, could gain but one impression of the campaign—that of a struggle between two well-led hosts, whose leaders, after watching one another cross a stretch of fenland for some weeks, at last met and fought and made peace on its edge. It is impossible to read into the history any incidents which justify belief in bases of operation sixty or more miles apart across forest country. It is still less possible to believe in them when the country is known or its features realised.

One important point however we must notice before going further. We have found it impossible to agree with the old theory which locates the site of the battle of Ethandun in Wiltshire, the difficulties in reconciling the accounts given by the authentic *Chronicles* being on that theory insuperable. How this site ever came to be selected seems at first sight inexplicable, but the mistake can be traced to its source and may be considered as to some extent natural.

There is only one apparent hint in the *Chronicles* as to where Ethandun is to be looked for, and that hint is given in the *Chronicle of Ethelwerd,* which was the most valued authority of the earlier modern writers such as Camden and his predecessors, Leland and Spelman. The passage is as follows in the original. The English has been given already.

"Interea post Pascha illius anni cooptavit bellum Aelfred rex adversus exercitus qui in Cippanhamme fuere in loco Ethandune, victoriaeque obtinent numen."

It has been overlooked that this is an account of a Danish victory at Ethendun, if Ethelwerd is to be followed literally. He goes on to say, "but after the issue of the battle the barbarians promise peace, beg a truce and bind themselves by an oath."

The whole account is confused, and worthless as an authority from beginning to end, but the connection of the two names has been quite sufficient to satisfy the old writers, who were content to find an Edington which would answer for Ethandun somewhere in Wessex in the Chippenham direction. Camden's lead has been followed without question until the original mistake has assumed the position of a statement of fact. We are quite aware that the reiteration of the mistake by well-known writers renders it almost heresy to suggest that they were wrong; but once the origin of the mistake has been pointed out, we can leave the chronicles, and the country involved, to settle the question. There is an Ethandun—Edington within sight of Atheleny, not so well known as the Edington marked by the White Horse, but close to Aller and Wedmore where Alfred made the truce with the Danes after the victory which wiped out the effects of the disaster at Chippenham.

So far as the following commentary on the "catena" is concerned, we have tried to interpret its statements with some regard for the obvious military necessities of the position in which the opposing forces were placed, as event followed event during the few weeks of the campaign, and with a personal knowledge of the actual topography of the district in which the struggle was carried on. At the same time we have thought it best to leave the controversial points which may be indicated for discussion in their own chapters.

It is clear that when the Danes withdrew from Exeter in 877 they had no intention of abandoning their hope of winning Wessex. Their plans had failed for the time, more by the mischance which had ruined their fleet than because of any Saxon successes, and there seems no reason to doubt that they expected, or sent for, reinforcements from over seas. They were ready to fall on Wessex again by the end of 877, although they had only left Exeter in August.

With the departure of the enemy at that date the Saxon levies would disperse after their wont, and Alfred and his thanes, having for the second time compelled the enemy to make such terms as he could and retire, evidently expected no immediate attack. Least of all would any movement of the Danes be looked for in mid-winter. The custom of the "host" was to find winter quarters and stay there until spring. Yet in the first weeks of 878 the Danes, probably perfectly well aware that they were unlooked for, and with their previous successful surprise attacks in their minds, "stole away" as they had done on Wareham and without warning occupied Chippenham. Possibly they had some hope of taking Alfred himself, as it is certain that he was in actual danger, at least during the time when he was in extremities amid the Somerset marshes round Athelney, where the loyalty of his personal retainers found him a refuge on his own Somerset estates.

Ethelwerd intimates that their starting place was Gloucester.

The expression used for the sudden invasion of Wessex in midwinter 878, is remarkable as being the same as that used in the record of the sudden seizure of Wareham which marked the beginning of the new attacks. In both cases the Danes are said to have "stolen away" on their objective— "her hine bestael se here into Werham" or to "Cippanhamme." In both cases the march was unexpected and very rapid, and was carried out by a mounted force, which at Wareham was strong enough to win its way to Exeter, and from Chippenham to raid all Wessex—"geridan

West-Seaxna land and gesetton." The Danes must again have quietly shifted their midland base to some point on the Wessex frontier, and thence made their dash across the country, utterly demoralising it, and leaving the way clear for their slower troops. It seems that Alfred fully appreciated the exploit, and presently defeated the Danes by their own tactics— an unexpected gathering and a swift march on the enemy.

Having once gained their footing in Wessex, it is clear that the Danes did not settle down in inactivity, whether they retained Chippenham as their base or not. In the shore space of time between Twelfth Night and Easter, which fell on March 23rd of that year, they overran a great part of Wessex, Hampshire sufrering in special. There can be no question that the invading host was very large, and at the same time mobile.

The weeks before Easter, to judge not only from Alfred's inactivity, but from the legends which grew up concerning his need for encouragement by supernatural signs, seem to have been times of indecision and helplessness, if not almost of despair. Yet one cannot overlook the fact that Alfred had available to the west of the Somerset fenland a force which could give a good account of itself, and with the advent of a fresh enemy did so.

Shortly before Easter, the sea-borne host reappeared, diminished in numbers indeed, but still formidable, if only by reason of its leader. Hubba, the brother of Ingvar and Halfdan, left his winter quarters in South Wales, and with twenty-three ships at least, one account giving the number as thirty, made a descent on the south shore of the Bristol channel. Alfred's western force, which we may call with Ethelwerd the Devon levies under Odda, met the invaders, and failed to prevent their landing. Hubba drove the Saxons into an existing stronghold, and there besieged them until, driven desperate by want of food and water, and apparently taking advantage of some oversight on the part of the Danes, Odda and his men made a sally, and cut the besiegers in pieces, slaying the redoubtable Hubba himself winning the magic flag of the sons of Lodbrok— a trophy whose loss must have had no small effect on the Danes of the fleet.

There has been much controversy as to the exact locality in South Wales whence Hubba sailed, and also as to the point on the southern shores of the channel at which he made his landing. The question is of the greatest interest, and perhaps of difficulty, but for the moment it may be dismissed. It is one which has served to obscure the broad outlines of the campaign, although the failure of the landing rendered it of secondary importance, so far as places are concerned. The important point is that such a landing was made to the westward of Athelney at the first moment when the ships could be taken from their winter quarters. It is enough to note that Hubba sailed from Wales, landed at some point on the coast of "Devon in Wessex" and that after his fall his force, or what remained of it, ceased to exist as an independent factor in the campaign.

But wherever the landing was made, its effects were at once evident. Immediately after Easter, and as a direct result of this landing, Alfred raised a "work" at Athelney, and from it fought against "the army," which as in other places can only mean the main host of the Danes, and in this case the forces under Guthrum.

This seems to be implied by the Anglo-Saxon test. See also Henry of Huntingdon in Catena p. 147.

Fortunately we know the exact position of this fen stronghold, and the reason for its erection are not far to seek. Guthrum was now aware that Alfred had a strong force beyond the Parrett, and must of necessity march on it; and Alfred was awake to the danger of the co-operation between the land and sea forces of his enemy. Those of Hubba's men who had escaped to their ships had joined Guthrum, and there was always the fear of the arrival of further sea-borne forces. A fortress therefore was needed which would dominate the fenland, and at the same time prevent the penetration inland of any Danish ships. The only possible reason why Alfred chose to remain in the fens after this victory is that the fenland had become the frontier of his last remaining cantle of Wessex. Guthrum was no longer far beyond the forest land, over sixty miles away across it, at Chippenham—but facing him, seeking a crossing place through the fen.

Roughly speaking, Alfred's frontier at this juncture was the old defensible line between Saxon and Welsh held by the Britons against Kenwalch. There is no record that the Danes ever crossed it into old Dyvnaint or into Dorset. Hubba's landing, if successful, would have completely turned the line of this frontier.

It is absolutely certain that as soon as the news of the defeat of Hubba reached Guthrum, he must have marched west at once to disperse the new gathering. Whether the Danes knew what had become of the Saxon king or not, they could not have left Odda's army alone to gather strength and become a rallying point for Wessex. It might be crushed by prompt action, for it certainly was not large enough to make it advisable for the great mass of Danes to retreat from Western Wessex to their original winter base. Hubba's ships may have carried at the utmost 150 men apiece. The average was probably less, and at the highest computation his force could not have been over 4500. This force had beaten Odda on landing, and only desperation on one side and rashness on the other had led to the defeat of the great captain. There should be no reason why the great Danish host should not be able to brush aside Odda and his men and end the matter, if they acted at once. To delay might make the affair more difficult.

The Danish line of march would certainly bring them along the Fosseway, and as soon as they reached the mid-Somerset marshes they would learn where Alfred was gathering men, if his personal hiding-place was still a secret. The fen fortress was, and still is, conspicuous for miles across the levels as the only elevation in their midst. It is the steep conical hill rising abruptly and isolated on the eastern bank of the Parrett, just below its junction with the Tone and the old mouth of the Cary, now diverted for the drainage of Sedgmoor. Across the river, and a mile to the south-west lies the low Isle of Athelney itself, running to the river's edge from which is an ancient causeway, traditionally, and no doubt correctly ascribed to the work of Alfred, at whose end the piles of an ancient bridge are still to be seen occasionally with the shifting of the mud of the channel at low tides.

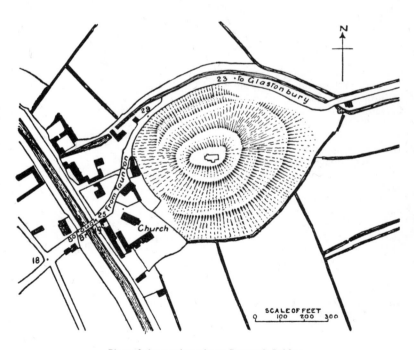

Plan of the earthworks at Borough Bridge.

The fortress itself, now known as Borough Mump and crowned with a ruined church, is defended by a triple line of earthworks. It is not certain that the hill is entirely artificial, though the local tradition says that it was so. More probably Alfred took advantage of a natural elevation of a kind which is not altogether infrequent in the district, though of smaller size than usual. The strategic value of the fortress is obvious, as it barred the way up the three rivers inland to Langport, South Petherton, Ilchester and Taunton against any such inroads as that attempted by Hubba, and at the same time was a point from which the whole extent of the fenland frontier could be guarded. As far as we know, Taunton to the westward was still intact, and the ancient crossings at what is now Bridgwater and, below that, at Combwich had their own guarded approaches. Between these the Borough fort was the link, made against no distant enemy, but in the face of one which was at hand. It was from this fortress that Alfred and his men fought daily battles against "the army."

It was impossible for the Danes to push forward against the Devon levies beyond the Parrett until this fortress, which could not be left on their flank, was disposed of with its builders. Guthrum must have been forced by circumstances to take up a position whence he could watch Alfred's movements while preparing to drive him from his stronghold and crush him.

The difficulty of the task before the Danes lay in the strength of Alfred's position. As Hereward the Wake showed William the Norman two hundred years later at Ely, there is no stronghold so hard to reduce as an island in the fens. Its surroundings are neither land nor water, and can be traversed neither on foot, nor in boats, except by narrow and winding ways which are hard for a stranger to find, and easy for the holders of the place to defend. The strange and swift ebb of the Parrett, which was the one waterway into the fenland fastnesses, would be of no use to the

The man from whom we had this tradition was unaware that the place was in any way connected with Alfred. He said that "they reckoned it was made in the days when men would work for a penny a day," and added that it was likely. The school children averred that it was made by the Danes, and said that, "Schoolmaster told them so." In his article on "Ancient Earthworks" however, in the Victoria County History of Somerset, Mr C. H. Bothamley expresses the opinion that the hill and its terraces are mainly natural, though the escarpments may have been made steeper artificially, Vol. II, p. 499. As far as we know the hill has never been examined with the spade.

Danes at Borough Bridge, as the deep mud of the banks would render landing in the face of an enemy, however numerically weak, out of the question. And it is certain that if there were any fear of an attempt to use ships, Alfred would have blocked the channel.

Yet the forcing of the fen could only have been a matter of time, even if it had been necessary to make a causeway from island to island until the work at Borough Bridge was reached.

Saxon manuscript drawing showing a king with his court.

Chapter 3

It is no matter of theory, but of definite chronicled statement, that some such fierce warfare as would result from Danish attempts to force the fen passages took place from Alfred's new stronghold, whence he fought untiringly against the army. Ethelwerd's addition that these battles were daily may be only a pituresque description, but he wrote for men who had not yet forgotten either the place or the details of the campaign. Neither statement can in any way be reconciled with warfare between bases more than sixty miles apart; and it must not be overlooked that in the days of Alfred sixty miles of forest country, broken and hilly, meant a great deal more than we have learned to consider it. The chronicle statement is only explicable on the natural deduction that the two forces were within reach of one another.

Neither is there any hint that this constant fighting had any effect other than to force the Danes to concentrate on the fen. Between Easter and Whitsuntide Alfred had no sufficient force for more than defence, though that defence showed that he was dangerous, and growing more so. There can be no doubt that Wallingford is correct in saying that Guthrum summoned his scattered men to his assistance. The winning of the fen needed a strong force, and a good position whence it could be attempted.

There are two points on the ranges of hills overlooking Athelney from the Danish line of advance, from either of which the Borough Bridge fortress is conspicuous: one being the hill called High Ham, south of Athelney, and the other the highest point of the Polden ridge to the eastward. The former lies nearest to Athelney, directly overlooking it, but it is far inland. Communications between it and the Danish posts eastward in Wessex would be liable to interruption, and until the stronghold at Borough Bridge had been forced, no co-operation with a ship force would be possible. At any rate it seems certain that the Danes did not occupy High Ham, as the church at Aller at the foot of that hill was not destroyed by them.

But the Poldens offered an ideal position for the Danish operations. Their long ridge reaches the Fosseway and the ancient roads through Glastonbury and Street at the indland end, and seaward sinks almost suddenly into the marshes of the Parrett and Brue where a great loop of the former river washed the base of a steep cliff at Downend, and formed with a creek, known later as "Downend Pill," a protected haven which no doubt would be of use. Almost opposite Downend, across the deep tidal water of the estuary where it narrows, was the ancient crossing at the "burh" which is now Bridgwater, which must be watched, or perhaps forced if possible; and lower down the estuary lies the tidal ford at Combwich, impossible to pass in the face of opposition, and guarded by its camp, but also needing watchfulness.

On the mid-ridge of the Poldens, and at the best point for observation and defence, is Edington hill, rising all but precipitously from the levels of Sedgmoor in such a way that its height of some 220 feet is almost imposing as seen from the fen, and so narrow that nothing more than a slight entrenchment would be sufficient for defence. Such entrenchments do exist even now, and are of the sort which would mark the lines of an observation camp well placed to overlook Athelney and the fen islands, Chedzoy, Weston-Zoyland, Middlezoy, and Othery, which lie in a chain nearly parallel with the Poldens, and must be gained before the fortress beyond them could be attacked.

Here however was not the Danish stronghold into which the invaders were driven from the field of Ethandun. It is the field itself, and the final refuge of the defeated Danes, strong enough and spacious enough to afford resources for a fortnight's siege, was elsewhere in the neighbourhood, though at no great distance.

The position of affairs just before Whitsuntide

was accordingly one of preparation on both sides, and John of Wallingford, though a late writer, no doubt helps us to realise it, whether his details are from tradition or, quite possibly, from records to which he had access. Gradually as the growing difficulty of the task before him became evident, Guthrum gathered his men. They are said to have come to him from the hill fortresses which he had occupied, the term "municipia" used being the same as that by which Alfred's hill-fortress at Borough Bridge is described, as if the Danes had been holding down Wessex by a series of strong posts on the line of great earthworks which from time immemorial had crested the Wessex hills from the Thames to Dorset. One by one as these posts were evacuated and their late holders went forward the Saxons would occupy them, watching this new move of their enemy, and waiting for news of Alfred, whose messages were spreading among them.

It is to this period that the old story of Alfred's visit to the Danish camp under the guise of a harper belongs. It is given by William of Malmesbury, and though the same story is told of other chieftains, notably of Olaf of Dublin, who is said to have gone in the same way into the Saxon camp before Brunanburh, the legend at any rate bears witness to what Alfred undoubtedly must have done in the way of finding out by spies what the movements of his enemy were to be. Sooner or later Guthrum would try to force the passage of the fen, with his whole host.

It will be admitted that the best time for a surprise attack on a watchful enemy would be at the moment when his attention was directed elsewhere. There could be no better time for an unexpected gathering of a new force than when the enemy has every reason to believe that every available man must be looking for attack on the point that he has threatened for some time. If Alfred could learn when Guthrum meant to swoop down on the fen from his hill position, his

This is pointed out by Matthew of Westminster, who thus corroborates John of Wallingford. Guthrum had held down Wessex by garrisoning her own ancient hill fortresses. (See Catena).

own plans could be accurately laid.

There is a very curious natural and physical reason which must have approximately fixed a time for any attempt to cross the fen. It has never been noticed, and probably would not occur to any but one who has had somewhat hard experience of the ways of the Parrett tides. Yet it must have entered into the calculations of the Danes, for the passage of the fens depended on what water was held up in them. At neap tides the drainage into the deep river channels is most free, the fen waters are at their lowest, and the fen paths are driest and most easily passed. It is certain that any force which had, as it were, to feel its way as it went across Sedgmoor and the other moors, must have waited for the time when that waste was in its best condition. Now as a matter of fact the week given by the *Chronicles* as that of the battle of Ethandun coincides with that of neap tides, which of course can be calculated from the full moon of Easter, which we already know. This may be only a matter of accident, and we do not insist on the point as of very great moment: but it is at the least remarkable that the week of neap tide was that chosen by Alfred for his attack on the Danes, which attack could be best carried out when the enemy was on his way to the fen. There was some definite movement of the sort expected by Alfred, as he took measures, personally or otherwise, to learn when it was to come off. Allowing time for Guthrum to call in his forces, as we know he did, the first favourable moment when the Danes could try to force the fen was during the low tides in the week chosen.

It is clear that, as his plans matured, Alfred sent messages through Somerset, Wilts, and Hants to bid the Saxons be ready to muster on a given day at a stated place for a direct and rapid march on the Danes at Ethandun. Once he had decided on the day, he would name it by his messengers, or, as the Rev. W. Greswell has suggested, signal for the gathering from the Quantocks, where one

Land of Quantock, p. 66.

ancient beacon-fire hearth seems to have been deliberately placed at such a point that its blaze could be seen from the Selwood hills, and from no intermediate height.

"Then in the seventh week after Easter, Alfred rode to Ecgbryht's stone, which is in the eastern part of the wood called Selwood, and thither came to meet him" the men of the three counties. So say Asser and the *Chronicle* in precise terms. Alfred must have left Athelney quietly, and almost alone, and ridden across the country he knew perfectly to the gathering place, as his men, who knew it equally well, converged on it from every direction in small parties. It seems almost superfluous now to note that the South African war was full of examples of similar gatherings, unsuspected and all the more dangerous, carried out by the men of the land.

There is not a word of any force marching from Athelney with the king to the Selwood rendezvous, which must have been the case had he been mustering all his available forces against an enemy posted some thirty miles eastward of the gathering place and out of reach of Athelney. There can be no doubt that the Devon men, who were not at the gathering, were left to oppose any move made by Guthrum from the Poldens against Athelney and to watch the line of the fenland frontier generally from the Parrett mouth to Taunton, and thence to Chard. Neither were the Dorset levies present, though the gathering place was actually on the edge of that county. Unless these levies also had some special duty to carry out, they would certainly have been summoned; but they were needed as guardians of the coast against reinforcements by sea, which were always to be dreaded, and probably also held the ancient camps which kept the old North Dorset border.

If this gathering had not been as sudden, and unexpected by the Danes, both as regards time and place, as the *Chronicles* imply, it must have been prevented. As the men composing it came

This is so evident that Mr Green has taken it for granted. In his History of the English People (Sect. V) he says, following the Wiltshire theory without examination, "still gathering his troops as he moved, he marched through Wiltshire on the Danes." This is rapid and picturesque, but there was no march from Athelney, and no gradual gathering of troops. The Chronicles are precise as to a gathering on a stated day at a named spot. The expression "through Wiltshire" resolves itself into a matter of ten miles across the county border. But this loose statement is on a par with the usual treatment of the events of the campaign, even by our best writers. They are absolutely unable to explain them on the lines of a Wiltshire Ethandun.

from the country ravaged by the Danes, unless it was carried out swiftly and secretly it would infallibly have been anticipated, probably would never have been recorded, or would only have found a place in history as a dispersal of an attempted rising of Wessex, before it became dangerous.

The exact position of Ecgbryht's stone we may leave for the present, as there is no question but that it is known within a few miles, and is probably well represented by the Stourton tower raised to commemorate Alfred's doings. The important point is that the gathering and the next march were masked by the Selwood forest land from Guthrum, whose eyes were fixed on Athelney.

There was no delay at the gathering, which was evidently marked by the utmost enthusiam, recorded in terms which certainly imply that Alfred's arrival at Ecgbryht's Stone was sudden, and the muster complete. On the next day the whole force marched to a place called Aecglea or Iglea, and there camped for the night.

This halting place is not known certainly. The name seems to be only a field name, of a type which is so common that wherever a field for Edington has been conjectured, there has been little or no difficulty in finding some name compounded with "lea" which will answer the purpose of the theorist. The only condition which must be fulfilled is that the place chosen must be within striking distance of the actual battlefield on the next day and therefore, as the battle commenced early, it should not be more than a few hours' march at the most. The question is discussed elsewhere, but we may say that the nearest approach to the actual name Aecglea which we have found is at Butleigh (the ancient Saxon "Budeclega") near Glastonbury, where the position fulfils the requirements admirably.

It lies some twenty-five miles from the Selwood gathering-place, and eight or ten miles from the

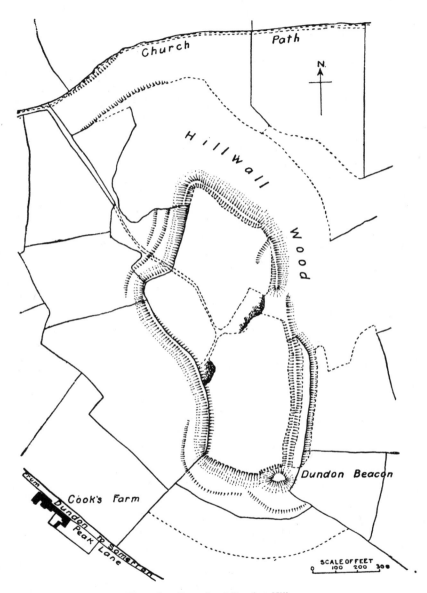

Plan of earthworks at Dundon Hill.

lines of earthworks on Edington hill. It is just off the main road from the Poldens to Glastonbury, and well masked from it by hill and woodland, while communication with Athelney would be easy. Less than three miles away, at the head of the Somertòn marshes, is the ancient camp on Dundon hill, isolated, and well adapted for an outpost.

Here again there was no delay. Through the dawn of the next morning a short march brought the king to the field of battle. The expressions used in the *Life of S. Neot* and by William of Malmesbury and John of Wallingford imply that he surprised the Danes, and seized a favourable position which they had neglected to occupy, though Simeon of Durham says that he found them ready for battle.

Both of these statements may be correct. The early march along the Poldens, favoured according to the *Life of S. Neot* by a fog, would, after but six or eight miles had been covered, bring him close to the Danish entrenchments on Edington hill. At the same time the road which he must have followed crosses, not more that a mile away, a higher shoulder of the ridge, whose point dominates by about 100 feet the Edington hill itself, forming what is exactly described as a "promontorium" by these chroniclers, and certainly being a point which the Danes would have held had they looked for attack by way of the hills of which they had made themselves masters. It is probably this point, whence the road onward to the entrenchments practically occupies the whole of the ridge, which Alfred took. Possibly the alarm which set the Danes in arms came from an outpost driven thence.

But if Alfred had deliberately timed his march to coincide with a Danish attempt to force the passage of the fen to Athelney, he would indeed find them drawn up ready for their advance, but on the lower ground at the edge of the marsh. In that case the surprise would be complete, and the advantage of position entirely in favour of the

Saxon host. An unexpected flank or rear attack is almost invariably successful in primitive warfare. And it must be remembered that Alfred needed every advantage which he could gain. He had to face successful and war-hardened troops with the levies of Wessex which had been so lately scattered and hopeless.

The battle seems to have been stubbornly fought and to have lasted long. Towards its end it must have been a rearguard action, ending in a rout of the Danes, who sought shelter in their stronghold, which we now hear of for the first time.

There is only one direction with respect to the battlefield on the Polden ridge in which a stronghold need be looked for. The hill crest is so narrow, and the fenland so close and deep at the foot of either slope of the ridge, that Alfred's advance from the direction of Glastonbury must of necessity drive the fugitives seaward to the end of the hills where they touch the river Parrett at Downend, above the little haven we have already mentioned.

Here has been a position easily and quickly made extremely strong, with the river and marshes on three sides, and only the connecting narrow neck of land requiring entrenchment or stockade, or both. The remains of ancient earthworks visible here and there have been considered as Roman until lately, and many Roman remains have been found in the immediate neighbourhood. The position has now been cut throught by the railway, and is scarred with the marks of the quarrying of generations, but there is not the least doubt that it has been of importance and strongly fortified. Human remains are very frequently found even now, and the making of the railway cutting is said to have disturbed great quantities of bones, within living memory. The cutting runs across the tongue of hill in almost exactly the position which would lie outside the entrenchments, where the main slaughter of the Danes took place after the gates were closed.

The expression used in the *Chronicle* that Alfred "pitched his camp before the gate" may be only a phrase for a siege, but it would exactly describe the position of the Saxon army across the Polden ridge, and is entirely compatible with the existence of one way only out of the stronghold, as would be the case at Downend.

Here the Danes turned at bay, and were blockaded for a fortnight. Their position was hopeless and explains the utter surrender, not only of this host, but of the almost accomplished Danish supremacy in England.

The only way of escape from the end of the Poldens was through Alfred's host, and so back to the Fosseway, and through the length of Wessex, which had risen upon them. The river to the west, and the Brue fens to the east were impassable. Even had there been vessels available in the little haven which the entrenchments guarded, the river channels are easily blocked, and we have no record of any attempt at escape in that way. Had Hubba's ships been brought up to this point by their remaining men, which is a mere matter of speculation, they were not enough for the defeated host, if the Parrett neap tides would allow of their immediate use. By the time the tides strengthened Alfred would have taken such precautions as would render the channel impassable.

It is extremely doubtful if a single fugitive found his way to Mercia with the tale of disaster and appeal for help, through the blockade. The width of hill crest to be watched is very small, and the fens, except to a native, trackless. It is one of the unanswerable difficulties involved in the acceptance of a Wiltshire site that no help came from the Mercian Danes across the Thames. Granted that every possible warrior had joined Guthrum, the Danish host must have been so immense that a siege of such a stronghold as a hill camp would require a still vaster force than we can imagine Alfred to have gathered. Yet a comparatively small army could hold the beaten host within the lines across the neck of the Polden peninsula, and Alfred's host was apparently not far from equal in numbers to that of his enemy. Probably as men came in it was larger toward the end of the siege.

The rest of the story is simple. After a fortnight's seige the Danes, worn out with hunger fear and cold were compelled to accept what terms Alfred chose to impose on them. The terror of thirst is not mentioned, as it must have been had the siege been that of a Wiltshire hill camp. Within the lines of Downend the water supply is remarkable, being due both to perennial springs and a brook at the hill foot. The part which the want of water played in the desperation of Odda's men in their fortress is specially noted, and the omission here is no doubt intentional.

The Danes swore once more to depart from the kingdom, but now there was a new development. Guthrum and his principal chiefs not only submitted to Alfred, but also to Christianity. Maybe the change of faith was not so sudden as it may seem. Guthrum had been in England for ten years, and must have learned from the Saxons around him.

As would be natural, the baptism of the chiefs took place within easy reach of their refuge. As the *Chronicle* points out Aller is a village in the fen, close to Athelney; and Wedmore, where the terms of peace were finally ratified, is a larger village, belonging to Alfred, situated on an island in the fens of the Brue and Axe to the eastward of the Poldens, where its position had no doubt saved it from devastation.

With the peacemaking, the Danes, undoubtedly disarmed so far as the rank and file were concerned, withdrew to Chippenham, their original base in the wasted lands which they could not harm much further. There they were allowed to stay until the end of the year, when they left for Cirencester, and so passed from

Wessex.

Probably they went back to Mercia gradually and not as a host, the last of them being gone only at the year's end. One may find reasons for their being allowed to stay so long, in Alfred's apparent certainty of Guthrum's good faith, in which he was fully justified, and in some wish to treat his new subjects generously. It is also possible that it was safer to let the host melt as it were from the land rather than to hustle them as a sullen and dangerous body over the border. His own Wessex levies might be trusted to watch them closely, for they had had a hard lesson in the danger of dispersal too early.

The foregoing interpretation of the story as told by Asser and the *Chronicles* is strictly in accordance with the facts they state. None of the statements have been distorted or read in any but their natural sense, and where the bearing is doubtful we have endeavoured to explain them in accordance with evident necessities. Read in this way the events of the Athelney campaign seem to fall into place with a coherence and significance which no other interpretation can give them.

These authorities have always been available, but it is astonishing in some ways, to note how little they have been profited by. They have been passed over by the history-writers who have been only too glad to leave "our barbarous Saxon ancestors" for Norman records, as hardly worthy of note.

Lately also, as if the fog in which the question has been wrapped were not enough, side issues have been brought forward and wrangled over as if they were essentials, rather than interesting details, of the campaign. We have done our best to avoid the least insistence on them, though we have little hope that our forbearance will be imitated.

Chapter 4

The question of the place-names mentioned by the chroniclers of this campaign demands most careful study. The identification of two or three of the most important sites is by no means easy, and it is round their names that previous controversies have mainly raged. We propose to deal with them in this section in the chronological order in which they occur in the story of the events of the year 878, and to examine them apart from any external considerations which might aid in their identification. These are dealt with in their place.

In this examination we have found the notes to Stevenson's edition of Asser's *Life of King Alfred* (Oxford 1904) an invaluable aid. They are practically the only serious attempt to study the names etymologically which has as yet been made, and our references to his work will be constant. In many cases indeed where we have seen no reason to differ from his views we have been content to state them without comment. Where we do differ from his conclusions, we have as far as possible examined the evidence independently, and have referred to such other authorities as we have been able to discover, in support of our own views.

About the first few place-names, Wareham, Exeter, and Chippenham, there is no question, and we need not dwell upon them. The district of Somerset (the "Summurtunensis paga," of Asser), Alfred's refuge in his first misfortunes, is also well known, being undoubtedly the country round and to the north of Somerton, the ancient chief town of the Sumorsaetas, including the marshes of the rivers Tone and Cary.

The place names involved up to the time of the flight into the woods and fenlands after the surprise by the Danes at midwinter are, therefore, of no difficulty. But with the arrival of the brother of Ingvar and Halfdan from Demetia we at once meet with a name which requires elucidation. Demetia itself is of course well known as the western district of the modern

Wales, including Pembrokeshire and part of Carmarthenshire but the landing place in Dumnonia, and the battlefield before the "Arx Cynuit" remain to be identified.

Cynuit (Asser and Flo. Wigorn.), *Kenwith* (Matt. West.), *Cynwith* (S. Dunelm).

The position of the fortress of Cynuit has been much disputed. W. H. Stevenson, says in his edition of Asser *(Life of Alfred):*

> The site of Cynuit is unknown. The name seems to represent an old Welsh form of "Cunetio," which still exists as a river-name in Wales, in the later form "Cynwydd." "Cunetio" is the older Celtic form of the river Kennett, O.E. *Cynete,* but no river of this name is known in Devon.

A site near Bideford in North Devon is widely known as that of this fortress owing to its adoption by the late Charles Kingsley, who refers to it in a picturesque passage in *Westward Ho!* But Mr Stevenson goes on to dissect the history of this never well authenticated tradition, and shows that it rests on no foundation of fact, but has merely an assumption of antiquaries.

With regard to other suggested sites, Stevenson proceeds to say in a footnote:

> Professor Earle's suggestion that Cynuit may be Countesbury is impossible phonetically and formally, since the latter name occurs in the *Exon Domesday,* as *Contesberia,* and as *Contesberie* in the *Exchequer Domesday.* A compound of *Cynuit* and *burh* as suggested by Plummer, "Countesbury, *quasi* Cynwitesbyrig" would not have had the gen. sing. -es. Bishop Clifford's attempt to prove that Cynuit was Cannington Park, Somerset, is one of the wildest freaks in his astounding paper *(Somerset Arch. and Nat. Hist. Society's Proceedings, 1877, p. 14).* In the *Proceedings* for 1876, part 2 p. 5, he alters the corrupt late form *Cynwith* into *Cynwich,* explains this as "King's town" (an unrecorded O. E. *Cynewic),* and identifies it with Combwich!

Dr. Clifford was certainly no philologist, but Stevenson's somewhat contemptuous rejection of the place on account of the peculiar deviations given by the Bishop does not rest on any examination of the older forms in which the name "Combwich" appears. There were other and more cogent reasons which led Dr Clifford to this identification beyond those of his derivations, and if only on that account, the name seems to repay study. Combwich appears in Domesday as "Comich" and "commit." In Kirby's *Quest* (1286) the spelling is "Comwych," phonetic variants of which occur constantly. Bridgwater documents, *temp.* Edw. IV, give the name as "Comwythe" and the Somerset Pleas (Roll no. 75, 27 Hen. III) as Cunyz, which is usually read as Cunyth, but may mean Cunyet, which approaches very nearly to the Cynuit of Asser.

If the theory put forward by Stevenson, quoted above, that the original Welsh form of Cynuit may still be represented by the river-name Cynwydd be correct, it is worth noting that the local mediaeval form Cunyth is practically identical with this Celtic original. At the same time it approaches more nearly to the Cynuit of Asser than any place-name yet suggested as representing it. In fact, we may say that had this name occurred anywhere within the boundaries of the modern county of Devon it would have been accepted without hesitation as the Cynuit of the Danish defeat. There is no reason at all to think that the brook which forms the Combwich haven, once a much more imposing body of water than at present, may not be responsible for the name. It is still "Combwich Brook" for its whole length.

Athelney—Ecgbryhtes Stone.

The position of Athelney itself, and the spot adjacent where Alfred threw up the work from which he waged war on the Danish host is undisputed, and need not be enlarged upon in this section.

With Ecgbryht's Stone, the mustering place of the force he raised with which to put the fortune of his kingdom to a decisive test, the case is

Bishop Clifford however professes to quote as his authority for the reading above the actual Latin text of Roger de Hoveden, which he gives as "occisi sunt ante Cimwich." What MS. or other warrant he had for this reading is difficult to discover. He may have misread his text, but is seems most unlikely that he deliberately falsified it to buttress up his argument, and it seems hardly fair to say that he altered it without pointing out this fact, especially as he is no longer alive to defend his reading. The c and t in some mediaeval MSS. are notoriously easy to confuse, and the mistake may not be Dr Clifford's.

The parallels between the older forms Comit and Cynuit, and between the later Domwythe and Kinwith, Cunyth and Cynwith, are suggestive.

somewhat different. It is true that we can locate it approximately, as we are told that it was in the eastern part of Selwood ("be eastan Sealwyda," A.-S.C.). This forest lay on the boundary between Wilts and Somerset, and extended southwards into Dorsetshire, and the stone probably stood near where the three counties meet on its eastern edge. Stevenson has exhaustively examined the various attempts which have been made to identify the exact spot, and shows clearly, as we think, that the name of Ecgbryht's Stone has perished. He points out that in maps dated 1804 a "boundstone" is marked at the point where the three counties meet near "Penzelwood" (*sic*) and that this would answer the conditions required for the trysting place.

Modern Somerset, *I*, p. *190*.

This "three-shire stone" is said by W. Phelps to be now covered by the water of a known pond. But if we take Penselwood as approximately marking the spot, any arguments based upon it cannot be far wrong. It is probable that the well-known Stourton tower, raised to commemorate the gathering, is hard by the very place where the levies met their king.

Aecglea or Iglea.

This place, that of the first halt at nightfall on the march to Ethandun, is another spot which has so far never been satisfactorily identified. The name is given as *Aecglea* by Asser and Florence of Worcester, as *Aeglea* in D and E MSS. of the A.-S. *Chronicle*, but as *Iglea* in the MSS. A, B and C of the latter, and in the *Annales Fani S. Neoti*. Another MS. of Florence gives the spelling *Ecglea*.

Modern identifications are many and diverse, varying according to the quarters in which the writers have wished to locate the site of the battle of Ethandun. Thus we find suggested in Wiltshire alone no less than five places, Winsley and Leigh, both near Bradford-on-Avon, Cley hill near Corsley, Highley near Melksham and Leigh near Westbury. In Berkshire the place, not now known, from which Eglei hundred took its name has been put forward; and in Hampshire Oakley near Basingstoke. In Somerset, Edgarley near Glastonbury, and Elleigh or Illeigh near Chard have their advocates.

None of these sites appears to stand the tests to which Stevenson has subjected them, and none has met with any very general acceptance. It is, therefore, hardly necessary to enter into a supplementary examination of their claims, but it is tolerably clear that wherever an Aecglea or Iglea is looked for it is possible to discover some place-name which will correspond more or less. The fact appears to be that an army of Alfred's time did not require as its halting place at night a town or village furnishing quarters and supplies. Each man carried with him sufficient for a night or two, and all that was sought was ground suitable for a bivouac. The name of such a place might be entirely descriptive, and if so would not be likely to leave much trace in permanent records, and might easily fall into disuse, or become altered beyond recognition as the conditions of the country changed.

It is not clear why the name appears under the two forms *Aecglea (Aeglea)* and *Iglea*. Stevenson, in an attempt to locate the battle of Ethandun in Wiltshire suggests that

the form *Aeglea* may be merely a misreading of *Ieglea*, which would be a more regular West Saxon spelling for Alfred's time than *Iglea*, if the first part of the compound is derived from *"ieg,"* later *"ig,"* "island," "watery land." The balance of evidence is certainly in favour of the form *Iglea*.

The place to which Stevenson wishes to apply this name is the seventeenth century Iley Oak in Warminster parish, Wilts, which appears in 1439 as *Ilegh*. His conclusion is that this Ilegh is the *Igleah (sic)* of the *Chronicle; that Aeglea* of Chron. D and E is either a miscopying of an *Ieglea* in a lost early MS. of the *Chronicles,* or arises from an erroneous identification of *Ieglea* with some other local name, and that the *Aecglea* of the Cott. MS., of the *Life,* and of Florence, is an attempt to rationalise the inexplicable *Aeglea* by substituting for the first member of the compound the word *Aecg,* a late spelling of *ecg,* "edge"—edge of a cliff.

Coming from such a source, this amazing piece of special pleading requires a word of notice. It rests on several assumptions, none of which is proven. Stevenson has assumed a derivation for the name, on which he has worked, has been further changed in order to "rationalize it." In other words, his contention is that chroniclers who knew the name of the place have altered the name they knew into one they thought might be easier for latter-day philologists!

Furthermore, the conclusion arrived at by Stevenson that the balance of evidence is in favour of the form *Iglea,* is equally open to question. This form stands almost alone, as it occurs in only one important MS. of the *Chronicles,* only supported by two of the less important copies and by the compiled *Annales,* while the *Aecglea* of Asser (who undoubtedly knew the Athelney positions) and Florence is corroborated by the *Aeglea* of the important MSS. D and E of the *Chronicles.*

It is possible that a name of the *Aecglea-Ecglea* type is involved in certain place-names of the district on the eastern borders of the Somerset marshes, where a chain of names compounded with "Leigh" stretches from near Somerton to Street, by Glastonbury. No argument can be based on the occurrence of this very usual nomenclature of course, as it stands; but a research into the older forms of the present "leighs" of this district has yielded some rather suggestive results.

The names centre round Butleigh, two miles from which on the S.W. is Bradleigh. Butleigh hill, Butleigh wood, and Butleigh bottom are connected with the village of that name, between which and Street, just south of the ancient road which leads along the crest of the Poldens, are Lower Leigh, Higher Leigh, and Leigh. Street itself appears as *Lega* in Domesday, and the manor of Butleigh itself is named under various forms which are worth examination.

The earliest mention of Butleigh is in King Ina's charter of 725 A.D., where it appears as *Budecaleth,* which is glossed, apparently by William of Malmesbury as *Buddecleghe.* In a grant made with the assent of King Ecgbert in 802 it appears as *Budecleg* and *Budeclege,* and in 971 it is written as *Budeclega* in a charter of King Eadgar.

In Domesday book it is entered as *Buduccheleia* (Exon D.B. *Bodecaleia)* and in the *Confirmatio Savarici* (circ. 1200) as *Budecleghe.* In the twelfth century records it occurs under various slight differences of spelling as *Budeclega* and in the fourteenth century as *Buddecle* and *Bodekaleya.*

It will be seen that the variations of spelling are practically very slight, and the name seems to be compounded with the verb *buan* to dwell, and a word of which the ninth century form is the *eclege* of 802 A.D., reappearing as *eclega* in 971. The D. B. name of Street *(Lega)* and the various Leighs still remaining in the vicinity suggests that *Eclega* may originally have been a name covering a considerable area, and that *Bud-eclega* was the name given to the place where, on higher ground than the other Leighs, the original hall with its surrounding cultivated lands stood at the modern Butleigh.

If this assumption be correct, it is possible that this district may represent the *Aecglea* of Asser, and the *Aeglea* of the *Chronicles.*

Ethandun

The battlefield of Ethandun was evidently so well known to the early chroniclers that, as in the case of the field of Brunanburh, it did not seem necessary to them to define its locality. The only apparent hint as to its position has been found in the careless misreading of Ethelwerd's summary of the campaign to which we have referred elsewhere. This is entirely misleading, and the only actual knowledge of the locality of the battlefield which can be gained from the *Chronicles* is that it was within striking distance of Athelney. The question of the site is complicated by the form of the name itself, which is of a simple descriptive type which might be looked for in any hilly country. It is written in the *Anglo-Saxon Chronicle* as Edandun and Epandun, and these forms are followed by Asser and the later chroniclers who took their material from either of these sources. The latest of these chroniclers, e.g. Hoveden and Simeon of Durham, use a transitional form Eddandune. Henry of Huntingdon spells the name Edendune, but Gaimar's Norman-French rhymed *Chronicle,* written about 1150, has Edenesdone.

The most obvious derivation of the name is from *"Haed-haeden-,"* the heathy, and *"dun"* a hill. An alternative from *"Haeden,"* the heathen, with reference to the defeat of the heathen, Danes, has been suggested, and a third, with the same reference, might be from the simple prefix *"Heden"* denoting battle.

Neither of these derivations seeming quite satisfactory, we submitted the question to Prof. Toller, who wrote,

"There is an adjective, though a rarely used one, *'ede,'* meaning waste, desolate. I think it possible that the name may have grown from some such form as 'Edan dune.' The Icelandic might be compared here, *e.g.* Eydi fjall, a wild fell, edi-land, desert land."

The recognised modern corruption of Ethandun is to Edington. There is fortunately no question as to this, the name, though it is nowhere given in Domesday Book, recurring in the case of Edington, near Westbury, Wilts, as Ethendune in a charter of 1280. It may be taken therefore that where an Edington is found the descriptive place-name of some waste hill position, Ethandun, has existed. At the same time it might be expected that places to which this name would apply would not be uncommon, and as a matter of fact, names which may have been derived from an Ethandun occur frequently in the south of England. Wiltshire, Somerset, Hampshire, Buckinghamshire, Berkshire, Kent, Surrey, and Northamptonshire all have examples, and in some counties, as in Wiltshire and Northamptonshire the names are duplicated.

The actual Saxon form "Ethandun" does not occur in Domesday Book. In the Wiltshire example already mentioned it is given as Edendone, while the Somerset Edington appears as Eduuinetone. Edinton or Edintune occur in other counties.

"Ethandun" is however mentioned three times in early Saxon documents. An Ethandun is left to his wife by King Alfred in his will. King Eadwig executed a charter at an Ethandun in 957: and an Ethandun was granted by King Eadgar to the abbey of Romsey in 968. There is however no reason for identifying either of these Ethanduns with one another, or with the battle-field, while there is good reason for believing that two at least are different manors. That at which King Eadwig executed his deed is not identifiable, and it may be a third.

The Ethandun of Alfred's will is a manor given to the queen with two other manors which are adjacent to one another, the grant being of "Lamburn, Waneting and Ethandun." The first two are now Lambourn and Wantage in Berks, and adjacent to these lies Eddington, all three being still royal property at the time of Domesday. This Eddington is represented in Domesday by "Eddevetone," which is probably an alternative or legal name used for closer identification, and is probably derived from the name of Queen "Eddeva." The present name, Eddington, which is the usual corruption of

Ethandun, cannot be connected with Eddevetone, but has persisted where the alternative form has disappeared. The Rev. F. W. Ragg, who edited the Berkshire Domesday for the *Victoria County History,* gives in a footnote against Eddevetone "probably for Eddenetone." The entry however would not seem to be a mere miscopying of v for n, as the name of the place occurs later in both forms. It is Eddevetona in 1101, and Eddevetone in the Pipe Rolls of 1167, but Edunetone in the *Testa de Nevill,* where the more ancient and persistent name recurs. There can be no reasonable doubt that this Berkshire Eddington is the Ethandun granted with the adjacent manors by King Alfred to his queen.

The remaining Ethandun of Saxon mention is undoubtedly the Edington near Westbury in Wiltshire, the "Ethendune" of 1280, which remained a Ramsey manor from the time of its grant by King Eadgar onward.

Very little help can be gained from these three names, as the fact of a victory gained by Alfred in his own kingdom does not necessarily render the battlefield royal property.

The Somerset Edington on Poldens occurs in Domesday under the name of Eduuinetone, the Exon variant being Edwinetona. The place was not a manor, but appears in the list of certain lands held in the great manor of Shapwick by Roger de Courcelles. This manor appears to have been Glastonbury property from very early times, as there is no record of its grant to the abbey. The name of the hamlet of Edington therefore appears almost exclusively in Glastonbury lists, but the Domesday form is never used. Its earliest appearance in Glastonbury documents is in the *Subjectio Savarici,* of 1199, where among the monks who signed appears the name of "Thomas de Edindone," the same name appearing a little later as "Thomas de Edintone." The name is Edinton in the *Rotuli Finium* of 1208, and it also appears as Edinctone, assuming the present form during the thriteenth century.

We pointed this out in a letter to The Athenaeum *of October 24, 1908.*

It is obvious that the Domesday name, Edwinetone, can have no connection with Ethandun directly, but while Edington is the known corruption of Ethandun through some "Edindone" form, Edwinetone is a possible expansion of Edindon or Edinton, the name in contemporary use. This expansion may have been due to an intention on the part of a careful scribe to set down what he believed to be the correct full spelling of an orally delivered "Ed'in-don," or may have been deliberately adopted in order to differentiate this Ethandun from the many others in existence. Whatever the reason for the Domesday form may have been, it is certain that it was never accepted by the owners of the place, and that it has left no trace.

Stevenson's opinion is that the Domesday form, Edwinetone, is for Edwinestone, an inference which is obvious. That some such name was for a time at least used by the Normans is evident from the "Edenesdone" of Gaimar, a record which should be conclusive as to the site of the battlefield. The modern form of Edwineston is Edston (Idston), which occurs elsewhere.

It should be noticed that the early form Edindone is practically identical with the form Edendone occurring in Wiltshire. This, according to Stevenson, is the correct Norman rendering of the Saxon Ethandun. There is no doubt that both these places bore the name of Ethandun, and the question as to which was the actual battlefield can only be decided by a close reading of the *Chronicles,* and a careful consideration of the strategic and other necessities of the case as set forth in them.

With regard to the appropriateness of the derivation of the name suggested by Professor Toller, it may be noticed that Domesday only accounts for about half of the 14,755 acres of the Shapwick manor. This is noted by Prebendary Eyton in his Domesday studies, where he points out that the balance must have

it may only be a coincidence, but there was an actual manor of Edwynston, now Idston, in Bucks, held by Glastonbury. The Rev W. Greswell considers that the name of Edwinetone for Edington has crept into Domesday by transference from some list of the abbey manors. Edington however must have been enumerated from a list of the de Courcelles holdings, as it was not a manor in itself. In that case it would be much more likely that the baron had an actual tenant of the very common Saxon name of Edwin, living on the spot at the hill foot northward where the present village of Edington stands, and giving his name to a homestead, which better represented the geldable property than the waste hill.

represented either royal forest, or unprofitable waste. The "waste hill" of Ethandun would most likely include the whole of the Polden range, where, as at Dundon, Pendon, Dunball and Downend, several other compounds of "Dun" still exist.

.   .   .   .

The original conjecture of Camden that Edington near Westbury was the battlefield has been recognised as untenable by students of the *Chronicles,* but the false lead given by the Ethelwerd misreading has been fatal. It may be said that every possible site bearing a name which in any way resembles Ethandun, within the Chippenham district, has been put forward as an alternative. Heddington, Eaton Down, and Yatton Keynell are all in Wilts. Yattenden and Eddington near Hungerford in Berks have also been advocated. The philological objections to these sites are very strong, and have been fully dealt with by Stevenson. In addition, none of these positions fulfils the first condition necessary to the site—that of being within the reach of action from Athelney. Hamdon, near Montacute, in Somerset, which does fulfil this condition, was suggested by W. L. Radford in 1904, but his derivation of the name from "Aet Handune" is too far-fetched, and the site for other reasons is improbable.

The earliest identification of Ethandun with Edington on Poldens is in Tindal's translation of Rapin's *History of England* (2nd edition, 1732), where the site of the battle is given in a footnote as "Edington in Somerset" without comment. The position was again put forward by Gabriel Poole at the Bridgwater meeting of the British Archaeological Association in 1857, and it was also strongly advocated, as mentioned elsewhere, by the late Bishop Clifford; but he so prejudiced his case by impossible etymologies that in spite of its common sense it met with no

In a paper read before the Somerset Archaeological Society at their annual meeting for that year. Proceedings *Vol. LI.*

more than scant consideration by the critics who had no knowledge of the country.

The testimony of tradition has long ceased to be of any value in the case of Ethandun. It may be safe to say that at the present time every possible Ethandun is credited with traditions of the defeat of the Danes on that spot. It might be hard to find any hill position in much-harried Wessex where at one time or another a battle has not taken place, and traditions of such fighting may have existed until the coming of the schoolmaster. But if they did exist they have been rendered useless by the theorising of local enthusiasts who have referred them indiscriminately to the one desired event. This is by no means an unknown method even to-day, and as an example we may suggest that the Bideford legend of the death of Hubba may have been evolved from a good actual tradition of one of the many Danish landings on the Devon coast. The Elizabethan mistake as to the Appledore in question started the notion that Hubba was involved, and the appropriation of the legend, so amplified by Kingsley has done the rest. Whatever the original legend, if any, may have been, it is now valueless.

Actual local traditions are priceless, but the "traditions" evolved by a system of leading questions are less than worthless. The results are repeated by the cross-questioned "oldest inhabitant," who has learned from them what he is expected to say to earn his shilling, and are thus perpetuated as what "they say." We have therefore thought it best to leave this source of information unexploited.

In the elucidation of the place-names Ethandun and Cynuit we have made full use of Mr Stevenson's notes to his edition of Asser. We have also been considerably assisted by a correspondence on the same subject in the Athenaeum, *extending with long intervals, from Aug. 18, 1906, to Oct. 24, 1908. In this correspondence Mr Stevenson and the Rev. W. Greswell were the protagonists, and one letter was contributed by the Rev. E. McClure and two by ourselves. A fair summary of the results of this correspondence, so far as the name Ethandun is concerned, may be found in an appendix to Mr Greswell's* Story of the Battle of Edington, *p. 90.*

Chapter 5

As we have already pointed out, this landing, though in actual results it was ineffectual, has some marked effect on the progress of the Danish campaign against Alfred, for the reason that any attack by a sea-borne force to the westward of Athelney, while Guthrum was master of the country to the eastward, was a new peril, specially to be met and needing new precautions against possible repetition. It should be hardly necessary to say that such a landing on any point of the Severn coast westward of the Parrett would, if successful, have been sufficient to place Alfred between two fires, and we do not consider that the actual locality of the place where this landing was made can have had any but an indirect bearing on the question of the site of the battle of Ethandun.

The whole expedition and its disastrous termination for the Danish chief is, however, so picturesque, and the identification of the landing place in modern Somerset so probable, that it has taken too prominent a place in the arguments between the rival upholders of the Somerset and Wiltshire sites of Ethandun and of the campaign which preceded that battle, the relatively small importance of the exact place being lost sight of, while the abortive invasion of a few days has been magnified into a long campaign.

This being the case we wish to make it thoroughly clear that, while we endorse Bishop Clifford's location of the site of the landing at the modern Combwich, we do not in the least insist on this identification as a necessary point in the argument for Edington on Poldens. It is an additional point in favour of that site in some ways, and we ourselves believe that Combwich is the most probable landing place yet suggested. Still, so long as it is allowed that a landing made in force by the Danes on the far side of Athelney must have had, as the *Chronicles* intimate that it had, its result in determining Alfred to defend the fen, besides drawing Guthrum westward, we are equally ready to accept any documentary evidence which might prove that the landing was elsewhere in Devon in Wessex, whatever that term may have meant.

Unfortunately, in stating that we support Bishop Clifford's identifications, it is almost necessary to say that we do so in spite of his extraordinary etymology. The bishop's knowledge of the country and the *Chronicles* needed no such backing as imaginative derivations of place-names could give, and they are superfluous. Were it not that the advocates of the Wiltshire theory have made full use of these mistakes as a very useful side issue with which to discredit the belief in a Somerset campaign from beginning to end, they might be disregarded.

To summarise the *Chronicle* accounts again, to save reference to the *Catena* it will be enough to say that Hubba wintered and ravaged in Demetia, and thence, just before Easter, crossed with between 20 and 30 ships to some point on the coast of "Devon in Wessex," marked by a fortress called Cynuit. Here he fell during a despairing sortie of the besieged Saxon force which had been defeated on his landing, apparently not more than a day or two previously. The Saxons captured the war flag of the "Sons of Lodbrok," but did not hold the field, and the Danes recovered the body of their leader and returned to their ships, thereafter joining Guthrum's forces. As a result of this victory Alfred built the Athelney stronghold, and Guthrum learned that the winning of Wessex was not yet complete. The actual Athelney campaign dates therefore from the fall of Hubba, which took place in the end of March. Later chroniclers state that the Danes buried the fallen chief in a known mound, the site of which is not clear.

There has been much controversy over the exact locality in South Wales where Hubba spent the winter, though the point is immaterial to a study of the subsequent campaign. Demetia comprised Pembroke, Carmarthen, and Glamorgan shires, and Hubba's winter quarters are usually supposed to have been in Milford Haven, where Hubbaston may still preserve his name, and where there were ancient Danish haunts and settlements. But it has also been argued that his wintering was in the Forest of Dean, as some sixteenth century commentators on Giraldus Cambrensis have derived the name of the "Denica Sylva" from the occupation of the district by Danes in the time of Alfred. Ethelwerd's statement that the Danes went from Exeter to Gloucester is probably accountable for the idea that they may have infested the neighbourhood, but the etymology is worthless, and the extension of Demetia to the Severn is not warranted by any recognised authority.

The suggestion would not be worth consideration but that this wintering in the Forest of Dean seems to be insisted on as necessary to a theory which imagines Hubba to have made constant descents on the Somerset coasts during the winter of 877-8, while Alfred was in hiding in Athelney, the idea at the back of the mind of the theorist seeming to be that starting point and landing place must necessarily be as nearly as possible opposite to one another. As a matter of fact the prevailing winds of spring in the Severn are north-west, and would rather favour a passage from Milford than from further up the estuary, though of course the latter point is the nearer to the mouth of the Parrett.

This theory that Hubba wintered in the Forest of Dean and thence in concert with "Hinguar" harried Somerset constantly during that winter, has been evolved by Greswell from some anonymous traditions printed by Thomas Hearne as an appendix to his edition of Peter Langtoft, and from a statement that Somerton was overrun "by the Danes, chiefly by Hinguar and Hubba," which is quoted in Collinson's *Somerset* from the heterogeneous collection of Elizabethan and other notes gathered under "Julius" in the Cottonian MS. Both these anonymous sources are worthless as historic authority. So far as the traditions are recorded by Hearne are genuine (and they seem to have their value) they should be referred to the Danish raids of 918. The Somerton statement means nothing more than that the place may have been raided by the Danes of Alfred's time, which is highly probable, seeing that Guthrum for some time held all Wessex east of the fens. But "Hinguar" was dead at that date, and Hubba was wintering, with all that that term means for his ships, in Demetia, and busy harrying that province. His landing in Somerset according to the authentic *Chronicles* was a matter of a few days, and purely local. His name and that of his brother are so constantly linked together in the earlier records of the period that the loose use of them to identify the Danish hosts of the time is understandable, and has no special force. There is no doubt that had Hubba penetrated so far inland as to reach Somerton, the *Chronicles,* which give so detailed an account of his landing and fall, could not have omitted to state so startling a feat.

The wintering of the ships of the period was a business which in itself was prohibitive of action until complete. Their build rendered annual repair, and in any case recaulking, imperative, and it will be remembered that the Danish fleet had encountered a severe gale off Swanage before the retreat from Exeter. "Wintering" is a definite and well-known term for the berthing of these ships for overhaul, under cover if possible, and it would be most unusual for a longship to be kept afloat during the winter months. There is not a word in the *Chronicles* to suggest that Hubba was anywhere but in Demetia until the spring of 878.

The question of where this landing of Hubba took place has been a matter of fierce dispute since Combwich was suggested by Bishop Clifford, though, except that his theory upsets a popular notion dear to tourists in North Devon, and that the Wiltshire theorists have their own reason for disliking it, it is hard to see why. The only indication of locality given by the

See Collinson's Somerset, Vol. III, p. 181, The Story of the Battle of Edington, pp. 20-32, and Appendix B in this volume, "Hearne's Reprint."

According to William of Malmesbury, Glastonbury was ravaged at this time, and lay waste and almost deserted until restored by Dunstan.

The first suggestion of a winter campaign and attacks on Athelney by Hubba was, curiously enough, made by Mr Stevenson, as an untenable part of a summary of what he imagined was the course of events set forth by Dr Clifford. Mr Greswell corrected the summary, and reminded Mr Stevenson that the suggestion was impossible, as Hubba was comfortably wintering in Wales, and waiting for the spring for his crossing (Athenaeum correspondence, Oct. 7, 1907, etc.)

Chronicles is the vague "in Domnonia" of Asser, and the wide "in Devonshire in Wessex" of the *Anglo-Saxon Chronicle,* with the name of the fort before which Hubba fell varying from Cynuit to Kynwith.

The popular idea that the landing took place near Bideford in Devon has gained acceptance owing to its adoption by Charles Kingsley in *Westward Ho!* There is no doubt that it originated in a sixteenth century confusion between Appledore in Devon and Appledore in Kent, where a Danish force did land in 893. The labelling in the Ordnance maps of a small earthwork in the neighbourhood as "Kinwith Castle," the location of a shadowy "Hubbastone" said to have been swept away by the tide, on the estuary of the Taw and Torridge, and the placing of a stone with a flamboyant inscription at a point chosen as convenient for the supposed defeat, are modern developments. Stevenson, in his edition of the *Life of Alfred* by Asser, has done good service to historic truth by showing on what unsubstantial foundations these Bideford "traditions" rest.

No doubt the acceptance of these localities has been in some measure due to the fact that, if the search for Cynuit is to be confined to the Severn shore of the modern county of Devon, it is difficult to see where else the landing can have taken place than in the estuary of the Taw and Torridge. Eastward of Morte Point the whole coast line up to the boundary between Devon and modern Somerset is rockbound and precipitous. There are few coves where even a single ship could be beached in safety, and none which would give space for a fleet of twenty or thirty sail. The only point which, so far as we are aware, has been suggested in this direction is Countesbury, near Linton, but the physical impossibilities of the landing have prevented the acceptance of this location.

But, like those of the older Dumnonia, the boundaries of ancient Devon were indefinite

The whole romance with every possible accretion is given as a matter of history in a popular book on Earthworks by J. C. Wall (Ancient Earthworks,*pp. 71-3).*

Earle, Two of the Saxon Chronicles, *note on the year 878. Professor Earle, who of course cannot accept the Bideford romance, based his suggestion on the possibility that some earlier form of the name might, if recovered, approximate to the Cynuit of the* Chronicle.

until very late, and in Alfred's time were wider than at present, a point which we have referred to elsewhere. The term "Devon in Wessex," which is used by the *Chronicle* where Asser uses "Domnonia," seems to indicate a part of the Dumnonian territory which had been incorporated in the royal domain in Wessex and brought under the same jurisdiction as that of the adjacent lands definitely known as those of the "Summurtunenses." In this district east of the present Devon boundary the coast line lends itself to a landing from Porlock to the estuary of the Parrett. At the latter point the rivers give open waterways into the heart of Somerset, and this is the strategic spot at which an expedition from Wales against Alfred would naturally have struck.

A landing made far to the west would have had no more than the results of a predatory raid; but if by the end of March the Danes did not know where Alfred himself was, there would be no more likely place in which to seek him than the great royal domain into which the tidal rivers of the Mendips gave free passage, and where a junction could eventually be made with the hosts under Guthrum already in possession of the most part of Wessex.

It must be realised that the force under Hubba was small, and that though it was efficient with the terrible efficiency of veteran seamen, trained to act under their captains, each man in his place, as an organised body under their chief, it was not large enough for an independent campaign when once the country was raised against it. Hubba in making his landing either dangerously underrated the force which he might have to meet, or intended to co-operate with Guthrum. There is every reason to believe that the latter was his plan, as wherever he landed to the west or north of Athelney, he was in unsubdued Dumnonia, which would rise, and did rise, against him. A landing so far to the west as Bideford Bay would eventually have meant a second sailing

Ethelwerd is responsible for the statement that the Saxon commander at Cynuit was Odda, "duke of Devon." His presence had been used as an argument against the location of the landing on the western shore of the Parrett estuary which is now included in Somerset: but even if "Devon in Wessex" did not extend so far in the time of Alfred, it is but a short march to the modern border, and there were no levies available from Somerset beyond the fens. The only Somerset men in arms at the date of the landing were the few retainers with Alfred in Athelney. Coast defence to the west of Parrett must of necessity have devolved on Devon. So we find Goda the Devon thane slain in 988 at Watchet in what is now Somerset.

eastward, if it were to be more than a raid; but to land in the Parrett estuary would mean that, if the worst happended, the way to Guthrum lay open across the great tidal inlet, whether it was safer to pass down the ridge of Mendip or along the Poldens, to the Fosseway. One of these ways Hubba's men may have taken after his fall. The fighting from Athelney did not begin until the Borough Bridge fort was made. Until Hubba was defeated there was nothing to render it evident to Guthrum that the Poldens must be held in force.

Little attention has been paid to the possibility of sites for a landing in the district between the Parrett and Exmoor, owing to the natural adherence to the modern boundary of Devon as the limit of search; but the probable identity of the ancient fortress known now as "Cannington Park" with the Cynuit of Asser and Kynwith of the later chroniclers, originally suggested by Bishop Clifford, has been recognised by all the exponents of the Somerset campaign, and so far as the resort to ridicule of the bishop's curious etymology is an evidence of a very weak case, by the adherents of the Wiltshire mistake. The fortress lies so close to the ancient tidal ford at Combwich that the name applies naturally to it, and it is on the western side of the Parrett, whence the access to Athelney is least difficult. There is no doubt that a successful landing here would not only have turned Alfred's main line of defence, the fen, but would also have barred his escape into the fastnesses of the Quantocks and Exmoor.

We have already dealt with the old forms of the name of Combwich and the probability that in the time of Alfred it was situated in a yet undefined district which would still be equally well described as in Dumnonia, Devon in Wessex, or in the land under Somerset jurisdiction. We believe that only a slavish adherence to modern boundaries could influence an otherwise unprejudiced student of the time to reject the identification, which is at the least common sense. It is by no means dependent on the philology of Dr Clifford, which seems to be the most cogent argument which its occasional opponents can find against it, next to the question of the modern county boundaries. The place has the disadvantage of being practically unknown, as it lies in no tourist track, and needs a special journey from Bridgwater if it would be seen and appreciated. But indeed, we might almost say the same of the whole Athelney district, even so good an authority as Stevenson having supposed that instead of the bold ridge of the Poldens, nothing but fen intervened between the Parrett and the Brue.

Athenaeum, *Oct. 5, 1907.*

The fortress at Combwich is evidently the only place where a force which had been defeated while trying to prevent a landing in the Parrett estuary on the western bank, could take refuge. It also answers exactly and in an unusual manner to Asser's description of the stronghold, written from his own personal inspection of the place, as Dr Clifford first pointed out. It may also be worth noting that in any case Asser must certainly have seen this fortress, at one time or another, on the way from Wales. It is surrounded with dry-stone walls of great thickness, after the manner well known in Wales and most uncommon in England, the only other example in the district being at Worlebury. It was certainly in existence in the time of Alfred, as the remains found in some abundance everywhere within the walls are, so far as pottery is concerned, of the date of Glastonbury Lake village, and of the same type, and therefore pre-Roman. Flint implements also occur, but the actual date of the building of the prehistoric walls remains to be proved.

A broad belt of water-meadows, intersected by the Combwich brook and by variouw "rhynes," marks an ancient arm of the Parrett estuary, from which the tide is now barred out by flood-gates, but within the last ten years these meadows have been flooded by an exceptionally high spring-tide. To the south of them on the hill on which the camp stands rises steeply and in places almost precipitously from the ancient shore-line, attaining a height of about 260 feet within the area of the camp.

As Asser says, the entrance to the camp is to the eastward, where a neck of land runs up from the south-east, and has been heavily entrenched across a carefully guarded passage way between opposing walls, now almost turfed over and indistinguishable at first sight from earthen ramparts. Elsewhere the stone walls are evident and still strong enough to explain why Hubba preferred not to risk an assault on the steep isolated hill which they encircle. The camp is waterless, as is recorded, the only spring being about half a mile distant, and commanded by what seems to have been the main position of the Danes, as the remains of men who have at some time fallen before the camp have covered the ground.

This position is on a small but steep hill belonging to the same outcrop of the mountain limestone through the red sandstone as the fortified hill, some 300 yards distant across a little valley. It lies between the fort and the Parrett, and commands the track to the tidal ford at Combwich, and the entrance to the fort. There must have been other posts of the besiegers to the south and west of the stronghold, where the encircling heights afford good positions, but the north was kept by the tidal inlet which ran toward the Quantocks, and a small force would be sufficient to blockade the place, unless very strongly manned.

The position between the gates and the river, where the ships would lie, is the natural place for the headquarters of a leader who brought his men from the sea, and here the whole hill top has been nothing more or less than a graveyard of an unusual type. Unfortunately the stone of the hill is valuable and it has been quarried for years, the

The camp is very little known and has been very imperfectly examined. Mr A. Hadrian Allcroft only mentions it as "a small and feeble camp" in a footnote to page 391, Earthwork of England. Mr C. H. Bothamley, in his article on "Ancient Earthworks" in the Victoria County History of Somerset, Vol. II, p. 75, describes it as a hill converted into a camp, probably for temporary occupation by scarping the sides some distance from the top. He also says that the area had been used as a place of interment and that large numbers of human skeletons had been found there. This is evidently a confusion with the burials on the Quarry Hill described below.

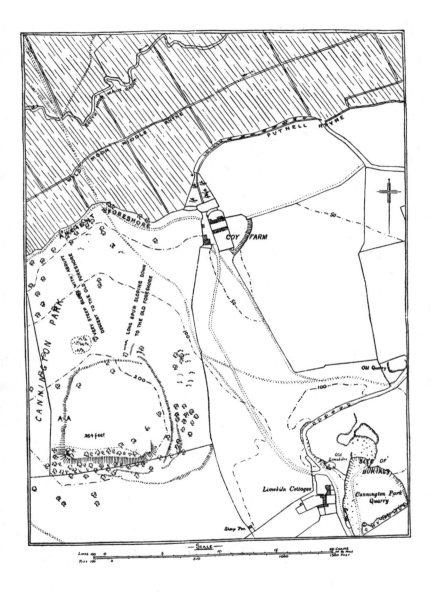

Plan of Cannington Park Camp showing the site of burials. The shaded area at the top of the plan indicates water-meadows formerly part of the tidal estuary of the River Parrett.

last graves being now in process of destruction as fresh headings are opened; but this work has been so rapid that the very large number of interments destroyed is a matter of common knowledge. The local tradition is that these buried men were "Danes," who were slain to the last man in some great fight, and as the battle is not ascribed to Alfred or to Sedgmoor, and is certainly not the result of the leading questions of local investigators, it may be safely taken as genuinely handed down. The remains are known everywhere in the neighbourhood as the "Danes' bones at the quarry hill."

When the writer first investigated the position together, the remains in sight at the quarry headings were very many, the long trenches in which they were buried running out on the ends of the cuttings at regular intervals, and showing the contour of the original excavations, which were shallow and conical as if dug in haste. Now and again too the quarrymen uncover pits into which the bodies had been thrown in no sort of order and in numbers. It has been by no means unusual to find skulls marked with the wound which must have caused death, and in some cases the stroke has been given from behind, as if during a flight and pursuit.

So far as is known no weapons beyond what might have been the point of a spear or sword have been found with the remains, though there are undefined statements that such were found at the first opening of the quarry in years past. A few bones are stained with the green colouration caused by bronze buckles or the like.

But see Appendix C, "Latest finds at Cannington Park."

Saga-Book of the Viking Club, *1908*, District Report for Somerset.

In 1907 what appeared to be the last remaining trench was laid open in order to record the arrangement of the burials and if possible to decide their date. The sketch appended will give a better idea of what was ascertained than much explanation. It shows the mode of burial, which is not of the British type of the date of the camp, but of the extended, east and west, arrangement common to the Gothic races; but, as will be evident, is by no means careful. A very curious find was here made, the skeletons of an old woman and a small child being placed between those of three men, two of whom were almost superposed, as has been found to the case elsewhere, one skeleton being found reversed on another in one place. To the south of these five interments the trench ran into one of the pits already mentioned, where an unknown number of skeletons had been found. The surface soil was considerably deeper in that direction, a chance which had apparently been made the most of.

Two more interments were uncovered in the small excavation marked to the south, and here with a burial, the most part of a food vessel of dark blackish brown pottery, which H. St George Gray, who was present, considers to be undoubtedly of Anglo-Saxon date. So far as we can learn, this is the only pottery recovered from the site.

The character and date of these interments are therefore quite compatible with the tradition of a Danish defeat, even the finding in the outermost trench of the victims of indiscriminate massacre carrying out the grim records of the times.

It may be of interest to note that the turf covering the burial trenches averaged 11 inches in thickness on the bare hill-top, and that an independent calculation, made without any knowledge of the number of men slain with Hubba, and based on the area known to have been covered by the trenches, resulted in an estimate of not less than 1000 burials on the spot. The statement of the *Chronicles* is that he lost 800 to 1200 men. The calculation took no account of the pits here and there. There is no historical evidence of any fighting, other than this raid, in Saxon times which would account for battle burials on so large a scale, but it tallies with the accounts of Hubba's overthrow. No doubt his ships were among the best of the

Danish fleet, as they had weathered the gale off Swanage, and we may put the fighting crews at about 100 men apiece, giving a force of 2000 to 3000 men, available for the landing.

As to the exact details of the disaster which befel him we have only Asser's statement that he was "perperam agens"—which intimates that he was in some way acting rashly, before the stronghold in which he had penned the Devon levies. Bishop Clifford's suggestion that he had weakened his force by sending raiding parties across the Parrett is not unlikely to be correct. In that case his ships would be stranded at low water on the far side, and until the short time of flood no help could reach him. The return of the raiders would make it advisable for the Saxon force, which must also have suffered heavily, to retreat, leaving the Danes masters of the field. According to Brompton, who probably preserved some tradition, this is what actually happened.

See Catena, *p. 147.*

Hubba's men joined Guthrum after recovering the body of their leader. Even without a chronicled statement to that effect it would be difficult to see what else they could do. The ships must have been short handed, and that was their best resort. They may have gone up the Severn to Bristol or beyond, and so to the Chippenham district, the known headquarters of the chief at the last advices, or into the Axe, and so along the Mendips to the Fosseway. It is not likely that they left their ships within reach of Alfred, and they remained as a menace of fresh landings wherever they may have been berthed.

The victory remained with Odda of Devon and his levies, though they had to retreat from the field of battle. That they once held it and took spoil of the slain may be confirmed by the absence of war-gear with the Cannington burials. After they had gone the Danes had time to bury their slain comrades in more or less orderly wise where they fell, but they probably took the body of their leader with them. The accounts of the burial of Hubba are late and confused, but they apparently imply that he was not buried on the field where he fell. It would be almost a point of honour with his men that they should prove that they were not so entirely beaten as to be forced to leave their chief to the Saxons, nor would they be likely to bury him where it was most probable that his mound would be broken by his enemies and despoiled of the arms and treasures which the men of the north buried with a hero.

There have been many endeavours to identify the site of this burial. The Bideford romance assumes that the "Hubbelowe" has been swept away by the tide. Bishop Clifford suggested a mound in Stockland Bristol, not far from Combwich, as possible, but deprecated its exploration except under the direction of experts. The curious etymology with which he backed his identification is irrelevant. This mound was dug into by Greswell, in co-operation with two temporary residents in the locality, and was found to be the mill-mound which local knowledge stated it to be.

A second mound, situated on a rise above the marsh which is known as Wick moor, once an inlet of the sea, and peculiar in its position and large size, had also been suggested as a possible burial place for the chief, especially as some distinctly Scandinavian traditions were attached to it. It was inspected and measured by Dr A Bulleid, F.S.A., and considered decidedly worth exploration, whatever it might cover, and the work was undertaken by the Somerset Archaeological Society and the Viking Club in 1907, under the full direction of H. St George Gray. It was found to be of late Stone or early Bronze Age, and the secondary interments discovered belonged to the same period. The Scandinavian traditions mentioned are fully accounted for by the existence of early northern settlements in the immediate neighbourhood.

The burial place of Hubba therefore still remains unknown. Gaimar and Brompton give the name of the mound in which he was placed

Mr Bazell has suggested to us that Hubba would probably have been buried on the summit of the knoll occupied by the burials and that this, with his mound, has been quarried away. If so this might account for a vague tradition that skeletons have been found at the quarry fully armed and euqipped.

The foot of the central millpost with its supporting framework was found in good condition, the opening of the mound being made from the top. Following Dr Clifford, who had compared the mound to the ship-burial tumuli of the north, the investigators at first thought that they had come upon the stem of the ship in which Hubba was buried. The mound is however hardly large enough to cover a decent sized boat, and they were unaware that ship burial was not a Danish custom. This mound breaking has never been previously recorded, though its negative result is valuable as disproving Bishop Clifford's suggestion.

See Catena, *pp. 146, 147.*

as "Hubbelowe," and state that it was in Devon. Gaimar however says that he was slain in "the forest of Pene," and Brompton refers the battle in which he fell to the Chippenham district. These accounts as stated above are late and confused, but it is possible that the body of the chief was actually carried by his surviving men to the Selwood district when they joined Guthrum, and that some tradition of the place was still known well enough to confuse the place of burial with the field of battle in Devon in Wessex, and *vice versa.* It can only be inferred from these two statements that the body of the chief was not buried on the field where he fell, but was taken to a distance. John of Wallingford also a late chronicler says that Hubba put to sea and was never heard of more, which sounds like a tradition learned from the locality whence the ships retreated, and bears out the impression that he was taken with his men on their way to join the main body of the Danes.

It may also be observed that had Hubba been buried in the neighbourhood of the fortress before which he fell, the fact would certainly have been recorded by Asser, who describes the fortress from personal knowledge. We are inclined to think this negative evidence decisive.

The Story of Heming, *translated by Sir G. W. Dasent. See "Orkneyinga Saga," in* Icelandic Sagas, Vol. *III of Rolls Series, p. 401.*

But it must not be overlooked that, as in the case of other famous chiefs, the burial of Hubba seems to have passed into a semi-mythical position. A MS. note to Roger of Hoveden (Arundel MS. 69) says that Ubba was slain "apud Ubbelawe in Eboracensi Colonia." This is certainly incorrect, but an Icelandic Saga dealing with the battles of Stamford Bridge and Hastings says that the burial howe of his brother Ivar stood on the shore in Cleveland in Yorkshire, and that every invader who landed there was doomed to defeat.

Ivar probably died in Ireland, but it is clear that legend was busy with the "sons of Lodbrok" very early, and the story of Hubba's burial in "Ubbelawe" is probably rather more legendary than traditional. It may be noted that the name is Saxon in form, not Danish, "howe" being the more northern term for a burial mound.

It seems highly unlikely that any further light will ever be thrown on the matter, though the hope of finding Hubba will probably continue to lure on enthusiastic searchers to further fruitless research. It is only to be hoped that any such undertakings as the exploration of a possible mound will be properly carried out and recorded even if the results are, from the point of view of the searchers, negative.

Chapter 6

This is unnamed in any of the *Chronicles* being called in the Anglo-Saxon texts "paet geweorc" and in the Latin "arx" simply. It is therefore most unlikely that any town was in question. It is not likely that the position on Edington hill itself meant, as if it had been so fortified as to be considered a "geweorc" the battle would be described as the storming of the fortress. The details, however, distinctly show that the Danes were driven from the field for some distance, flying to their stronghold, which was evidently their headquarters and food depot. Its extent must have been large, and its water supply good. At the same time it must have been well placed for defence, and not difficult to blockade, if too strong for Alfred to attempt to storm.

Something more than a mere hill fort such as may be found almost anywhere on the Wessex hills must therefore be looked for; and if there were no other reasons to prove that it was within a few miles of Athelney, the choice of Aller and Wedmore as the places where the final peace-making was to take place would settle that question.

There are two positions within a few miles of Edington hill, neither of them hill forts, or places to which any definite name would be attached by the *Chronicles*. Both have been fortified from early times, and either would easily be strenthened by a force needing a headquarter station which would be within reach of Edington and yet safe from attack by the Saxons from Athelney.

The position suggested originally by the late Bishop Clifford was the old Roman station of "ad Pontem," which is presumably marked by the present town of Bridwater, placed at the one available bridge position at the head of the estuarine water of the Parrett. Here the ancient road from Exeter through Taunton eastward crosses to the Poldens and so runs down them to Glastonbury, and apparently led in some more direct line to "Uxella" on the Axe, now a lost site. No doubt, if "ad Pontem" is rightly located here, the Roman works which protected their bridge were still in existence and strong in Saxon times, and possibly the bridge was still available.

The town was up to Norman times only known as "the burh," and this absence of definite name for the place seems to coincide somewhat with the *Chronicle* accounts, though one would have expected that the term "burh" would have been used, as already a known designation of the old works.

The points in favour of this ancient "burh" being the fortress of the siege are that it would be fairly easy to defend, being kept on one side by the Parrett, and on two others by brooks and fen along their courses. The fourth side, where the western road passes to the foot of the Quantock ridges, might well be barred by stockading between the two watercourses, but the Roman works would be the main stronghold. There would be no difficulty in water supply, even for a large host, and room for cattle enough for the siege would be found. The distance from Edington is about four miles—not more than will account for the statement that the battle was fought over a long tract of country. Siege would be of the nature of a blockade by occupation of the heights by which the position is commanded, but would not be difficult. Alfred had already besieged the Danes successfully twice—at Wareham and Exeter—without the advantage given him by their previous defeat after a pitched battle.

Bishop Clifford's suggestion need not therefore be discarded. It is based on personal knowledge of the place, and perhaps the only weakness of the theory lie in the doubt as to whether Roman works of sufficient strength were available, and whether the bridge was in use. We have no record of any crossing of the river, and in addition it may be noted that to cross the river was to pass to the side most open to attack by Alfred—the west. Yet of course it might be a wise precaution on the part of Guthrum to hold the main crossing of the river against western levies such as that under Odda. And it may be worth while to recall that the later defences of the town lay on both banks of the Parrett.

But the more probable, and indeed we may say almost certain position of the Danish stronghold was at the end of the Poldens, at the point later known as Downend.

The Polden Hills touch the inland heights along which the Fosseway runs, at their southern end, and at their northern extremity run out into a long tongue of high ground between the fens of the Brue and Parrett, the headwater of the estuary of the latter river sweeping across its levels from the Quantock side in a wide curve to the very foot of the steep. Here the deep water of the channel runs below a cliff-like bluff, though not now so close to the rising ground as it has been within living memory. Embankment and drainage work have slightly set the river, in its narrowed course, away from the hill.

Here was the creek which was known as "Downend Pill," the term "Pill" being the west-country name for a tidal inlet forming a small haven. Apparently it ran across the very end of the headland, where excavation has proved that some sort of embanked basin, now silted up, once existed.

From Downend an ancient road runs along the Poldens, connecting with the main road across Edington hill, while another track led along a ridge of firm ground across the marshes to the tidal ford at Combwich. There was also a way across the levels to the "trajectus" at what is now Bridgwater. The promontory is well calculated for defence and has always been considered to show marks of Roman earthwork. It is not certain that the entrenchments visible are of that date, but Roman remains, as well as remains of even earlier date, are commonly found in the vicinity. There is no doubt that the advantages of the hill, with its well-protected haven, have been recognised and made use of from very early times.

The position at Downend is therefore one which would be of the first importance to the Danes. Eastward it was in direct communication

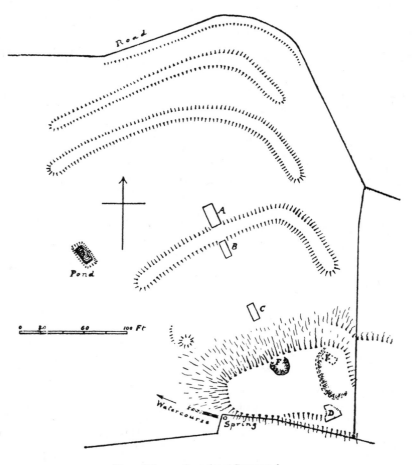

Plan of the earthworks at Downend.

with the heart of Wessex and Mercia, and it had its haven where any Danish vessels could lie in perfect safety. Even if no defences were already available, which seems unlikely, very little labour would be required to throw up such a "work" across the neck of the promontory as would be sufficient to render it impregnable if strongly held. Water is abundant, and the area protected would be amply sufficient to satisfy the requirements of a fortnight's blockade. It would be impossible for Alfred to raid this headquarters from Athelney without forcing the passage of the river at some point first, and the only available crossings beside that at Borough Bridge are the present site of Bridgwater, and the tidal ford at Combwich, either of which would be impracticable for a small force.

With regard to the probable existence of fortifications at Downend in the time of Alfred, we can only say that they are hardly likely not to have existed. Since the position here was first suggested as a likely amendment of Bishop Clifford's choice of Bridgwater, the researchers of the Rev. W. Greswell in the mediaeval charters of the district have shown that Downend was a place of importance and had its stronghold in early Norman times, when it is mentioned as "Burgh de capite Montis," and had special jurisdiction as a separate hundred.

In the article on the "Battle of Ethandune" (Rev. C. W. Whistler, Antiquary, *July - August, 1901).*

"The Sequel to the Battle of Edington," Rev. W. Greswell (Somerset Arch. Soc. Proceedings, *Vol. LIII, 1908).*

Excavations instituted here by Greswell in 1908 for the exploration of the curiously regular mound at the end of the promontory and the earthworks in a field below, known as the "Bailey field," produced abundance of early Norman and some possibly earlier pottery, but beyond these traces of ancient occupation no definite conclusions could be drawn as to fortification positions. The earthworks seemed to be the remains of embankments enclosing a small haven, probably the Downend Pill already mentioned, long silted up with the change in the river channel. So far as the mound could be explored, it seemed to be composed of refuse tipped from the quarries which have been extensive and destructive on the ridge. The surface of the whole promontory has been so much altered and disturbed that practically nothing of its original features have been left. The field name and the charters however are sufficient evidence that strong works have existed here, and there is no reason to suppose that the Normans were the first to make the most of the position. It would be, and apparently was, of importance to the Romans, commanding the way from the Polden road to their "trajectus" and to "Uxella," and was the point at which the pilgrims to Glastonbury from beyond Severn would disembark.

The excavations mentioned, although Mr Greswell was responsible for the undertaking, and was present at them, are not referred to by him in his book, *The Story of the Battle of Edington*. Although the results were negative and so far disappointing the omission is rather unaccountable. They are however fully recorded in the volume of *Proceedings of the Somerset Arch. Society* for 1909. The survey of the position gave little hope of finding any marked remains of ancient work, hardly any of the original surface of the ground remaining. This in itself is a loss which should be recorded.

"Excavations at Downend, near Bridgwater, 1908," by A. G. Chater and A. F. Major. Proceedings, *Vol. LV, 1909. The lettering on the subjoined plan refers to these excavations.*

Greswell's researches have further elicited the suggestive existence of a creek in this vicinity once known as "Viking's Pill." He says

> the place-name occurs several times, and was well known in the reign of Henry IV, at the time when the *Placita* or Pleas were written. . . . This Viking's Pill, from the local description given in the charter can most clearly be identified with a place known better in after centuries as Downend Pill, or perhaps Walpole, close by, at the foot of the Polden hills.

The discovery is apparently a proof that the Downend haven and position has been at some time the known port used by Scandinavian seamen, whether as traders, settlers, or raiders of the usual type, but we cannot follow Greswell

The Story of the Battle of Edington, pp. 32-4.

Only some four are
known, and these
occur in the D.B. for
the eastern counties.
One of these is
doubtful.
Lincolnshire and the
Danes, *Rev. G. C.
Streatfield, 1884, p.
101.*

*Mr Greswell himself,
in* The Antiquary *for
January, 1912, p. 40,
points out that
Danish place-names
are rare in the locality.*

in his unhesitating reference of the name to the
campaign of 878. The men of Guthrum are not
designated Vikings in the *Chronicles,* where the
name only occurs occasionally. Names
compounded of "Viking" are extremely rare in
these islands, and we are not at all sure that the
obvious etymology is the correct one. If it is, the
name if far more likely to be a personal
appellation of some well-known seaman whose
ship frequented the little port, and who possibly
had his own ship-garth in some small inlet under
the hill. We have elsewhere given reasons for
believing that the Scandinavian settlements
existed in West Somerset from early times.

Turning to the question of a Wiltshire site for
the fortress of the siege, which of course must be
close to Ethandun, the whole Chippenham
district is available, if once we are prepared to
disregard the necessity for finding a position near
enough to Athelney to allow of the two forces
being within reach of each other, and able to
carry on the constant warfare stated by the
chroniclers to have been waged against the army
from Athelney. Names bearing at least a
superficial resemblance to Ethandun are common
in the district, each with some variant of the field
name "lea" within reach as a possible "Aecglea,"
while the name of Ethandun itself or its
corruption postulates hilly country, while hilly
country in Wiltshire also postulates a hill fort.

None of these sites has any real claim to
represent Ethandun, as not one of them is within
seventy miles of Athelney as the crow flies, and
but for the initial misreading of Ethelwerd which
we have noted would never have been thought of
as possible. None of the Wiltshire sites suggested
has anything but a waterless chalk hill fortress
near it, and this in itself is prohibitive of a siege
lasting for a fortnight in summer. Two Wiltshire
sites however are usually named in the text-
books as the scene of the battle, and they should
not be left unmentioned, as one instinctively
cleaves to the old school teaching, however

contradictory it may have seemed even at the time one learnt it.

The name of Heddington (near Calne) is accountable for the choice of "Oliver's Castle" near at hand, though for this "Ethandun" the town of Chippenham itself is usually put forward as the fortress. But the Wiltshire site which is now usually claimed as that of the fortress is the ancient fort of Bratton which overlooks Edington near Westbury, the "Ethandun" in Wiltshire whose claims we go into elsewhere.

Bratton Castle is well known, as it is marked by the "white horse" of doubtful antiquity which is boldly carved on the turf of its western declivity. This horse is of course loosely claimed as the work of the victorious Alfred, and is no doubt, as Professor Earle says, partly the reason for the identification of this Edington as the battlefield. The camp itself is of the usual hill promontory type, very strongly defended by the extremely steep downs on three sides as well as by the earthworks. The fourth side, where the promontory merges into the wide downland summit, is less strong by nature, but has the usual entrenchments, which were, when in use, no doubt fully adequate for the defence. Probably they would be augmented by stockading.

Two of the Saxon Chronicles, *note on the year 878*.

The situation is imposing, but the camp has drawbacks which are entirely against its acceptance as the fortress of the siege. It is absolutely waterless, and no water is within reach even of a sortie in force, as the downs are chalk. No large force could hope to hold out there for more than a day or two—any more than could Alfred's western levies stand a waterless siege of two days at Cynuit in the springtime. The acreage of the enclosure is considerable, but hardly seems spacious enough to allow of any accumulation of cattle sufficient for the needs of a fortnight, even on short rations both for herds and men.

There is no question that both Oliver's and

Recent explorations in Oliver's Castle revealed no trace of occupation in Saxon times. See "Oliver's Camp, Devizes," by Mrs M. E. Cunnington, Wilts Archaeological Magazine, *XXXV.*

Bratton Castle were in existence and strong in 878, and either of them would be pitched upon offhand as likely sites for a required fortress near a theoretic Edington, but imposing position and propinquity are not all that is required in the fortress of the siege. It will be necessary to seek for some more possible position if a Wiltshire site is insisted on. Chippenham itself has been suggested, but if it had been the Danish "work" there is no doubt that the *Chronicles* would have named it.

By way of conclusion, although we believe that it must be clear enough why we consider that the *Chronicles* are right, and that Athelney and Ethandun were within touch of one another, and that the actual existence of an Ethandun within sight of the fortress of Borough Bridge must be explained away before any other site can be discussed, it may be as well to summarise the main objections to any Wiltshire site for Ethandun and the fortress of the siege.

The distance, about seventy miles from Athelney, is, to begin with, too great to allow of the constant fighting recorded, and this objection is unsuperable. There was no possible reason why, with his enemy at that distance from him, across forest country, as forest was in his days, or at the present day either for that matter, Alfred should have remained in hiding in the fen. It cannot be supposed that Guthrum and his host were so terrified at the small successes of a few desperate Saxons in the fenland that they fled to their winter base, and there huddled together to wait for attack, allowing the beaten Saxons to gather within a few miles of them as, and when, they would. It would have been possible for them to have wiped out the straggling detachments on the way to the gathering in detail if they were so close at hand; and the general movement throughout the raided country could only have remained unknown if carried out beyond the radius of their foraging parties. Had the battle been anywhere in Wiltshire, it would have been a practical confession of weakness to allow the defeated Danes to remain in Chippenham. But if it took place in the neighbourhood of Athelney, to insist on their retreating for seventy miles through country already raided was in itself a condition which showed that they accepted defeat. There is no reason which will account for the voice of the two fen villages, Aller and Wedmore, as the scene of the last stages of the peacemaking unless they were close at hand.

Any position in Wiltshire would of necessity involve a sortie in force from the besieged camp, with every prospect of a further successful retreat to the Mercian border. The sortie from Cynuit was quite successful, though made by a very small force, and after making every allowance for the losses the Danes had suffered and for demoralisation due to their defeat, it remains inconceivable that they can have been penned up anywhere within reach of Mercia without an attempt on their part to win their way through, or on the part of the Mercian Danes to gather forces and raise the siege. There is no suggestion of any such attempt in the *Chronicles.*

Index

88, 95, 104, 131, 136, 139, 140, 141, 142, *142*,
144, 145, *149*, 150, 155, 156, 160, *161*, 166, 167,
170, 174, 179, 182, 183, *183*, 188, 189, 190, 195,
196, 197, 198, 201, 202, 204, 205, 207, 208, *208*,
209, 213, 220, 221, 226, *227*, 228, 229
Anglo-Saxons, 17, *24*, 54, 77, 89, *107*, 110, *111*,
112, 116, *138*, 213, 220
Anton or Test, Valley of the, 18
Appledore, 144, *144*, 203, 208
Arthur, *13*, 28, 62
Ashdown, 58
Asir, 127, 128
Assandun, Battle of, 157
Asser, 39, 47, *138*, *142*, 161, 167, 183, 190, 191,
192, 196, 197, 198, *203*, 208, 210, 211, 212, 216,
218
Athelney, 45, 47, 49, 97, 168, 169, 172, 174, 176,
179, 180, 183, 184, 186, 189, 190, 193, 198, 202,
204, 205, 206, *208*, 209, 210, 211, 224, 226, 228,
229
Athelstan, 94, 98, 102, 138, 142
Augustine, Saint, *84*, 103, 115
Avalon, Isle of, 62, 65, 76, 104
Avebury, 163
Avon, 18, 19, 20, 54
Avon, River, 25, 29, 32, 34, 40, 42, *57*, 149, 155
Axe, River, 37, 44, 56, 63, 86, 99, 189, 216, 220
Axminster, 86, 93, 99
Axmouth, 52, 86
Aylesbury, Vale of, 33
Babcary, see also Caric, 66
Badbury Rings, 19, 20, 24, 29, 40, 41, 52, 85, 163
Badon, Mount, (Mons Badonicus), 9, *13*, *24*
Baldred, King, 65, 66, 70, 106
Bamfleet, 144
Barbury Hill (Beranburh), 33
Barnstaple, 97
Basingstoke, 195
Bath, 9, 34, 54, 156, 164
Bawdrip, 68
Beandun (Bampton), Battle of, 35
Becary (Beokerie), 61
Bede, 15, *26*, 58, *77*

Bedford, 33
Bedfordshire, 163
Bedwin (Biedanheafod), Battle of, 64
Bennett, Rev. J. A., *55*
Bensington (Benson), Battle of, 94, 100
Beokerie, 59
Beorhtric, King of Wessex, 95, 139
Beornwulf, King of Mercia, *96*
Beranburh, see Barbury Hill
Bergen, 94, 124
Berhtwald, 59, 61
Berkshire, *15*, 17, 18, 33, 35, 142, 163, 195, 199, 200, 202
Berkshire, *15*, 17, 18, 33, 35, 142, 163, 195, 199, 200, 202
Bideford, 192, 203, 208, *208*, 209, 217
Bieda, landing of, 15
Birinus, first Bishop of Winchester, 36
Bishop's Hull, 80
Björkmann, Prof., *112*
Blackdown Hills, 57, 78, 80, 86, 88, 90, 99, 104
Bleadon, grant of, 86
Bodmin, 98
Bokerly Dyke, Grim's Ditch, *19*, *22*, 32, 40, *40*, 42, *52*, 52, 142, 143, 163, 164
Boniface, Saint, 59, 93
Borlase, Rev. W., 98
Borough Bridge, 45, 46, 176, 177, 179, 181, 210, 224, 228
Bothamley, C. H., *177*
Bradford-on-Avon, 54, 55, 59, 61, 103, 105, 194
Bradleigh, near Butleigh, 196
Branscombe, 86
Bratton Castle, 227, 228
Breamore Down, 22
Brean Down, 45
Breguoin, Mount, Battle of, *13*
Brendon Hills, 51, 57, 79, 88, 120
Brendon-Quantock valley, 88, 92
Brent, 62, 86
Brent Knoll, 45, 141
Brian Boroimhe, King of Ireland, 151
Brice, Saint, Massacre of, 154

Bridget, Saint, Chapel to, at Glastonbury, 61
Bridgwater, 10, 45, 46, 48, 49, 50, 51, 64, 66, 67,
    68, 69, 71, *71*, 73, 82, 123, 179, 180, 193, 211,
    220, 222, 224, *225*
Brihtric, son of Elphege, 157
Bristol, 216
Bristol Channel, see also Severn Sea, 166, 173
Britford, *30*, 32
Britons (British), 12, *13*, 13, 18, 22, 23, 24, 25, 27,
    28, 32, 34, 35, 36, 37, 41, 57, 61, 64, *66*, 75, 76,
    77, 78, 79, *82*, 84, 85, 92, 98, 101, 102, 103, 104,
    105, 109, 110, 111, 120, 121, 123, 143, 175
Brittany, 149
Brögger, Dr. A. W., *138*
Brompton, John of, 142, 216, 217, 218
Bronze Age, 109, 110, *110*
Brue, River, 37, 45, 46, 47, 51, 56, 61, 65, 180,
    188, 189, 222
Brunanburh, Battle of, 93, 138, 181, 197
Buckinghamshire, 155, 199
Bugge, Dr. Alexander, *112*, 113, *116*
Bulleid, Dr. A., 217
Burford, Battle, 92, 100
Burh, 221
Butleigh (Budeclega, etc.), 184, 196
Buttington, 144
Buzbury, 40

Cadbury Castle, 57
Caerleon, Battle of Arthur at, *13*
Calne, 227
Cambridge, 135, 161, 162, 163, 164, 165
Camden, W., 47, 202
Camelford, 95
Cannington (Cantuctune), 67, 68, 69, 73, 82, 155
Cannington Brook, 72, 74
Cannington Park, 51, 73, 125, 127, 128, 129, 192,
    210, 212, 216
Canterbury, 142
Cantucdun (Quantock, Cannington), 67
Caric (Castle Cary, etc.), 66
Carmarthenshire, 192, 205
Cary, River, 45, 176, 191

Clearbury Ring, 20, *22*, *23*, 24, *24*, 29, 30, *30*
Cleveland, 218
Cley Hill, 194
Clifford, Bishop, 192, 193, *193*, 202, 204, 205, 206, 210, 211, 216, 217, 220, 221, 224
Clist, 153
Cnut the Great, King of Denmark and England, 134, 154, 156, 157
Codex Wintoniensis, 24
Codrington, T., *41*
Coins, *138*
Collen, J. W., 90
Collingwood, Professor W. G., 118, 161
Collinson, Rev. J., *68*, *91*, 206
Columbton, 86
Combwich, 45, 50, *51*, 56, 72, 122, *122*, 123, 124, 125, 126, 127, 128, 129, 177, 180, 193, 204, 207, 210, 211, 212, 216, 222, 224
Combwich Brook, 75, 210, 222
Commail, British king, 34
Compton Dundon, see Dundon
Condidan, British king, 34
Cornwall, 38, 39, *77*, 96, *96*, 98, *98*, 102, 103, 106, 107, 119, 138, 140, 151
Corsley, 195
Countesbury, 192, 208
Courcelles, Roger de, 200, *201*
Cranborne Chase, 19, *22*, 29, 32, *32*, *33*, 40, *40*
Crediton, 93
Creech St Michael, 46
Crewkerne, 78
Cromwell, 41
Crook, also see Cruca, 68, 69
Cruca (Cruce), 67, 68, 69, 70, 75, 76
Cunnington, Mr and Mrs B. H., *33*, 228
Cutha, see Cuthwulf
Cuthberga, Saint, Abbess of Wimborne, 84
Cuthred, King of Wessex, 92, 105
Cuthwulf (Cutha), 33, 34, 35, 95, 101
Cwichelm, King of Wessex, 34, 35
Cynegils, King of Wessex, 35, 36
Cynewulf the Atheling, 88, 90
Cynewulf, King of Wessex, 92, 94, 95, 105

Cynric, King of Wessex, 13, 15, 27, 29, 33
Cynuit, seige of, 168, 192, 193, *195*, *203*, 205, 208, *208*, 210, 227, 229
Cynwydd, 192, 193

Damerham Knoll, 20, 22, 23, *24*, 24, 31
Damnonia, see |Dumnonia|
Danelagh 143, 148, 150, 154, 162, 163
Danes, 27, 38, 42, 57, *57*, 84, 93, 96, 97, 98, 100, 101, 103, 106, 107, 109, 112, 116, *116*, 118, 119, *119*, 121, 122, *122*, 123, 125, 126, 127, 130, 131, 132, 133, 134, 135, 136, 137, 138, 139, 141, 142, 143, 144, 146, 148, 150, 151, 152, 153, 154, 155, 157, 159, 160, 161, 162, 163, 164, 165, 166, *170*, 172, 173, 174, 175, 177, *177*, 178, 179, 181, 182, 183, 184, 186, 187, 188, 189, 191, 203, 204, 205, 206, 207, 208, 209, 212, 214, 215, 216, 218, 221, 222, 223, 224, *226*, 228, 229
Daniell, Rev. J. J., *98*
Dartmoor, 80, 81, 87, 93
Davidson, J. B., 78
Dawkins, Professor Boyd, 56
Dean, Forest of, 206
Demetia, the, 166, 168, 191, 205, 206, 207
Denmark, 110, *138*, 141, 154, 166
Deorham, Battle of, 9, 30, 34, 36, 37, 40, 53, 54, 102, 103, 116
Derwent, 13
Devizes, *142*, 155, *228*
Devon, 38, 39, *39*, 52, *77*, 78, 79, 81, *81*, 82, *82*, 83, 93, 94, *95*, 96, *96*, 97, 98, 99, 103, 106, 107, 119, 124, 138, 141, 148, 150, 152, 156, 159, 168, 173, 174, 177, 183, 203, 205, 207, 208, 209, 216, 218
Domesday Book, 46, 54, 57, 66, 67, 68, *68*, 69, *75*, 81, *81*, 83, 120, *126*, 193, 197, 198, 199, 200, 201, *201*
Domnonia, see Dumnonia
Dorchester (Oxon), 36
Dorchester, 36, 41, 52, 53, 139, 165
Dorset, 32, 37, *39*, 40, 42, 52, 55, *55*, 83, 84, 85, 86, 93, 95, 96, 79, 99, 106, 123, 140, 142, *143*, 151, 156, 159, 175, 181, 183, 194

Ecglea, see Aecglea
Eddeva, Queen, 199
Eddington (Berks.), 200, 202
Edgarley, 195
Edinburgh, 111, *111*
Edindone or Edintone, Thomas de, 200
Edington on Poldens, *122*, 180, 184, 185, 199, 200,
    201, 204
Edington, 220, 222, 224, 228
Edington (Wilts.), 171, 198, 200, 202, 227
Edston, 201
Edward the Confessor, King of England, *39*, 99
Edward the Elder, King of Wessex, 67
Edwynston, Edwineston, 201, *201*
Ellandun, Battle of, 106
Elleigh, 195
Elworthy, F. T., 80
Ely, 177
Emma, Queen, 154
English Channel, 10, 40, 86, 93, 102, 138, 140,
    144
Episford, battle at, 13
Essex, 96, 144
Ethandun, 38, 57, 97, 134, 135, 157, 170, 171, 180,
    182, 194, 197, 198, 199, 200, 201, 202, 203, *203*,
    204, 224, 226, 227, 228
Ethelnoth, Ealdorman (Duke), *170*
Ethelwalch, King of Sussex, 58, 89
Ethelward, son of Ethelmar, 157
Ethelwerd, 139, 140, *161*, 166, 170, *170*, *172* 173,
    179, 198, 202, 206
Exe, River, 152, 154
Exeter, 51, 93, 94, *94*, 96, 97, 138, 139, 144, 145,
    152, 154, 161, 165, 172, 191, 206, 207, 220, 221
Exmoor, 64, 75, 79, 80, 81, *81*, 82, *82*, 87, 98, 120,
    210
Eyton, R. W., 68, 83, 201

Farinmail, British king, 34
Ferramere, 59, 61
Fethanleag, Battle of, 34, 35, 36, 102
Firth of Forth, 111
Flat Holm, 150

Florence of Worcester, 38, 39, 64, 96, 150, 155, 194, 196
Fordingbridge, 20
Forester, T., 155
Fosbury, camp at, 18
Fossway, The, 50, 51, 52, 56, 57, 62, 66, 76, 80, 86, 93, 99, 122, 175, 180, 210, 216, 222
Fowey, 135
France, 10, 135, 146
Freeman, Professor E. A., 11, *11*, 64, 70, 75, 78, 80, 89, 93
Frey, 128
Frisian, 148
Frome, River, 151, 156
Frome, Valley, 33, 40, 42

Gafulford, Battle of, 95, 103, 105, 106
Gaimar, 198, 201, 217, 218
Gall-Gael, The, 114, 118
Gaul, 11
Gautelf, River, *26*
Geoffrey of Monmouth, 115, 116, *116*
Gerent, King of Dyvnaint, 77, 78, 79, 83, 84, 86, 88, 89, 90, 91, 93, 99, 104, 105
Gidley, 86
Gildas, *24*, 28
Gillingham, 55, *55*
Glamorganshire, 205
Glastonbury, 45, 46, 47, 51, 55, 58, 66, 71, *71*, 78, 82, 86, 104, 180, 184, 186, 195, 196, 200, *201*, 207, 222, 225
Glastonbury Abbey, 37, 58, 59, *59*, 60, 61, 62, 63, 65, 66, 67, 76, 86, 103, 104, 130, 200
Glastonbury, John of, *59*, 65, 66, 67
Glastonbury Lake village, 211
Glein, Battle of King Arthur at, *13*
Gloucester, 34, 155, 166, *167*, *170*, 172, 206
Gloucestershire, 33, 36, 92, 109, 155
Goda, the Devonshire thane, 38, 150
Godenei, 59
Godmans Cap or Frankenbury Camp, 20
Godney, 61
Godsal, Major P. T., *26*

Godwine, 64
Germund, 115, 116
Gothenburg, 109
Gower, 118
Gray, H. St. George, 71, *82*, 109, 213, 217
Green, J. R., 101, *183*
Greswell, Rev. W. H. P., *57*, *68*, 79, 81, 182, *201*, *203*, *207*, 217, 224, *224*, 225, *226*
Greylake, 47
Grim's Ditch, 22, *22*, 23, *23*
Guinnion Castle, Battle of King Arthur at, *13*
Guorthemer, see Vortimer
Guthrum, 97, 116, *116*, 134, 146, 160, 161, 162, 165, 169, 174, 175, 177, 179, 181, 182, 183, 184, 188, 189, 190, 204, 205, 209, 210, 216, 218, 222, 226, 228

Haigh, D., *9*, *111*
Haldon (Howel Down?), 98
Halfdan (Healfdene), 160, 162, 166, 167, 173, 191
Half Mile Ditch, Cranborne Chase, 32
Hamble River, 17
Hamdon, 202
Hamdon Hill, Roman fortress at, 40, 51, 57, 66, *66*
Hampshire, 9, 10, 15, *15*, 17, 18, 22, 23, 28, 40, 89, 142, 150, 153, 154, 155, 157, 168
Hamworthy, 41, 163, 173, 182, 195, 199
Harald Fairhair, *26*
Harbin, Bates, 67, 68
Hare Path, 70
Hare Knap, 70
Hasting (Hasten, Hasteinn), *170*
Hastings, Battle of, 218
Haverfield, Professor F., *56*
Heahmund, Bishop of Sherborne, 142
Healfdene, 83
Hearne, Thomas, 206, 207
Hebrides, *113*
Hedda, Bishop of Winchester, 65, 70
Heddington, 202, 227
Hengestesdun (Hingston Down), 140
Hengisl, Abbot of Glastonbury, 65

Hengist, 111
Henry of Huntingdon, 15, *15*, 24, *39*, 64, 78, 92,
    99, 140, 150, 166, 174, 198
Hereward the Wake, 177
Hertfordshire, 163
High Ham, 44, 179
Highley, 195
Hill Forts, 12
Hobhouse, Bishop, 66
Hod Hill, 32, 40, 41, 43
Holderness, 129
Holt Forest, 40
Horlake, near Athelney, 47
Horsa, 111
Hoveden, Roger de, 38, 198, 218
Howel, King of Cornwall, 98, 102
Hroald, 149
Hubba, son of Ragnar Lodbrok,   144, 160, 161,
    166, 173, 174, 175, 177, 188, 203, 205, 206, 207,
    208, 209, 210, 212, 213, 216, 217, 218
Hubbaston, 206, 208
Hugo, 154
Hull, Miss Eleanor, 114, 116
Humber, River, 38, 141
Huntspill, *69*
Hwiccas, Kingdom of the, 36

Iceland, 218
Icknield Street (Via Iceniana), 52, 163
Idston (Edwineston), 201
Iglea, 184, 194, 196
Ilchester, 44, 52, 55, 57, 177
Iley Oak (Ilegh), 195
Illeigh, 195
Ilminster, 44, 78
Ine, King of Wessex, 62, *64*, 77, 78, 79, 80, 82, 83,
    84, 86, 87, 90, 91, 104, 105, 120, 197(a)
Ingvar (Ivar), son of Ragnar Lodbrok,   83, 134,
    160, 166, 173, 191
Inkpen Beacon, 17, 18
Inysvitryn, Island of, 37
Ireland, 109, 113, *113*, 114, *114*, 115, 116, 118,
    119, *119*, 122, *122*, 141, 151, 161, *161*, 218

242

Iron Age, 65, *128*
Ivar Vidfadme, 160, 161, 218

John, King, charter of, 81
Jutes, 15, 28, 58, 112

Keenthorne, 127
Kemble, J. M., *149*
Kennet, River, 17, 192
Kent, 66, 77, 94, 96, *138*, 141, 142, *144*, 148, 156, 199, 208
Kentwine, King of Wessex, 59, 62, 64, 65, 66, 67, 69, 70, 71, 74, 75, 76, 77, 78, 80, 82, 86, 92, 104, 105, 130
Kenwealh, King of Wessex, 36, 53, 54, 55, 56, 57, *57*, 58, 59, 61, 62, 63, 64, 66, 78, 82, 84, 89, 90, 103
Kenwith (Cynuit), 192, 208, 210
Kerslake, T., 55, *55*, 94
Keynsham, 155
King, J. R., *93*
Kingsley, Rev. Charles, 192, 203, 208
Knap Hill Camp, *33*

Lambourn, 199
Land's End, 98, 140, 151
Langport, 10, 45, 46, 48, 55, 177
Langtoft, Peter, 206
Lanprobi, 55
Lantocai, see also Street, 65
Lappenberg, Dr. J. M., *9*, 162
Lega, Legh, see also Street, 197
Leigh, near Bradford-on-Avon, 194, 195, 196
Leland, J., 93
Lewes, Rape of, 89
Lilstock, ancient sea inlet, 123
Limene, River, *144*
Limenemouth, 144
Lincolnshire, 129, *226*
Linton, 75, 208
Litton, 86
Llanrhidian, 118
Llongborth, Battle of, 10

Nadder, River, 30, 32
Nansen, Dr Fridtjof, 110
Natanleod, *13*, 15
Nately, 15
Nennius, Battles of Vortimer, *13*, *24*
Neot, Saint, 97
Neroche, see Castle Neroche
Noon's Barrow, 90
Norfolk Broads, 47
Norman, son of Leofwin, 157
Normans, 41, 49, *58*, 59, 71, *142*, 190, 201, 221, 224, 225
Normandy, 152, 156
Northamptonshire, 199
Northmen, 160
North Petherton, 49, 56, 68
Northumbria, 35, 36, 38, 39, 96, 100, 101, 102, 106, 107, *138*, 143, 144, 145, 146, 157, 160, 162
North Wales, 151
Norton Fitzwarren, 51, 57, 71, 72, 76, 80, 88, 120
Norway, 94, *110*, 112, *112*, 113, *113*, 114, 115, 116, 118, *122*, 123, 124, 131, 132, 135, 136, 137, 138, *138*, 139, 140, 151, 152
Norwich, 154
Nunna, King of the South Saxons, 77, 78, 90
Nydam boat, 11
Nyland Hill, 61, 62

Oakley, 195
Ockley, Battle of, 142
Odda, Earl of Devon, Dorset and Somerset, 99, 173, 175, 189, 216, 222
Odin, 128
Odstock Down, *19*, 20, 30, 31
Offa, King of Mercia, 94, 95, 96, 139
Offa's Dyke, 95, 107, 149
Olaf, King of Dublin, 181
Olaf the Saint, King of Norway, 138
Olaf Tryggvason, King of Norway, 135, 151, 152, 156
Old Burrow Camp, Exmoor, *82*
Old Sarum, 18, 19, 20, 24, 29, 30, 32, 33, *33*, 34, 52, 54, 55, 102, 154, 157, 163, 164

Oliver's Castle, 227, *228*
Olney, 157
Olrik, Professor Axel, 112
Oman, Professor C., 9, *15*, *58*, *96*, *142*
Ordnance Survey, 24, 90, 122
Ordulf's Monastery at Tavistock, 151
Ormiegill, Caithness, 110
Orosius, 10, *10*, *112*
Osric, Ealdorman of Dorset, 141
Otford, Battle of, 94
Othery, 46, 180
Ottar, 149
Over Stowey, 73, 74
Oxfordshire, 35, 92, 94

Padstow, 150
Pallig, 152
Parrett, River, (Pedridan), 39, 44, 45, 46, 48, 50,
    50, 51, 54, 55, 56, 57, *57*, 62, 63, 64, 65, 66, *66*,
    70, 71, 72, 76, 81, 82, 83, 86, 106, 122, 123, 124,
    127, 141, *142*, 144, 176, 177, 180, 182, 183, 187,
    188, 204, 106, 209, 210, 211, 212, 216, 220, 221,
    222
Pedridan, see Parrett
Pembrokeshire, 192, 205
Pen, Pen Hill, Pen Knoll, Pen Mills, 56
Penda, King of Mercia, 35, 36, 58, 94, 103
Pendon Hill, 46, 202
Pene, Forest of, see also Selwood, 218
Penger, see also Pennard, 65, 66
Penhoe, 153
Pennard (Penger), 66, 76
Penselwood, 54, 55, 57, 134, 156
Peonna, battle at, 54, 55, 56, 58, 59, 61, 63, 105
Phelps, W., *122*, 194
Picts, 10, 35, 102, 107
Pitt-Rivers, General, *19*, 32, *33*, 40, 42
Plainsfield, 74
Plummer, C., 192
Plymouth, 96, 141
Polden Hills, 45, 46, 47, 48, 49, 50, *51*, 62, 65, 66,
    68, 71, 76, 86, 104, 122, 123, 179, 180, 183, 186,
    188, 189, 197, 202, 210, 220, 222, 225

30, 32, 33, *33*, 34, 38, 40, 41, 44, 49, 52, 53, 54,
55, *55*, 56, *57*, 58, 59, 61, 62, 69, 70, 71, 75, 76,
79, 83, 84, *84*, 85, 86, 87, 92, 94, 96, 100, 102,
103, 104, 105, 110, 111, *111*, *112*, 115, 119, 120,
121, 122, 123, 126, 129, 132, 133, 135, 137, 138,
140, 143. 144, 145 146, 148, 149, *149*, 152, 154,
156, 157, 160, 161, 162, 163, 172, 175, 181, 182,
184, 187, 188, 189, 190, 199, 200, 201, *201*, 213,
216, 217, 218, 220, 221, *227*, 228

Scandinavians, 10, 109, 110, 112, 116, 118, 120,
124, *126*, 127, 128, *128*, 129, 130, *138*, 217, 225,
226

Sceorstan, see also Sherston, 157

Scilly Isles, 98

Scotland, *110*, 112, *119*, *122*

Scots, 10, 35, 102, 107

Searobyrig, see Old Sarum

Seaxburh, 64

Sedgmoor, 47, 48, 74, 176, 180, 182, 214

Selwood, 39, 42, 49, 51, 77, 83, 84, 144, 157, 168,
183, 184, 194, 218

Severn, River, 33, 42, 44, 53, 89, 109, 149, 151,
206, 216, 225

Severn Sea, 82, *82*, 102, 104, 110, 118, 120, 138,
139, 141, *142*, 144, 204

Severn Valley, 34, 103

Shapwick, 200, 201

Sheppey, 96, 159

Shepton Mallet, 51

Sherborne, 55, 57, 63, 84, 141

Sherborne Abbey, 55

Sherston (Sceorstan), Battle of, 38, 134

Shetland, *110*, *113*

Ships, 10, *11*, 124, 125, *128*, 133, 134, 136, 137,
139, 140, 141, 142, 144, 146

Shore, T. W., 89

Shropshire, 58

Sidbury Camp, 18

Sigtrygg Silkbeard, King of Dublin, 122

Silchester, 17, 19, 34

Solent, 148

Somerset, 9, 10, 33, 34, 38, 39, *39*, 40, 42, 44, 46,
51, 52, 54, *77*, 78, 80, 81, 82, 86, 89, 91, *94*, 99,

102, 106, 109, 110, 119, *120, 122*, 126, 1*26*, 138, 139, *142*, 153, 155, 156, 159, 167, 168, 172, 173, 175, *177*, 182, 191, 194, 199, 200, 202, *202*, 204, 205, 206, 208, 209
Somerton, 45, 46, 106, 141, 186, 196, 206, 207, 210
Sorbiodunum, see Old Sarum
Southampton, 17, 18, 142, 150, 151
Southampton Water, 18, 58, *58*
Southlake, near Athelney, 47
South Petherton, 44, 56, 57, 63, 66, 82, 88, 91, *91*, *142*, 177
South Saxons, 15, 35, 77, 89, 90
South Wales, 53, 150, 166, 173, 174, 205
Sowi, 46, 86
Stamford Bridge, Battle of, 218
Stawell, 46
Stephens, Professor G., *111*
Stert, 124
Stevenson, W. H., *142*, 190, 192, 194, 195, 196, 201, 202, *203, 207*, 208, 211
Stilicho, 10
Stockland Bristol, 217
Stoke Courcy, 67
Stolford, *75*, 123, 124, 126, 128
Stone Age, 109, 110, *110*
Stour, River, 25, 26, 40
Stourton, 184, 194
Strathclyde, 35
Streatfield, Rev. G. C., *226*
Streatley, 163, 164
Street (Lantocai or Legh), 56, 65, 66, *66*, 122, 180, 196, 197
Strenwald, 151
Stubbs, Bishop W., 59
Stuf, 15
Sturminster, 86
Sumner, Heywood, *22*, 23, *23, 30*, 32, *41*
Surrey, 58, 77, 91, 96, *142*, 199
Sussex, 58, 77, 78, 88, 89, 90, 91, 96, 152, 155
Swanage, 165, 207, 216
Sweden, 109, 112, *112*, 113
Sweyn, King of Denmark, 134, 154, 156

Tamar, River, 97, 98, 151
Tapp, Dr W. M., *82*
Taunton, 44, 45, 49, 64, 66, 71, 78, 79, 80, 82, 86,
    87, 88, 89, 90, 91, 98, 99, 105, 106, 120, 122,
    177, 183, 220
Tavistock, 151
Taw, River, 93, 208
Teignmouth, 98
Teington, 152
Tennerley Ditch, Cranborne Chase, 32
Thames, River, 17, *25*, 33, 38, 94, 100, 101, 142,
    144, 146, 152, 155, 157, 160, 163, 188
Thanet, 13, 141
Thor, 128
Tindal, N., 202
Toller, Professor T. N., 201
Tone, River, 45, 46, 66, 70, 71, 78, 79, 176, 191
Torridge, River, 93, 208
Trat Treuriot, Battle at, *13*
Trigonshire, 98

Uxella, 37, 50

Viking, see also "Wicinga", *11*, 11, 12, 13, 28,
    112, *116*, 122, 124, 132, 134, 138, *138*, 139, *146*,
    217, 226
Viking's Pill, 225
Vortimer (Guorthemer), 13
Waelas, 70
Walbury Camp, 17, 18
Wales, 36, 38, *94*, 101, 102, 106, 111, 118, 126,
    130, 139, 174, 192, *207*, 209, 211
Wall, J. C., *208*
Wallingford, John of, 179, 181, *181*, 186, 218
Walpole in Pawlett (Wallepille), 68
Walter de Douay, 49, 67
Wansdyke, 33, *33*, 34, *40*, 42, 54, 163
Wantage (Waneting), 199
Wareham, 41, 84, 135, 142, 154, 157, 161, *161*,
    162, 163, 164, 165, 172, 191, 221
Warminster, 195
Warne, Sir Charles, 26, *41*, *143*
Wash, The, 38